THE OPPOSITE OF CHEATING

TEACHING, ENGAGING, AND THRIVING IN HIGHER ED

James M. Lang and Michelle D. Miller, SERIES EDITORS

THE OPPOSITE OF CHEATING

Teaching for Integrity in the Age of AI

TRICIA BERTRAM GALLANT
AND DAVID A. RETTINGER

University of Oklahoma Press : Norman

This book is published thanks in part to the generosity of Edith Kinney Gaylord.

Library of Congress Cataloging-in-Publication Data

Names: Bertram Gallant, Tricia, 1970– author. | Rettinger, David A. author.
Title: The opposite of cheating : teaching for integrity in the age of AI / Tricia Bertram Gallant and David A. Rettinger.
Other titles: Teaching for integrity in the age of artificial intelligence
Description: Norman : University of Oklahoma Press, [2025] | Series: Teaching, engaging, and thriving in higher ed ; volume 4 | Includes bibliographical references and index. | Summary: "Outlines workable, implementable measures, backed by research, to help teachers better understand why students cheat and to prevent cheating and enhance learning and integrity by creating classes that center human interactions for students' personal and professional growth"—Provided by publisher.
Identifiers: LCCN 2024027751 | ISBN 9780806194950 (hardcover ; alk. paper)
| ISBN 9780806194967 (paperback ; alk. paper)
Subjects: LCSH: Education, Higher—United States—Evaluation. | Educational tests and measurements. | Cheating (Education) | Learning and scholarship—Moral and ethical aspects. | Integrity.
Classification: LCC LA227.4 .B4748 20225 | DDC 378.1/70973—dc23/eng/20241106
LC record available at https://lccn.loc.gov/2024027751

The Opposite of Cheating: Teaching for Integrity in the Age of AI is Volume 4 in the Teaching, Engaging, and Thriving in Higher Ed series.

The paper in this book meets the guidelines for permanence and durability of the Committee on Production Guidelines for Book Longevity of the Council on Library Resources, Inc. ♾

The manufacturer's authorized representative in the EU for product safety is the Mare Nostrum Group B.V., Mauritskade 21D, 1091 GC Amsterdam, The Netherlands, email: gpsr@mare-nostrum.co.uk

3 4 5 6 7 8 9 10

CONTENTS

ACKNOWLEDGMENTS

This is not the first book that has called on educators and higher education institutions to change their approach to the cheating problem. This book is almost what we'd call the third in a series. The first came from Tricia's plea to treat academic integrity as a teaching and learning issue.[1] The second was Jim Lang's operationalization of Tricia's call with specific examples and strategies he gleaned from the research, his own teaching, and the teaching practices of others.[2] And, of course, these three books stand on the shoulders of many, many giants.

We cite several of those giants throughout this book. Others include teachers who helped us question what education might be. For David, those include J. Frank Yates at the University of Michigan, William Reilly at Great Neck North High School, and Walter Kintsch at the University of Colorado. For Tricia, those include Linda Wood and Al Lauzon at the University of Guelph, and Terri Monroe at the University of California, San Diego.

The other giants are those who aided us on our academic-integrity practitioner and researcher journeys. For Tricia, they include her dissertation committee (Lea Hubbard, chair; Patrick Drinan; Cheryl Getz; and Adrianna Kezar), as well as her UC San Diego colleagues and Academic Integrity Office team members (students and career). For David, that includes Gus Jordan, who introduced him to the topic, and his colleagues at the University of Mary Washington—faculty, students, and administrators alike. No other institutions would have given us the opportunities to explore academic integrity in quite the same way.

We would both like to thank our colleagues and friends in the world of academic integrity, particularly at the International

Center for Academic Integrity: Courtney Cullen, Valerie Denney, Daniela Gallego Salazar, Jean Guerrero Dib, Christopher Lang, Amanda McKenzie, Jennie Miron, Christian Moriarty, Greer Murphy, Gonzalo Pizarro, Camilla Roberts, Jason Stephens, Blaire Wilson and many others. Special credit goes to the dedicated people who spend their careers as practitioners in this field; their work is not always easy to cite in traditional ways, but their influence is felt nevertheless. Thank you for being the change we hope to see at our institutions.

We would also like to thank our personal circles. David thanks Julie, Ellery, Dad, and all the California Rettingers. Tricia thanks Jamie along with all of her family and, at UC San Diego, her amazing team and colleagues for supporting her during the writing of this book and for always challenging her thinking. We'd also like to send a "good dog" to Barley, Pebbles, and Hershey.

INTRODUCTION

Cheating is out of control. According to a post by u/PissedOffProfessor on Reddit, "The number of students that have been caught cheating on exams is absolutely incredible." Pissed Off Professor argues that students are "brazenly" using generative artificial intelligence (GenAI) despite risking failure in the course and that it's become completely "normalized." Our observations confirm that there are a lot of posts about cheating on Reddit and that it's becoming a serious problem. If people say so on Reddit, it must be true. A quick glance at r/Professors points to a cheating epidemic, one that began during the COVID-19 lockdowns of 2020–21 and flared to catastrophic levels by the November 2022 introduction of ChatGPT and GenAI more broadly.[1] Higher education instructors have reason to be concerned;[2] cheating is a problem and it is largely ignored within our institutions.

It was fall 2004 when the story broke at the University of Southern California (USC).[3] Elena Martinez, an army reservist from a modest background, was the freshman roommate of one of the richest college students in America—Paige Laurie, the granddaughter of a Walmart founder. After Martinez agreed to complete one paper for Laurie to help solidify their relationship, she quickly became Laurie's personal contract cheater: Martinez would do all of Laurie's academic work for her in exchange for money that Martinez desperately needed to pay for school and life expenses. Despite this financial arrangement, Martinez could not afford to continue at USC, so she dropped out and moved back home. Martinez continued to cheat for Laurie for a period thereafter, but eventually quit the gig and revealed the entire scheme on ABC's *20/20* TV show, causing Laurie to surrender her USC degree.

At first glance, this story appears to provide evidence for the fears expressed by Reddit professors: "Students [are] behaving badly,"[4] and there's little instructors can do to change that. It's true that some people who enroll in higher education institutions have no intention of learning at all and so will likely be undeterred by instructor choices. Our Australian colleagues Cath Ellis, Kane Murdoch, and Shaun Lehmann refer to such people not as students but as "enrolled persons."[5] Enrolled persons engage in academic fraud, contract cheating, and other behaviors that are inconsistent with the educational purpose of assigned coursework. We hope that such persons constitute a minority of those enrolled within academic institutions. The remaining cheaters are students whose behaviors can be shaped. So, what is the secret solution to eliminating cheating among those students once and for all? There isn't one solution, but there is a right approach.

A Teaching and Learning Approach

To err is human, as Alexander Pope once wrote, and as long as intructors are teaching human beings, there will be cheating. But there are partial solutions aimed at preventing, addressing, and remediating acts of academic misconduct. This book is about a teaching and learning approach to academic integrity; specifically, what you can do to teach with and for integrity in online, hybrid, and in-person classes.[6] There are no simple answers, but we aim to provide workable and practical strategies that should help you better understand why students cheat and therefore how you can prevent cheating while enhancing learning and integrity.

Enhancing learning and integrity is, after all, *The Opposite of Cheating* and is premised on an optimistic, growth-oriented approach to addressing cheating. Let's start by explaining what we mean by cheating. We intentionally chose the word "cheating" as the simplest, most common vernacular for a host of choices like academic misconduct, academic integrity violations, academic integrity breaches, and plagiarism. As you continue reading, you'll see there are contours and nuances to what we refer to as cheating. We do not intend a moral judgment by using "cheating," since we know that these behaviors have a host of causes that go well beyond dishonesty.

Our focus on learning and integrity does not mean that we are pollyannaish about the challenges and threats to learning and test-taking with integrity in the age of AI. Nor does it mean that we oppose consequences for actions that are dishonest or create an unfair advantage for one student over others. It does mean that we believe, and hope we'll inspire you to believe, that through thoughtful and intentional choices, integrity and learning can thrive despite the many forces that are reshaping the educational system.

These thoughtful and intentional choices are rooted in understanding how individual students, their environment, and assessment design intersect in ways that will produce either scenarios for cheating or scenarios for learning. This is not to say that what you do as the instructor is the final, or even the most powerful straw, that will break the proverbial camel's back. In organizational and human behavior, there is no great and powerful Oz who can manipulate their way to the preferred end of the story. While you are not all-powerful, neither are you a pawn or a victim. You have agency and choices. You can choose how you teach, grade, and interact with your students. You can choose how you show up to class and for your students. You can choose your assessments and their design, as well as how you give feedback to students. You can choose how you respond to cheating when it occurs despite your efforts. While your choices may not always achieve a cheat-free classroom, they will give you freedom from wondering whether you could have done more and relief from having to deal with an avalanche of cheating.[7]

The teaching and learning approach we take in this book is built on ten baseline principles:

Principle 1. Cheating is a natural and normal human behavior, most often enacted as a way to survive or as an error in judgment. Everyone does it, and the vast majority of students cheat a little. A few cheat a lot, and these students should be treated differently from the occasional cheater. For the most part, cheating is not something students do intentionally to dupe you, deceive you, or insult you.

Principle 2. Inviting you to prevent and respond to cheating is about encouraging you to extend your role as an educator, not asking you to become a "police officer."

Principle 3. Knowledge is constructed not received; therefore, as the instructor you are not the deliverer of knowledge but the facilitator of learning.

Principle 4. Students learn from mistakes, errors, and failures and it's instructors' job to create a culture accepting of errors. This also implies that redemption, even from serious errors in judgment, is both possible and desirable.

Principle 5. Higher education has a moral obligation to society not just to produce graduates, but to graduate ethical citizens and professionals who have the necessary knowledge and skills to contribute positively to a democratic society.

Principle 6. Students' decision to cheat is not caused by internal factors only, but by an interaction between internal and external factors.

Principle 7. Students do not enter higher education with fixed moral mindsets or intellectual ability; students can grow and learn in all areas.

Principle 8. Cheating by itself is not a problem to be fixed. It is a symptom of a number of other problems, primarily with pedagogy, the culture of higher education, and a mismatch between students' and instructors' expectations.

Principle 9. Cheating behavior is constantly evolving based on available technology, trends in assessment, and other cultural factors, but the reasons for cheating remain consistent. So, tackling the reasons, rather than the behaviors, is the solution.

Principle 10. Strategies for reducing cheating and enhancing learning should be multipurposed—enhancing other benefits such as student success, inclusion, and equity.

Who *The Opposite of Cheating* Is For

This book is for everyone involved in higher education, but particularly for the faculty and staff whose voices we hear in workshops, after talks, and on social media. Like the Reddit professor we quoted at the beginning of this chapter, these voices predominantly express frustration, anger, sadness, and offense over the state of academic integrity. They often ask for advice on how to respond to a student who has cheated, how the student could be so clueless, and what they (the professor) could have done differently. These colleagues realize that academic life has changed, especially in the classroom, and that they must find new strategies for adapting as well. This book is for them.

This book is also for the hardworking higher education staff who partner with faculty to reduce academic misconduct through training, pedagogy, and implementation of integrity policies. We hope that the ideas we share in these pages can inspire faculty and staff alike to see academic integrity as a team effort and, along with their students, work toward integrity as a goal. To that end, we have highlighted concrete strategies for preventing, detecting, deterring, and responding to academic cheating throughout the chapters. Some of these will be new to a given reader while others will be reconsiderations of familiar ideas in the context of making cheating the exception and integrity the norm.[8]

Finally, *The Opposite of Cheating* is also for institutional leaders, accreditors, and others in higher education who are responsible for ensuring that higher education delivers on the promise of authentic learning that we make to society. While the strategies we present are geared toward instructors, enhancing academic integrity and protecting the value of the university degree should not be their responsibility alone. Therefore, you'll notice some suggestions for administrators at the end of each chapter. We mean this to be a call to arms for academic leaders. Only a few of you lead colleges and universities in countries where there are national agencies that partner with you to help ensure higher education quality. Only a few of you lead institutions in countries where there are systematic and coordinated efforts to respond to the massive contract cheating industry. Only a few of you lead institutions with offices or organizations dedicated to academic integrity,[9] whether they be in the form of an academic integrity office like at University of California, San Diego (UC San Diego), or in the form of a student-led honor system like that at University of Mary Washington.

Instead, most of you lead institutions in which academic integrity is the sole responsibility of the individual instructor. As a result, thousands of colleges and universities are fundamentally ignoring cheating. We ask that you read this book to learn what instructors can do to help students be authentic learners (and thereby protect the integrity of your institution's degrees). Then, we ask that you take action to enhance institutional support for teaching and learning and to reduce institutional constraints on teaching and learning to support your faculty in their efforts. Support means providing learning assistance infrastructures, rewarding instructors for good teaching, making decisions that are in the best interests of student learning (rather than in the interests of enrollment or graduation rates and grade point averages), and designing quality online learning opportunities (rather than rushing to create remote classes simply to provide access). Reducing institutional constraints means building active and engaged classrooms, hiring more full-time instructors who are a part of the campus community, addressing students' basic needs (e.g., financial, food, housing), and offering faculty paid opportunities to implement the suggestions in this book.

In other words, while this book is focused on what instructors can do to deter cheating, the content is for anyone who cares about the integrity of teaching, learning, assessment, and the higher education degree.

Advice for Reading *The Opposite of Cheating*

Begin by reading chapter 1, then you can read the rest of this book in any order you like. The first chapter sets the stage: understanding why students cheat is fundamental to embracing the teaching and assessment strategies that we recommend you try.

The remaining chapters focus on applying these principles in practical ways, so feel free to flip to the chapter that addresses your most immediate concern. For example, if you are interested in learning more about how to talk to students about academic integrity and cheating, continue on to chapter 2. However, if you are really intrigued by the practical elements of how to protect the security of your assessments you might want to jump to chapter 6. Chapters 3 and 4 are about course and assessment design, respectively. You could read them together or separately, and you could read them before or after reading chapter 5, which walks you through general strategies for how you might engage with the students in your classroom. Finally, chapter 7—which focuses on how to respond to cheating—might be attractive to read immediately if you have an urgent need to respond to a cheating incident. If so, go ahead and jump to that chapter but otherwise, we suggest you wait until you have had time to focus on yourself and what you can do differently to prevent cheating and enhance integrity and learning.

The strategies within each chapter vary in their difficulty, required workload, and reach. Some you will find easy to implement because they take little time and, after reading this book, you will find you have the necessary knowledge and skills to administer them. Other strategies take a little bit more time or effort, but you will have sufficient background to implement them and may well choose to do so. Perhaps these strategies are ones that you can plan to complete as a small summer project or at a faculty development event. Finally, there are strategies that will require a lot of your time and effort because you will need to learn more details through reading other books or studying the research behind the strategy before you spend time crafting and implementing it. Perhaps you will need to apply for a teaching grant or attend a series of faculty development workshops to master these strategies.

Of course, whether you perceive a given strategy as easy or quite challenging to implement is highly individual. Your discipline; the size of your courses; the amount of teaching support you are provided; your teaching background; and your knowledge of pedagogy, course design, and assessment design will shape your reactions to the proposed strategies—and so they should if you want your choices to be meaningful within your specific context.[10] The point is that in each chapter, we provide a range of strategies, from those that may seem immediately doable to those that feel aspirational. That way, you can pick and choose what is right for you to try now and in the future.

The Learning Objectives

Our goal for this book is to help instructors begin rethinking their approach to learning with integrity and subsequently to change their teaching habits accordingly. One-time modifications to a syllabus or lecture are relatively easy, but systematic, week-by-week shifts in pedagogy require that we instructors retrain ourselves to work differently. Changing our teaching and assessment habits—the things we have always done and that used to work—can be difficult and stressful. The process is even worse when we feel we are forced to make the changes because of external events not of our own making. But keep two facts in mind: (1) disruptions to education occurred before the COVID-19 pandemic and the explosion of GenAI (remember calculators, the internet, and grammar checkers?), and (2) students have been cheating forever. Yes, in the age of AI, the prevalence of cheating may be accelerating, but the need for academic teaching to adapt has been present for decades. *The Opposite of Cheating* aims to equip you to make positive, proactive changes on your own terms, rather than feeling forced into rapidly reacting to external forces—which in the end, might do more harm than good.

The strategies we recommend are theoretically grounded in teaching and learning research and are presented as practical and manageable ways to combat academic cheating. We provide resources for promoting authentic learning on a deep level and for enhancing relationships among instructors, students, and their institutions in ways that will positively impact everyone. As a result, we offer many ideas that will be familiar to regular readers of the teaching and learning literature, and especially to those who work in teaching and learning centers. For those readers, the book will help you envision and articulate the web of factors connected to cheating and academic integrity. For those readers whose day jobs focus on academic integrity, you'll gain some practical and tangible advice for helping faculty to make integrity-focused changes. And for those readers who are just beginning to think about cheating as a problem and teaching strategies as a solution, welcome aboard. We hope we'll present the strategies you need not only to stay afloat, but to reach your destination.

1

WHY STUDENTS CHEAT

David has a daughter who loves to cook. Once when she was small, she asked to use a sharp knife to help prepare dinner. Incorrectly believing that she was old enough to do so, David shortly found himself driving to the emergency department one Sunday night. If you ask him on a typical day, David will say that he's a good and careful driver. He probably would have acknowledged that he'd be more aggressive in some situations than others, but only within reason. That Sunday night, the people sharing the road might have said otherwise. David found himself making left turns from the center lane around slower vehicles—which was definitely not within reason.

What does this have to do with cheating? Simply put, most students understand that cheating is wrong, or at least against the rules,[1] but evidence indicates that they cheat anyway. Like David, many students recognize that they might "cut corners" in some situations but don't believe that they would compromise their values. Yet they do. Students have a "price" for cheating, just as David had for reckless driving. That price is lowered by stress, limited time, and fear of failure. The price is raised by a wish to live a values-based life, a desire to learn, and a fear of being caught and receiving consequences. One way to frame this book is that it offers instructional strategies that raise the price of cheating.

Of course, the preceding description of the conflicted student doesn't apply to all students. Some would never cheat under any circumstances, whether for fear of being punished or because they value their education too much. Others see rules as being for other people and consider cheating to be a major component of their academic strategy. As educators we owe it to those students who would never cheat to do our best to curtail cheating so that the learning and credentialing system is fair. Students who cheat routinely (likely high scorers on the "dark triad" of personality traits: sociopathy, Machiavellianism, and narcissism) are unlikely to change their behaviors, so we owe it to our institutions to detect and report cheating in order to protect our institution's credentials from being devalued due to fraud.[2] Lastly, there are the students in the middle who are susceptible to making a bad decision to act dishonestly once in a while, in particular situations. This book is a guide to helping them by providing the fairest academic system possible.

There are many strategies that we can implement to help our students learn with integrity. To do this most effectively, we first need to answer a series of important questions about cheating that all boil down to one big one, "Why do students cheat?" Because this book, like others in the Teaching, Engaging, and Thriving in Higher Ed series, focuses on concrete, manageable solutions to difficult problems, this chapter is not intended to be a complete literature review on the topic of cheating. There are a number of good sources on this topic, written by us and by other authors.[3] This chapter, modeled after a style of literature summary used by Eric Anderman and others,[4] is meant to be an introduction to the research that bears on the recommendations made in the rest of the book. It's also intended to serve as a reference for those chapters, so pull out those sticky notes to mark the sections that you find most useful.

Self-Efficacy: Do They Think They Can Do the Work?

Try to remember the last time you sat down to complete a novel, high-stakes task. For example, imagine sitting down to begin writing the key chapter of your first book. This is something academics are expected to be able to do, but some revel at the prospect while others stress out. One reason for these varied responses has to do with an individual's beliefs about their own ability to complete a task to their satisfaction. Psychologists refer to these beliefs as *self-efficacy*.[5] Self-efficacy is a relative of self-esteem but is more closely connected to a single task or domain and focuses more on one's confidence in performing specific tasks than on overall self-worth. The relationship between self-efficacy and cheating is somewhat intuitive. Students who believe that they can complete academic work successfully (by their definition) are less likely to cheat. This relationship is most important when students face new tasks or when they do not view the pedagogical strategies as supportive.[6]

Let's consider two philosophical approaches to pedagogical strategies. In the first, Professor R is trying to get students to take the course seriously and "put in the work" to be successful. R therefore writes scary language into the course syllabus, talks in class about the importance of hard work and the failure rate in previous semesters, gives a quiz after the first week of class, and ensures that the class average is very low. R's motivation is well intentioned—he wants his students to learn and believes that fear is a great motivator of hard work. The fear-based strategy may be helpful for those students whose self-efficacy is very high and who need situational motivation to help them engage with the material. However, it is detrimental for those students who aren't sure they can do the work. Now imagine Professor D, who acknowledges that the material appears difficult, but points out that's why the students have an instructor and coursework to help them master it. Professor D starts out by sharing a story of his own struggles with the material and speaking about strategies for success. D's first assignment is designed to generate student effort and ultimate success (more on how to do this later in the book), which helps his students envision a path to mastering and completing the course.

In our example, Professors R and D are the same person separated only by time. David figured out that helping students develop a belief in their own abilities does not require reducing intellectual rigor. Instead, activities designed to build students' belief that they are capable of learning the material support more advanced work later. This is just one example of teaching the students we have, not the students we used to have or wished we had or used to be ourselves. If you find students are anxious about completing assignments or about understanding tricky concepts in your discipline, address not just their learning strategies but also their beliefs about their ability to learn. If they don't believe that they can learn and grow as learners in your discipline, they are vulnerable to taking shortcuts that you might consider cheating.

It's reasonable to ask, "Why is a student's self-image my problem?" The research on self-efficacy argues that it becomes your problem as soon as it interferes with student learning because student learning is the main goal of instruction. We would also argue that it is our problem because instructors can contribute to the shaping of students' self-efficacy. Consider the idea that girls aren't good at math or science. Stereotype threats like these can lead minoritized students to fear that they will fail to achieve in certain subjects, thereby reinforcing the disparaging stereotype. For example, the negative messages girls receive from an early age about their lack of scientific and mathematical ability have been shown to lower their performance on such tasks.[7]

Some academic disciplines have a long-standing culture of exclusion. "Some people are simply not cut out for our field," the belief goes, and courses are built to weed out such people early. Stereotype threats and self-efficacy beliefs are connected to Carol Dweck's notion of possessing a *fixed mindset* about learning in which students tell themselves, "I can't learn" and instructors tell themselves, "the students can't learn." The opposite is a *growth mindset* that says learning is possible.[8] It's difficult to switch mindsets but worth the effort, since research shows that students who possess a growth mindset are less likely to cheat and more likely to engage with their learning.[9] And instructors who possess a growth mindset are more likely to try a variety of instructional strategies to reach all of their students. Therefore, if it is within instructors' power to influence students to develop a healthy set of self-efficacy beliefs and a growth mindset for the course material, we educators should do that, if for no other reason than to reduce cheating.

A fundamental feature of a growth mindset is a positive approach to failure. Dweck and her followers have famously argued that students should be taught the mantra, "I can't do it . . . yet."[10] Students who approach failure as a learning experience (growth mindset) rather than as a referendum on their intelligence (fixed mindset) are, in this view, more coachable and more willing to take on challenges. Having a fixed mindset amplifies self-doubt because these students believe they cannot accomplish a particular task, that they will never be able to, and that failure is evidence that they are less intelligent than they wish they were.[11] This is a terribly vulnerable place for any person, and students with self-doubt about their work and a fixed mindset may choose not to engage with any task they find threatening. The result may be noncompliance behaviors such as missed deadlines, absences, or academic misconduct. For students in this situation, the possibility of being caught cheating is less painful than the guarantee of failure if they don't. The research on mindset belies the commonly uttered myth that "if students spent as much time doing the work as they did cheating, they would have succeeded." That correlation just isn't true for all students, at least not for succeeding to the level they desire.

In sum, students' beliefs about their ability to engage with course material are crucial. Those who believe they can do the work, or that they can learn to do the work, are less likely to cheat than those who have little belief in themselves. Pedagogical strategies that address these beliefs either directly or indirectly can have a powerful effect on students' behavior and, ultimately, on their learning.

Expectations: Do They Know They're Cheating?

Anyone who has taught first-year students in the past ten years probably has a story like the following. In a first-year seminar David taught, there was a solid to very good student. This student engaged in class discussions, completed work on time, and wrote effective short responses to weekly assignments. When the first writing assignment was due, a draft of a short research paper, the student submitted a pastiche of lightly paraphrased abstracts from relevant papers. Each source appeared on the works-cited page, but no in-text citations were included. David called the student in for a chat because the draft was a de facto example of plagiarism. During the discussion, the student appeared dumbfounded and explained, "This is exactly what they taught me at my (high-quality suburban) high school. I got A's on research papers there." It was David's turn to be dumbfounded. Of course, it's possible that the student wasn't exactly telling the entire truth, but the sheer frequency of stories like this lends credence to the explanation. In combination with recent changes to the writing curriculum, at least in the United States,[12] it is very possible that the student did not, in fact, know how to use research properly in written work.[13]

Between the two of us, we've seen more than 15,000 cases of academic dishonesty, and "I didn't know it was cheating" is one of the most common explanations students give for their behavior. It is fair to say that not all students who make this argument are speaking entirely in good faith. However, it is also fair to say that not all instructors make their expectations clear, nor do all K–12 schools teach research, paraphrasing, or academic integrity at the level that collegiate instructors expect, nor do the teachers address cheating or plagiarism when it occurs. Students don't always enter our institutions with the academic knowledge and skills that we anticipate.

Students seem to have particular difficulty in identifying plagiarism. While some types of plagiarism are easy for students to identify (straight-up copying and pasting, for example), others are much harder (such as when they have done minimal paraphrasing).[14] In fact, even faculty disagree on proper paraphrasing. Roig presented professors with examples of paraphrasing ranging from word-level substitutions to complete rewrites and asked them whether they would consider each example plagiarism. He found "moderate disagreement" about which ones were appropriate and which were not. When Roig asked a different faculty group to demonstrate paraphrasing, 25 to 30 percent appropriated text from the source.[15] This activity is worth repeating with your own students and colleagues. It's also worth doing the same thing with a GenAI tool like ChatGPT to see how the resulting paraphrased paragraphs compare to those generated by humans. You might find the outcome enlightening and a little disheartening. These findings are worth remembering when a student claims that they honestly thought they were paraphrasing properly. Perhaps this task is not as straightforward in the doing as it seems in theory.

Plagiarism isn't the only behavior difficult for students (and perhaps faculty) to identify. Waltzer and colleagues found that students also expressed uncertainty about many blatant examples of cheating.[16] In fact, when presented with vignettes describing behaviors such as unauthorized collaboration and use of inappropriate resources, students failed to identify cheating in 54 percent of them. This failure to recognize inappropriate resources is likely to become more pronounced with the advent of GenAI and the ways in which those tools not only appear authoritative and legitimate, but also obscure the sources they use.

The rules and expectations around collaborative work also commonly create confusion for students. Guidelines for appropriate collaboration can vary from course to course, and even within the same course. We've seen syllabi for programming classes in which some assignments are intended to be done completely in isolation, while others are open-note with internet use permitted and still others allow teamwork. It's not hard to imagine that a student could honestly confuse which rules apply to a particular assignment or situation.

It is also true that the line between appropriate tutoring and collaborative misconduct can be unclear to students lacking experience with well-executed tutoring. Students want to help one another, and often want to do so with integrity, but they don't always know how. We have both seen cases in which a well-meaning student shared a paper with a classmate, believing that the classmate had already submitted the assignment or at least had already completed their work. On its face, this is a potential violation of an academic integrity policy, but it could also be an honest misjudgment made from a place of empathy.

In at least some of the cases where students commit academic misconduct, they give it no moral consideration at all, because they don't realize they're doing anything wrong (though see chapter 7 for ways to help them become more ethically discerning). In short, there is substantial ambiguity and confusion about the rules of integrity among students at the high school and college levels.

Values: Do They Think They're Doing Something Wrong?

"Rules are made to be broken." "If you're not cheating, you're not trying." These sayings are so ubiquitous that it's hard even to find their source. Obviously, we're not endorsing these beliefs, but they're useful to reach a full understanding of reasons why students might cheat. Actually, they're useful to remind us why *anyone* might sometimes behave in a certain way even when they know that it's wrong.

Tricia, for example, often reminds audiences that while all of us consider ourselves to be safe (or at least not reckless) drivers, most of us violate the speed limit on a regular basis. Why? Clearly, we know the rules are in place and we understand the logic of road safety. We speed because we want to, we're in a hurry, everyone else is doing it, it's fun, or the risk of getting caught is low. As David's story at the beginning of the chapter shows, we're able to provide rather good rationalizations and justifications for speeding, even though our actions are doing the very thing we're trying to prevent—endangering ourselves or others.

In American football, it's against the rules for players on offense to grab the jerseys of their opponents. This infraction, cleverly referred to as "holding," usually results in a ten-yard penalty. Holding is against the rules, yet it happens two or three times per game in the National Football League (or at least that's how frequently it's enforced).[17] Perhaps students view cheating the same way that you view speeding or football players view holding. It's against the rules, but in a transactional way. Sometimes it's worth the risk of a ten-yard penalty for the benefit of interrupting a competitor's play. It's worth the risk of speeding for the benefit of getting your child to the hospital even a minute or two sooner. Yet, faculty see cheating as something more akin to reckless driving (changing lanes often while speeding) or putting laxatives in the opponent's water supply, behaviors that are egregiously against the rules, violate community trust and our sense of fairness, and potentially even cause physical harm.

From a research perspective, there is evidence that students don't think cheating is morally wrong to the same extent as their instructors do. Donald McCabe and colleagues' classic work showed a substantial gap between student and faculty ratings of the severity of cheating behavior, particularly the use of (new at the time) electronic devices to cheat.[18] Waltzer and colleagues found that 87 percent of students in their sample were uncertain about whether it was wrong to engage in acts that they identified as cheating.[19] Students who think cheating is a "gray area" or a not very serious act tend to self-report greater engagement in cheating.[20]

Moral Disengagement: Why Is It So Easy to Violate Our Own Morals?

Our colleague Jason Stephens, a moral development psychologist, calls the decision to cheat despite the rules a *judgment-action gap*.[21] In his research, he gave students a list of behaviors (some cheating, some not) and asked them to identify whether each behavior was a personal choice, against the rules but not really wrong, or wrong "regardless of laws or rules" (i.e., morally wrong). Using this rubric, Jason found that most students do see cheating as morally wrong, not just against the rules. Those who consider it to be a personal choice are comparatively more likely to cheat, and those who rate cheating as morally wrong are much less likely to do it.

So, many students know that cheating is wrong and believe that they shouldn't do it. However, as we've seen, they don't always recognize a cheating behavior when they face it. In other cases, they know that their behavior would be cheating and therefore wrong, yet they do it anyway. Why? It happens because humans are remarkably able to set aside their values when they deem that the situation requires it. Psychologists call this ability *moral disengagement*, and criminologists label the method of morally disengaging as *neutralizing*.[22] There are four common types of neutralizing, all of which may sound familiar, either because you've heard them from a student or you've used them yourself in your own life.

- **Denial of responsibility.** The student justifies their behavior by claiming that they didn't cheat intentionally or that the behavior was an accident. To quote the musical *Chicago*, "And then he ran into my knife! He ran into my knife TEN TIMES!"
- **Denial of the victim or denial of harm.** The student believes that cheating is a "victimless crime" and that their actions benefit them while harming no one.
- **Condemnation of condemners.** The student blames the professor, the academic integrity office, or the university more broadly for their behavior. The student believes that the instructor doesn't like them, the instructor is grading unfairly, or the system is rigged against them.[23]
- **Appeals to higher loyalty.** The student uses loyalty to rationalize cheating. Imagine a student in danger of failing a course who asks a friend for help with an assignment. Imagine that student is a friend, teammate, or compatriot who expects loyalty from the friend. When someone feels loyalty toward another person, it becomes much more difficult to deny help to that person, leading to neutralization.[24]

The key point to recognize is that the power of neutralization lies in the fact that the neutralizer believes what they are saying, which is different from deliberately making excuses that even the excuser doesn't believe. The process of neutralizing enables *ethical fading*, in which the moral aspects of an action or decision fade into the background. When ethical fading happens, people are better able to engage in an unethical act without feeling remorse or guilt or harming their self-perception as a good person.[25]

Neutralization can occur any time a student engages in an action that contradicts a moral or ethical standard they hold. As you consider changes to your course or your assessments, keep in mind the power of neutralization and, in particular, the perception that students may have of instructors' actions. A recent attempt to reduce cheating in a coding class was quite successful statistically, but students reported increased neutralizing attitudes.[26] One even said, "The professor put more effort in trying to find 'cheaters' than in actually teaching the class." We're concerned by this finding because it indicates the techniques may have reduced cheating in the short run but antagonized students, who will be better able to neutralize their attitudes in the future. The sweet spot, then, is to reduce cheating and improve attitudes toward learning without increasing neutralizing attitudes and alienating students.

Contract Cheating Services: What Messages Are Students Receiving?

As we have discussed, in order for students to identify a behavior as wrong, they first have to be able to identify the behavior as cheating or plagiarism.[27] The contract cheating industry seems to understand this reality better than those of us within higher education, and they leverage it to their advantage. Look at any contract cheating site, defined as a site where students can hire someone to complete academic work (in part or in total). On those sites, you will see deft use of euphemisms referring to their services as "homework help," "tutoring," and "expert help." They also expertly use rationalizations to justify the use of their products, positioning themselves as just another service like ride-sharing or food delivery:[28]

- "Fast. Simple. Always with you."
- "Get help and become one more happy . . . client."
- "Learn with us. From first day to finals, get homework help, exam prep & writing support—tailored to your courses."
- "Our top-level essay writing service will take away all your education-related worries."
- "We've built our paper writing so that every student can relieve their academic stress and ace their semester without being left penniless in the process."

The use of the word "help" is particularly brilliant because that term is often used in higher education when advising students about how to be successful in school. Look at university websites.

Cornell University emphasizes that "successful students ask for help!" University of Michigan reminds students that "academic success requires asking for help." And Columbia University encourages students, "Ask for help when you need it."[29] By casting the use of their services as getting "help," contract cheating services neutralize the morality of the situation and stimulate the act of cheating. More simply said, "euphemistic language can make harmful conduct respectable."[30] Of course, students can use euphemisms (aka neutralizing words) themselves to engage in self-deception, but perhaps it is more powerful to hear them from others and to see them repeated on multiple websites. The power lies in the ability of the metaphor to transform "morally wrong behavior into socially acceptable actions."[31] My university encourages me to get help, I need help, and these sites are offering help when I need it. And it's not just contract cheating sites that offer to complete entire assignments for students anymore. GenAI chatbots are integrated directly into the platforms that students use to complete their work. Imagine how difficult it is for a traditional-age college student, or an older student returning to college after a long hiatus, to resist that "help me write" button in Google docs, for example. Blank page syndrome be gone! (We'll address the appropriate [and not so appropriate] uses of cognitive offloading in chapter 4. For now, we're merely pointing out that technologies and companies are leveraging natural help-seeking behavior to convince students to make use of them.)

It is this help-seeking behavior that leads even honest students to believe that it is acceptable to hand over their thinking and doing to another human or a machine. GenAI tools are easy to use, many are free, and all are available 24/7. Contract cheating companies are as easy to find as typing "write my essay for me" into a search engine, which leads students to sites that help them disengage their moral injunction against cheating. Other students are recruited or, dare we say, even seduced into contract cheating by nefarious actors. As recruiting strategies, contract cheating companies advertise directly to students through emails sent to their .edu email addresses, create fake study groups on social media (think WeChat) or discussion platforms (think Discord Channels), partner with legitimate companies (e.g., "get a subscription to our company with your Sallie Mae loan"), and even host on-campus events.[32] This is why Australian higher education institutions have blocked access to many contract cheating websites.[33] Now, if a student receives an advertisement for a cheating service, at least they're not receiving it at their official university email address and they can't access the website on university-provided equipment or broadband. This is one way to communicate to students that the action is unethical and the university does not support or approve of it. It also aims to limit the power of euphemisms to trigger ethical fading. Some colleges and universities tried the same approach to countering ChatGPT when it was first released in 2022. However, they quickly realized that although the contract cheating industry and large language models (LLMs) can result in the same outcome (students outsourcing their thinking and doing), a ban is not the answer for addressing technology that will be integrated into students' daily and professional lives.

Peer Effects: What Are the Cool Kids Doing?

Are you interested in what your students think about cheating and what influences them to cheat? Ask them. In one of David's courses, he did just that. Specifically, David asked, "Is your behavior influenced by the behavior of your peers?" Students' answers were enlightening. First, they said that when they see a lot of people cheat, it minimizes the seriousness of the behavior ("It's not that big of a deal") and may even make those who don't cheat feel like suckers. Second, they said that seeing even one other person cheat might influence them, especially if that person was someone was worth emulating. For example, an upper-class student might influence a first-year student, or a successful student might influence one who is struggling. Third, witnessing a single successful cheating episode might shake up automatic patterns, leading a normally honest student to consider cheating as an actual option. Finally, the students explained that every time they see a peer cheat and get away with it, that makes cheating seem like a better idea.[34] While parents and educators might like to think that we are more powerful influences on student behavior than peers are, it's more likely that student cheating encourages student cheating, just like peers can influence any number of other behaviors.[35]

The research evidence for this phenomenon is substantial. For example, there are findings from both psychology and economics that seeing other students cheat is a risk factor for cheating oneself.[36] In surveys, students who believe that their peers often cheat report cheating more often themselves.[37] Those who believe that their peers think cheating is acceptable are also more likely to cheat. Thus, peer effects seem to be among the most important influencers of cheating, even more so than moral values.[38]

You might be thinking "Great! Then nothing I do will matter if peers are the most powerful influencer of student behavior!" Do not despair. Good teaching can still influence student behavior. A set of unpublished data collected by students at the University of Mary Washington showed that good teaching could reduce students' belief in a "culture of cheating."[39] Another example involves engineering professors at UC San Diego, who in the middle of emergency remote teaching during the COVID-19 pandemic decided to introduce oral assessments in their classes. The mere introduction of oral assessments convinced students that their peers were unlikely to cheat, that integrity would be maintained, and that they could focus on learning.[40] We discuss the implications of both these studies in more detail in later chapters.

Fundamentally, better teaching creates a culture of authentic learning, which reduces cheating. Students often look to one another to decide how to behave, but they do also look to the teacher, and when they see a focus on learning being modeled and learning occurring, this can make a big difference in their choices. Every time educators help a student to learn authentically, that student will contribute to the beliefs of peers and potentially influence their behavior toward integrity.

Narcissism: Do the Rules Apply to Me?

Do you know someone who is generally friendly as long as they get what they want? Someone who is happy only when they are the center of attention? There's a good chance that this person tends to flout the rules and say things like, "It's not cheating if you don't get caught" or "The rules don't apply to me." These descriptions apply to the traits of narcissism, Machiavellianism, and sociopathy, or the *dark triad* of personality traits. While the dark triad is not a diagnosis per se, people who have these traits tend to require positive reinforcement (narcissism), are willing to use other people or situations for their own advantage (Machiavellianism), and have little regard for the effect of their behavior on others (sociopathy). These traits, particularly sociopathy, are associated with higher levels of self-reported cheating.[41]

Unfortunately, there isn't much that we as instructors can do to change fundamental personality traits in our students. Understanding these traits does however help us to reduce cheating. These traits are not an all-or-nothing proposition, so students who are only mildly narcissistic, for example, may still be influenced by their learning environment and by the beliefs they hold about a particular course. Even the most hardened sociopaths are less likely to cheat if they believe that cheating is counterproductive, so thoughtful course design can influence their behavior. If simply doing the work is the easier, cheaper, or less stressful course of action, or if they believe that they will be caught and that the punishment will be severe, a student with dark triad traits may opt not to cheat or choose to avoid your classes. While the focus in this book is on prevention, as humans, students will still sometimes cheat and so we must act accordingly.

Motivation: What's the Point?

Someone we know told us the story of a student named John. John was very accomplished in his extracurricular activities and was a solid student. However, John struggled in a particular upper-level course. He attended office hours every week, prepared meticulously, and yet only earned a B– in the course. The instructor assumed that John would never enroll in a similar course again. Yet, much to the instructor's surprise and delight, John appeared on the roster for an advanced seminar on the same topic the following semester. The instructor saw John before class and commented on how delighted he was to see John in class again, thinking that it was a surprise given his earlier struggles. John said something to the effect of, "I know I didn't do that great in your last class, but I think I almost got it, so I didn't want to stop trying." John's dedication to mastering the material represents the extremely important role that one's motivational orientation plays in school and beyond.

As John's case illustrates, a student's motivational purpose influences all aspects of their academic life. Some students enroll in school or in a particular class because they love the material, love learning, or respect the teacher. These motivations are referred to as *mastery goals,* or motivations that lead to a desire to master the material for its own sake. However, most students (also) care about the extrinsic rewards of higher education. Grades lead to a degree, and a degree is a ticket to a better job and ultimately a better life. These motivations are often described as driving *performance goals,* or the "desire to demonstrate competence."[42] Performance goals are driven by but are different from *extrinsic goals.* Extrinsic goals define success by external benchmarks, whereas performance goals define success by competition with other students. Extrinsically motivated students want an A (not to *produce* A-worthy work) and want to get a good job (not to *earn* a good job). Mastery, extrinsic, and performance goals are not mutually exclusive. Most students who have a desire for learning also want to have a good job when they finish their education. Both groups are likely to want to do well relative to friends, peers, and familial expectations.

Recently, David asked a group of students why they were in college. Most of them answered that they wanted to get a job and make good money. This isn't surprising. He asked them why they chose not to become plumbers or learn another skilled trade, which is a much surer way to financial security than most options that a psychology degree provides. Their answers were more subtle. Some mentioned their parents' expectations, others said that they didn't want to do "hard work," and yet others talked about "return on investment and wealth ceilings." A few even mentioned learning marketable skills. Not one student mentioned learning for its own sake, competence as a citizen, or well roundedness. This very unscientific poll highlights the extrinsic and performance messages that motivate a small sample of students in the United States. It should serve as a reminder that our students aren't necessarily motivated by the same things that we were, and that we should create learning environments with their actual motivations in mind. More on this in the following chapters.

Students shouldn't really be blamed for their focus on extrinsic goals such as grades and degrees, rather than on learning or growing personally and professionally. According to *US News & World Report*, tuition and fees at major universities increased by more than 100 percent between 2003 and 2022, while workplaces continue to demand higher education for many positions.[43] This confluence of factors leads students and their families to feel that they have little choice but to pursue higher education, even if it does not suit their interests or situation. The pressure to succeed in order to justify the financial and opportunity costs of postsecondary education is high. In India in 2015, for example, there was massive cheating on university entrance exams as depicted in a famous photo of supporters scaling the walls of a testing center to pass information to their test takers.[44] For these prospective students, a place at a prestigious university can represent the opportunity to change the fortunes of their entire family, so it's easy to see why parents succumb to the pressure to give their children a literal leg up. These sorts of pressures, even on a much lesser scale, can lead students to internalize performance and extrinsic goals and neglect the relatively subtler joys of mastering new material.

The lesson of this story is that students who are motivated by jobs, grades, and praise from others are likely to cheat.[45] Conversely, students who wish to learn for the sake of learning report that they are unlikely to cheat, and they actually do cheat less.[46] Interestingly, healthy competition in classes where students are also expected to develop mastery can lead to improved learning outcomes with little increase in cheating. However, when students' motivations are to avoid looking bad, losing face, or seeing themselves as inferior to peers, they are likely to cheat more often, especially in the absence of mastery goals.[47] In sum, the goals that students have for their education and the messages that teachers and institutions send them can make a big difference to their behavior in class.

Procrastination: Where Did the Time Go?

In a large number of cases we've seen, students cite desperation in the face of deadlines as a contributing factor to academic misconduct. Evidence supports this intuition. Across many studies, students who report more procrastination also report cheating more often.[48] Students themselves cite failures of time management as a major factor in actual instances of cheating.[49]

Of course, some time-management issues aren't related to procrastination per se. Students in the twenty-first century are, in fact, busier than their predecessors were. For example, as of 2016, the US Bureau of Labor Statistics reported that the average college student spent 3.5 hours on educational activities and 2.3 hours in paid employment on a given day.[50] According to the Center on Education and the Workforce, 70 to 80 percent of students reported having a job during college, with 40 percent of undergraduates working full time or more.[51] The same report indicated that 19 percent of working learners were also caregivers to children. Time pressure is a substantial contributing factor to academic cheating, whether it is caused by a lack of time management or simply a lack of time.[52] As educators consider ways to address these concerns, we must be mindful that the students we teach today are experiencing different stressors (as a group) than their predecessors were.

Instructor Effects: What Is It about Chemistry?

Do you have a colleague who appears to be a "cheating whisperer," someone who can detect plagiarism without any effort and who seems to spot cheating even behind their back? Most institutions have some instructors like this, and there are two nonexclusive explanations for why. One is that they really are psychic or otherwise attuned to misconduct in their courses. The other is that their classes bring out dishonesty in students, so there really is more for them to spot. Conversely, we all have colleagues who boast that their students can't, won't, and in fact never do cheat in their classes. While we hope that they're right, we suspect that they are probably overly optimistic (or even a bit naive). Assuming that there really are differences in the amounts of cheating that take place in various classes and that the differences can't be explained solely by the factors we've already discussed, what are the most likely reasons for them?

In 1999, Pulvers and Diekhoff conducted an important study of student-instructor interactions as they relate to misconduct.[53] The authors asked students to rate their courses on a set of scales measuring the classroom environment, and the results showed that students were less likely to report cheating or rationalize dishonesty when they felt that

- they had individual relationships with their instructors;
- they had the opportunity and desire to engage with the material inside and outside of class;
- they had formed cohesive relationships with at least some of their classmates;
- the course was enjoyable overall;
- their time was well spent; and
- the course was well organized.

These qualities seem similar to the recommendations often given in a new instructor workshop. There appears to be nothing magical about reducing cheating. Good pedagogy, at least as perceived by the students themselves, makes a difference in reducing cheating. It bears repeating that we are *not* recommending simply being nice to students or making the coursework easier. We *are* recommending being nice—because why wouldn't you be?—but, of course, never at the expense of student learning. We are also advocating for making the class logistically easier, not by dumbing it down, but by designing it mindfully with student learning at the forefront. When students are supported through their learning challenges, they will often opt for authentic learning over cheating.

Cost-Benefit Analyses: Is Cheating Worth the Cost?

Students who do cheat don't cheat all the time.[54] Why do students choose not to cheat, then? The answer appears to be a process of self-regulation in which students weigh the benefits of cheating against the potential longer-term consequences. For the most part, students are susceptible not to threats of dire consequences, but rather to the likelihood of being caught and shamed or punished. As with the parenting of children or pets, threats don't work as well as consistent responses to undesired behavior.[55]

We acknowledge that the decision to (or not to) cheat is ultimately made by a given student at a particular moment. At the same time, that decision is influenced by that student's perceptions of the consequences inherent in each situation. Economists, decision scientists, and learning theorists alike understand that the environment and our perception of it shapes our choices. Many external factors can increase the chances that a student will cheat, and many of these factors interact in complex ways with the psychological factors we've been discussing. For example, a student who consistently believes that cheating is wrong may not be as susceptible to environmental changes as a student who is somewhat ambivalent in their values. Unfortunately, this also means that students who have made cheating an academic strategy are unlikely to be swayed by changes in their environment.

Yet most students are sensitive to the academic costs and benefits of their behavior, particularly when grades are on the line. Given the currency that grades have in society today, some students may be willing to trade other goods, such as time, reputation, or even money, for an increase in their grades. For some, time is their most precious resource, while for others it's money. Outside of the context of misconduct, there are constant tradeoffs among these resources. For example, one student might trade spending time at a talk by Douglas Adams in the Michigan Union Ballroom for time working on a statistics course (to pick a not-at-all-random example) or might hire a (legitimate) tutor at their own expense to help them pass chemistry. Within the realm of misconduct, students often must decide whether to risk a lower grade by performing their work honestly or risk sanctioning or loss of reputation for the chance of earning a higher grade by cheating.

Students are not particularly sensitive to the severity of consequences for cheating.[56] Rather, the likelihood of being caught has more influence on student cheating than does the severity of the consequences once caught.[57] In a survey of students, David and his colleagues found that severity of consequences did not impact self-reported cheating rates at all. In a classroom setting, Dench and Joyce found that warning students that they had been caught plagiarizing on an earlier assignment reduced plagiarism on future assignments by 65 percent.[58] In sum, the old adage that "1,000,000 times 0 is still 0" remains true. No matter how severe the possible sanctions, students are only sensitive to them if they believe that there is a high chance of being caught.[59]

However, there is some nuance to the impact of sanctions, depending on the sanction type. Charness and colleagues found that people are less likely to cheat when sanctions are morally based (rather than financial).[60] Although these are small experimental studies, they highlight a really important point: students are sensitive to the social and moral repercussions of being caught cheating just as much and sometimes more than the academic repercussions. This brings us back to the power of peer norms: if students believe that cheating is morally repugnant to their peers (in honor code schools, for example), then the fear of violating those norms is a more powerful disincentive to cheating than fear of being caught by the professor.[61]

Final Thoughts

Students are human beings, which means they are complex and their motivations and behaviors are hard to predict, explain, or control. Students might cheat because they don't believe that they can earn the grade they want. They might cheat because they fail to realize their behavior constitutes cheating. They might cheat even though they understand the behavior is against the rules because they don't find the rules morally convincing or because they can neutralize the immorality of their behaviors. They might cheat because their peers are doing it (or they believe their peers are doing it), and anyway, they have run out of time, grades are too important and, well, their teacher sucks. A small handful might cheat because they possess one or more of the dark triad of personality traits. And all might cheat if they think there is little likelihood of getting caught or that no one would actually disapprove of their behaviors if they were caught. Or, more likely, cheating results from a combination of two or more of these factors.

But do not despair! There are solutions, and the good news is that many of the strategies to make cheating the exception and integrity the norm are also multifunctional. That is, most of the things we'll advise you to do in the remaining chapters are not just good for integrity, but also for learning, and they might even make your job of teaching more enjoyable.

2

COMMUNICATING INTEGRITY

Consider this scenario. A student posted your assignment prompt to ChatGPT and asked it to produce an outline for an essay. They then used that outline and asked ChatGPT to generate some ideas for each section, which they then incorporated into their essay without attribution. Did that student cheat? What if the student had posted the prompt to ChatGPT, asked it to write the essay, then submitted the output as their own work? Would that be cheating? What if the student instead gave the assignment to a human—a contract cheating provider—who produced an essay that they then submitted as their own. Did that student cheat?

Once you have reached your own conclusions, survey your colleagues in your academic department. What percentage agree with your determination? What about colleagues outside your academic department but within your disciplinary sphere (e.g., other engineers, other social scientists)? What about colleagues within your discipline but employed in other higher education institutions, both within your country and around the world? Our guess is that you would not achieve 100 percent agreement in your department, let alone across your institution or your discipline.

After decades of surveying students and faculty about cheating, the research is clear. There is no unanimous, shared definition of cheating on which one can rely. Take this 2002–10 snapshot from a leader of this research, Don McCabe. His data were based on more than 100,000 survey responses, which remained very

TABLE 1 Percentage of students and faculty who rated a behavior as moderate or serious cheating

	Undergraduate students (%)	*Graduate students (%)*	*Faculty (%)*
Cut-and-paste plagiarizing	59	71	85
Copying from another student's test or exam	93	96	98
Collaborating on assignments meant to be completed individually	37	59	84
Using crib notes during an exam	90	95	98

Source: Data from McCabe, Butterfield, and Treviño, *Cheating in College.*

stable over the period of his study, though they haven't been updated since. McCabe and colleagues presented a list of behaviors to undergraduate students, graduate students, and faculty, and asked them to rate the degree of cheating in each behavior as not at all, trivial, moderate, or serious cheating.[1] Table 1 presents the percentage who rated the behaviors as moderate or serious cheating. More recent findings are also concerning, since students report that cheating using GenAI is less objectionable and ethically more acceptable than similar behaviors like plagiarizing from another student or hiring a human for contract cheating.[2]

There's a tremendous amount of variance in judgment, not just within but between groups. Why does this matter? As we explained in the last chapter, students are more likely to cheat when they do not recognize a behavior as cheating or when they do not see the behavior as morally wrong. Also, due to the lack of agreement among faculty, students receive mixed messages, which can make neutralizing easier for students; for example, "If working together is so wrong, how come my math professor lets us do it?"

It's easy to say that college and university students should already know about academic integrity since they have been attending school for twelve years. However, with every teacher having different rules about cheating, how could they possibly know what *you* consider cheating unless you tell them? When students perceive inaction by teachers and institutions in response to cheating, they begin to doubt their own knowledge and beliefs about cheating. Let's be clear. Students have not only received mixed messages about cheating their entire academic lives, but they have also never been taught how to make decisions when faced with an ethical dilemma (such as "to cheat or not to cheat"). We address the ethics education vacuum in chapter 7. For now, let's concentrate on how teachers can consistently and effectively communicate with students about academic integrity. We use the word "with" purposefully. Rather than communicating *to* students about integrity, communicate *with* them.

The very first time you address academic integrity is likely in the syllabus. In fact, most faculty start and stop talking about academic integrity in the syllabus. So, before we get into how to communicate integrity, let's consider how talking about integrity in your syllabus can go oh so wrong.

The Syllabus: Don't Miss a Golden Opportunity

Let's start with an example from a computer programming course. In this syllabus, the students are informed that they have weekly programming assignments that are due every Sunday by 11:59 p.m. Programming assignments 1–4 must be done individually, but students can choose to do assignments 5–9 in pairs. When students choose to do assignments in pairs, they are each to submit the same assignment with both their names clearly indicated on it. There are no other guidelines for working in pairs. The syllabus ends with "don't cheat by working with other students when you are submitting an individual assignment and don't cheat by using Co-Pilot to write your program for you."

What are students learning about academic integrity from this syllabus? Very little. There are many unanswered questions. For example, is academic integrity being upheld if the students take turns doing their paired assignments, say, Jorge does assignment 5, Xinyi does assignment 6, Jorge and Xinyi do assignment 7 together, then Jorge does assignment 8, and Xinyi does assignment 9? What if Jenny decides to do her assignments on her own, but when her program doesn't work, she asks a classmate for help in debugging it. Is that what "working with other students" means? Or, in the same scenario, Jenny asks Co-Pilot to help her debug her program. Co-Pilot didn't "write" her program for her so is she upholding academic integrity?

This kind of ambiguity creates problems at many levels. First, students may try to do their work the right way but still unintentionally violate course policy. Second, students may come to resent their instructor's cavalier attitude toward misconduct because they wish the rules were clearer. In our experience, decisions about academic misconduct often seem clear to instructors but mysterious and unfair to the students. This can lead to resentment and provide a rationale for misconduct. Third, students don't understand the pedagogical reasoning for such a complex set of rules, so the rules feel arbitrary, capricious, and perhaps disrespectful of their autonomy. When students feel disrespected, neutralizing attitudes become more prevalent and misconduct is easier to justify. Furthermore, faculty may feel that students should simply ask when a rule is unclear, but students don't always realize that they have a different understanding of the rules than their instructor does (until they are reported for an integrity violation).

Let's look at another example syllabus, this time from a math class. In this syllabus, students are told that homework assignments are to be done individually yet the homework questions come from a textbook for which there are readily available solution manuals. The syllabus contains a vague statement about academic integrity, something like "Please do not cheat. You know all about academic integrity from the tutorial you had to take in your first year. If you've forgotten that, here's a link to the policy. It's up to you to take responsibility and complete your work with integrity. If you don't, I will catch and report you and you will receive an F in the course." Despite this warning, some students proceed to complete their first assignment by copying their answers from the solution manual. They receive full points with no accusation of cheating. So, the students do the same thing on the next assignment. Again, full points and no accusation of cheating. And this pattern of behavior continues. Do the students realize that they are cheating? Do they understand why it is wrong? Which message is being reinforced: that cheating is unacceptable or that it doesn't matter?

Let's look at one more example. This time from a writing-intensive course. In this syllabus, the instructor is very clear about what constitutes plagiarism. In fact, the instructor provides a five-page "how not to plagiarize" guide that explains why, when, and how to cite, with many examples and tips. The instructor is also very clear that plagiarism is a serious academic integrity violation that, if it occurs, will be reported to the academic integrity office per the university's policy and will result in a 0 on the assignment in question. Winnie understands the rules of citation in principle, but she struggles with writing in the language of instruction. So Winnie decides to write her paper in her native language then uses software to translate the paper into the language of instruction. Finally, she gives her paper to a friend to edit, to make it sound better. Winnie is very proud that she understands the course readings and that she formed and communicated her ideas in her paper. She cannot wait to see the good grade she'll receive. Imagine Winnie's shock when her paper is returned with a big fat F and a note from the teacher reading, "I don't believe that you wrote this paper. You either plagiarized, used ChatGPT, or contracted with someone else to write it. I'm reporting you for cheating." Should Winnie have known that using translation software was cheating? Is it, in fact, cheating, based on university and course policy? What about the editing assistance from a friend? Does it matter how much editing—editing content versus grammatical errors—the friend did? How would the student know that?

The syllabus, or your course website, provides an initial opportunity to effectively communicate with your students about academic integrity. While it's important to make your syllabus as clear as possible, you cannot stop there. Think of the syllabus as the beginning, not the end, of the conversation about academic integrity with your students. Before we discuss the strategies for having these conversations, we want to make it clear that communicating about academic integrity is not the sole responsibility of individual faculty members. The institution has an important role to play as well to ensure that there is continuity and unity in the messages students are receiving about academic integrity. Institutional communication about academic integrity also sets a cultural tone for students that instructors can use to connect a given course to a larger set of values. At a minimum, higher education institutions should create a course or tutorial (online or in person) to teach all incoming students about academic integrity. See, for example, Epigeum's course on academic integrity, the Academic Integrity Course at the University of Auckland, or the Academic Integrity Tutorial at UC San Diego.[3]

An institutional tutorial should, at the very least, cover the most commonly misunderstood academic integrity violations and the core values or integrity code that the institution wants students to uphold. Judgment scenarios, quizzes, and videos of students talking about academic integrity are core pedagogical tools for such tutorials. Beyond tutorials, institutions should maintain channels of communication about academic integrity policies and practices that provide students with easy ways to have their questions answered (even anonymously). Institutions should also offer ongoing academic best practices training through writing centers, academic success coaches, and other student-focused units of the institution. Individual instructors must then build on that cross-disciplinary introduction to ensure that students understand what is and isn't academic integrity in their particular course and with their particular assessments (because decisions about cheating are intimately connected to the course or program learning objectives).[4] So, now let's turn to how you could communicate academic integrity in the classroom.

Define Academic Integrity and Its Opposite—Cheating

Consider this story about Susan, a student in Tricia's Academic Integrity Seminar. Susan said to Tricia, "So I wrote my paper and then I sent it home to my mom like I always do. But when my mom sent it back, it was really different and so I asked her, 'Mom, you didn't go on the internet for any of this stuff, did you?" and my mom said no. But then Turnitin said that my paper was 40 percent plagiarized." A tear started rolling down Susan's face. Tricia asked her, "So, what's the lesson learned?" and Susan said, in all seriousness and without a hint of sarcasm: "Check the work my mom does?"

It turns out that all her life, Susan had been trained essentially to coauthor her assignments with her mom to ensure an acceptable grade. Through this practice, Susan learned to care only about the product that was produced; the means behind the production didn't matter, nor did the learning meant to be reflected in the product. Was Susan a cheater, or was she a child who was trying to please her mother with what she thought mattered—getting the grade? Susan knew that copying from the internet was wrong but was incapable of recognizing that having her mother contribute to her assignment was also wrong. Of course, we don't excuse Susan's behavior, but the response to it should reflect this context and the goal of helping Susan become an authentic learner.

Students enter your classroom with all types of past experiences, experiences that have shaped their beliefs, attitudes, choices, and behaviors. So, on day 1, define academic integrity and cheating in the context of your class. Do so in writing (whether in a syllabus or on the online course platform) and orally. As it should be clear by now, it is insufficient simply to say, "Don't cheat. It's bad." Yet, if you examine higher education syllabi posted on the internet,[5] you will see statements that offer generalized definitions of cheating and the punishments that might ensue, such as these:

- Cheating is wrong. If you do it, I'll catch you and fail you in the course.
- No student shall engage in an activity that undermines academic integrity or facilitates academic integrity violations by others.
- Changes in policy give instructors little choice but to report plagiarism to the Academic Integrity Coordinator. You should know the university's policies on academic misconduct by now.

- As academic integrity is a cardinal scholarly virtue, it is important that an apprenticeship program implement policies that support the development of academic integrity. Hence, there are consequences for those who flout this virtue (more on these consequences below).
- Academic dishonesty is considered a serious offense. Students caught cheating will face an administrative sanction, which may include suspension or expulsion from the university. It is in your best interest to maintain your academic integrity.

When such statements are not followed by a clear definition of the most misunderstood cheating acts, or a definition that counters the external messaging students receive that cheating is an acceptable strategy, they do little to change students' mindsets or behaviors. While students already generally perceive cheating to be wrong, the behaviors they identify as cheating may differ from those you or your peers identify. Therefore, you have to define what cheating is.

What Cheating Is and What Academic Integrity Is

Of course, you cannot list every behavior that might violate academic integrity in your class. You'll likely miss some. Also, listing every prohibited behavior doesn't help your students develop their ethical reasoning skills. At most, it would teach them to know the rules and obey them—not exactly the types of critical thinkers that higher education institutions seek to develop. So, cataloging cheating behaviors for your students is not necessarily the goal.

Instead, we suggest that you talk about academic integrity according to the International Center for Academic Integrity's Fundamental Values statement, which can be phrased as "the courage to uphold honesty, respect, responsibility, fairness, and trustworthiness even when it's difficult to do so."[6] Then give some vivid examples of the behaviors that would uphold those values and the behaviors that would undermine them. For example, using the work of another person or a machine (e.g., GenAI) and passing it off as your own would not be honest. Using a nonauthorized aid on a test would not be fair to your peers in the class who are not cheating. Giving a false excuse for missing an assessment undermines trust. And so on. These are just examples, because you would, of course, use ones that are specific to your class. A syllabus for a composition class that doesn't include tests would not have to address test-taking behavior, and a syllabus for an introductory math class likely wouldn't need to review essay writing.

Although an exhaustive catalog of misconduct is not helpful, we strongly recommend highlighting the most common integrity pitfalls in your courses. Because life doesn't have a soundtrack like the creepy music that signals incoming peril in an after-school special, it's important that you help students develop their own internal warning system to avoid difficult choices. Take a look at each graded assignment in your class—how have students undermined integrity on those assessments in the past or expressed confusion about the ethical boundaries of completing them? In our collective experience, students typically have been unsure if and how they could reuse their own work and how they should (or should not) work with other people (and more recently with machines) in the process of learning, studying, and completing their assessments.

The use of machines or technology to complete assessments deserves special mention, given the rapid evolution of GenAI since November 2022. While we do not recommend a complete prohibition against using GenAI tools for a number of reasons we discuss in chapter 6, we understand that some faculty may still have legitimate reasons for banning its use in some cases. So, if you want to prohibit GenAI, be clear about the prohibition and the reasons for it (and be prepared to secure that assessment as discussed in chapter 6). If you do not want to ban its use, you'll need to talk about the ways that students can and cannot use GenAI in their work. Start with the learning goals of the assignment and the reasons for asking students to do the work. Then let them know which parts require their direct effort and which can be aided by GenAI tools.[7] Once students understand the point of the assignment, they can use their judgment to meet the spirit of it, even if the letter of your assigned rules is unclear. These principles cannot be uniformly defined for all assessments or all classes. You will need to figure them out for your own courses, likely by playing with GenAI tools using your own assessments. It might also be useful to talk with your students about how they are already using GenAI tools to discern whether they might be using them in ways that would amplify rather than hinder their learning. Consider reviewing the assessments and their associated learning outcomes with the students, discussing with them when and if it would be acceptable to use GenAI on each assessment while still achieving the learning outcomes. You can use their input and your new insights to finalize your GenAI policy. Perhaps you don't incorporate all of their ideas, but you will be better able to explain the rationale for your policy. If you do allow GenAI use on your assessments, we recommend requiring that (1) students retain the history of their engagement with the tool, (2) acknowledge which tool they used and for what portion of the assignment, and (3) reflect on the use process, commenting on how it helped or hindered their learning.[8] This is especially important since AI detectors can't determine which AI tool was used or *how* it was used. Information about the student's process can be very important from the standpoint of promoting learning and determining whether the student fairly and honestly demonstrated their learning.

Why Academic Integrity Matters

Now that you have defined cheating and academic integrity, it's critical to talk about the why. Why should students care and why should they act with integrity when cheating may help them reach their short-term goal (i.e., an A in the class)? Let's be frank. Our global education system has converted diplomas into commodities in the work marketplace, which means that grades, credits, diplomas, and degrees are what people covet, not the knowledge and skills (or integrity) they are meant to represent. Grades are currency in the knowledge economy. Secondary school students need them for admission into tertiary institutions. Undergraduates need them to be accepted into graduate school. And employers still use a university education as a minimum application requirement for most positions, though that is changing as they discover that college graduates are often not sufficiently knowledgeable or skilled.[9]

To counter the ever-prevalent and much louder cries of extrinsic motivators such as grades, we must talk about why academic integrity matters, and we must stimulate intrinsic motivations to learn and be honest. Why does integrity matter in the daily and future lives of our students? It's best if you can personalize the answer or anchor it in your discipline, if possible. Here are some ideas for talking about the why:

- We learn better together when we can trust one another. You trust me to design a useful and engaging curriculum. I trust you to learn and then honestly and fairly demonstrate your learning according to the rules and standards. You trust each other not to create an unfair environment by cheating. Think about your own personal relationships. Are you friends with anyone you can't trust? Likely not. We care about trust, so let's act that way in this class.
- Grades are currency in today's society, but only if they accurately reflect your knowledge and abilities; if you cheat to get the grade, then you have cheated your own personal and professional development.
- Have you ever experienced an unfair class or test? Me too. Let's make sure we don't feel that way in this class.
- In the world of Generative AI, there are uniquely human skills that you will need to develop while in college: a distinct personal voice, presentation skills, creativity, empathy, situational awareness, and moral virtues.[10] Focusing on developing these skills will position you to succeed far better than you will if you focus simply on the grade. Here's how the activities in this class will help you work on these skills if you engage with them with integrity.
- I know many of you wouldn't choose to take this class if it wasn't required. If you do your assignments as designed, you'll develop the following skills in this class that will help you in school, work, and life. . . .

- A diploma might get someone their first job, but competence is what helps them keep that job and get future jobs. Don't waste the opportunity to learn the skills that will get you ahead at work and in life.

Ideally, make talking about academic integrity a two-way conversation with your students. Ask them questions about when they have been dishonest or been lied to and how it felt. Or ask them if they've ever let someone else down or been let down by someone. You can keep this fairly light by using reasonably commonplace examples, such as promising someone you'll help them move and then cancelling at the last minute, or telling your parents you were at one friend's house when you were really somewhere else. Use their answers to make connections with your policies and practices, highlighting that your values are actually closely aligned with theirs. Students (mostly) want to do the right thing when they know what it is and when they are reminded of their values.

How You Will Handle Integrity Violations

Students (like most human beings) are notoriously bad at long-term thinking because they are hardwired primarily to "respond to clear and present danger,"[11] and because they think of themselves as moral and therefore not likely to cheat.[12] Even so, it is important to be clear that you will respond to cheating and specify what you will do. Talk about your professional and ethical obligation to respond per your institution's policy. Talk about the consequences previous students have received for cheating in your class (or in the course in general, including in sections taught by others).

Talking about consequences in the form of a powerful story (with pseudonyms, of course) may linger in some students' minds and deter rash decisions because stories linger and are more meaningful than directives, for example.[13] If you don't have your own stories, you can use examples from popular culture like the story of Jayson Blair, the *New York Times* journalist who sabotaged his career by routinely and habitually plagiarizing and fabricating information for his stories.[14] Or, tell the story of Lance Armstrong, who ruined his reputation, had his wins stripped from him, and erased his future ability to participate in competitive racing because he was found to have cheated by using banned substances while racing. Use diverse stories that will be representative of the students in your class and their career or life goals, because the idea is to trigger their emotions and help them identify with the characters, which helps them to retain the story (and lessons learned) in their own minds.[15]

Whatever you decide to state in writing about your response to integrity violations, be sure you are willing and able to follow through with it. We have encountered many faculty who want to appear "tough" in their syllabus so they state that any student caught cheating will be given an F for the course. Yet, when a student cheats on an assignment worth 2 percent of the total grade, they regret their tough stance and want to simply give the student a 0 on the assignment in question. While that does feel like the fairer decision, it also means that by going against their own policy, the instructor undermines their trustworthiness. As a result, students might be less likely to believe the instructor's other policies or promises. Furthermore, it means that the instructor will need to backtrack on the policy for all their students or risk a (rightful) accusation that they play favorites. The moral of the story is this: don't put anything in writing that you are unlikely or unwilling to do.

Finally, give some thought to when you will have these conversations. It's tempting to speak with students about academic integrity at the outset of a course, when many instructors have a "syllabus day" to ease into a new semester. It's great to get the ball rolling early, but this isn't really the best time to have the only serious conversation about the topics we've just covered. First, students don't see themselves as cheaters, and so probably won't apply general lessons to specific situations. If people expected that they would run out of time, they might start tasks earlier, yet this lesson is notoriously difficult to internalize. Second, students are most likely to cheat when they don't understand the material or the assignment. Therefore, talking about misconduct whenever you assign a high-risk activity helps them to behave appropriately under stress. The lessons from week 1 will be a distant memory by week 10, when a difficult assignment challenges their integrity. Finally, integrity is about trust and relationships, which are nascent at the beginning of the course. After some time has passed, students will (you hope) begin to trust you as an instructor and be better able to internalize lessons about integrity. When a level of connection has developed, they will also be more likely to ask you hard questions about which behaviors you consider to be cheating and which ones you don't.

Use Integrity Nudges

After that initial conversation, what's next? Anything of value bears repeating, especially because the forces promoting ethical fading (e.g., advertisements for contract cheating firms) do not stop after day 1. Traditional honor code schools in the United States have understood this for centuries. In traditional honor code schools, students learn an honor pledge, are expected to memorize it, and recommit to it on every assessment. They may learn this during the application process or at the welcoming convocation, where they have to publicly commit to the honor pledge (as at the University of Mary Washington). Then they see the pledge posted everywhere—perhaps even in every classroom, on every syllabus, and on every assignment or test.

There is nothing magical about an honor pledge, though. Your school is not Hogwarts, so the exact wording isn't what's important. It's the intent, the reminder that students live in a community that upholds trust and the other fundamental values of academic integrity. Thus, a school doesn't need to have an honor code to implement integrity pledges. Non-honor-code schools around the world have adopted the idea of using pledges as mechanisms for committing students to the practice of academic integrity. Integrity pledges can be especially useful in asynchronous courses, since they can be automated as part of the assignment structure. Following are examples of pledges from three universities:

- **Academic integrity pledge.** I affirm that I will not plagiarize, use unauthorized materials, or give or receive illegitimate help on assignments, papers, or examinations. I will uphold fairness and honesty in my work and the work of others.—University of Pittsburgh (USA)[16]
- **Honor pledge.** I recognize the importance of personal integrity in all aspects of life and work. I commit myself to truthfulness, honor, and responsibility, by which I earn the respect of others. I support the development of good character and commit myself to uphold the highest standards of academic integrity as an important aspect of personal integrity. My commitment obliges me to conduct myself according to the Marquette University Honor Code.—Marquette University (USA)[17]
- **Academic integrity pledge.** We act with integrity and professionalism and uphold the highest ethical standards. We are committed to transparency and accountability.—University of Queensland (Australia)[18]

Integrity pledges like these are intended to nudge ethical sensitivity in students and trigger their inherent sense of morality,[19] thereby reducing the temptation to cheat even when cheating opportunities occur. That is the theory anyhow. It stems largely from the work of Don McCabe and colleagues regarding honor codes and pledges, although behavioral economists have shined much of the recent light on the use of nudges to shape and influence behavior. There are two main premises behind the effectiveness of nudging: (1) human behavior tends to be based on "fast thinking," thinking that is based on heuristics and known/familiar patterns, so it is intuitive, nonreflective, and often not conscious; and (2) the environment and the people around us are powerful shapers of our behaviors. Nudging serves to interrupt this fast thinking and induce deliberate and deep thinking that can sway the person in a different, more desirable, direction.[20] Picture a student who is facing an assessment due date. They quickly jump to resolving this pertinent question: "How can I get this assignment done in time?" They unconsciously go through their playbook formed by past experiences until they find a strategy that works to meet the goal of getting the assignment done and submitted. They may also simultaneously be having conversations with their classmates about the assignment, thereby being influenced by the peers' strategies. An effective nudge delivered at just the right time may shape the student's action away from cheating and toward integrity.

However, the empirical research on the efficacy of integrity nudges is mixed. Some of the empirical research suggests that nudges can be effective for reducing cheating.[21] It turns out however that one of the most convincing empirical studies was based on falsified data,[22] and at the time of this writing, other studies on nudging conducted by the involved authors are under review.[23] Other researchers have found that academic integrity pledges seem to have no impact on student behavior, except, counterintuitively, when the impact is negative; that is, pledges can lead students to perceive that cheating is common and therefore acceptable.[24] Tricia and colleagues found that nudges may only work if they are salient;[25] timing, content, delivery method, and sender may all influence the effectiveness of an integrity nudge. Research by Bryan and colleagues supports this finding.[26]

Bryan and colleagues conducted an elegantly simple experiment to study the nudge effect, by putting people in a situation where they have an opportunity to cheat for money. Interestingly, when participants were asked to choose a number between one and ten, more chose an odd number (typically three or seven) than an even number. The researchers used this baseline information to create two experimental conditions to test whether they could nudge participants to tell the truth about their number choice, even when there was a monetary incentive to lie. The researchers would know participants were lying if the ratio of odd to even number choices changed markedly from the baseline measure. Their previous research had shown that self-referential nouns ("cheater") were more effective than verbs ("cheating") at nudging.[27] So, in this study, participants were randomly assigned to one of two conditions. In the first condition, they were told that the researchers were studying the prevalence of *cheating* using a game that allowed the researchers to estimate the overall amount of cheating without knowing whether each individual participant was cheating. In the second condition, participants were given the same study explanation except the verb "cheating" was replaced with the self-referential noun "cheaters."

The researchers predicted that people in the "cheater" condition would be more likely than those in the "cheating" condition to tell the truth (that is, pick an odd number at the same rate as in the baseline) in order to avoid being labeled with that negative noun. Sure enough, fewer people cheated in the noun than the verb condition. While the nudge proved effective, the researchers wondered whether the face-to-face context might have influenced the effectiveness of the nudge. When they repeated the experiment in an online study, they found the same effect: the self-referential noun ("cheater") decreased cheating behaviors. This is a good reminder that basic psychological principles can often be just as relevant in online contexts and courses, sometimes even more so. Finally, the researchers repeated the online experiment again, but this time added a control group (where no discussion of cheating occurred) and found that giving people the label "cheater" reduced cheating behaviors to zero. It is relevant to note that nudges using "cheating" had no positive influence on behavior; those participants cheated just as much as those in the control condition.

In this simple experimental study, integrity nudges were only effective when they were salient. Saliency is enhanced if the nudge is self-referential, easy to understand, and striking, and if it presents an opportunity for acting.[28] Bryan and colleagues showed us one way to make the nudge self-referential, but asking students not to be cheaters in your class may not be palatable. So, what are some other options? Since perceptions of peer attitudes and behaviors are powerful influencers of student cheating, nudges that relay student-to-student messages may have higher relevancy. Consider this example. After discovering a significant number of students cheating in her class in the early days of emergency remote teaching during the COVID-19 pandemic, a professor at UC San Diego asked all the students in the class to anonymously submit the reasons why they don't cheat or why it hurts them when their peers cheat. The professor then collated those responses, looked for themes, and messaged them back to the class. The number of cheating incidents decreased for the remaining assessments. The moral of this story is to take advantage of any opportunities you find to reflect students' voices back to them, especially when they confirm the majority viewpoint that cheating is wrong.[29] Perhaps you could even co-create an integrity nudge with the students to make it more self-relevant (more on this next).

"Don't be a cheater and tell me you chose an even number when you didn't" is an easy-to-understand nudge that follows from the language in the Bryan study. It is short and to the point, which may be especially important in an academic setting where students are stressed and experiencing high cognitive loads at the times when they are tempted to cheat (for example, taking an exam, having a major assignment due).[30] It is also salient because it was presented right before the opportunity to act. What kind of nudge could be similarly easy to understand and yet striking in the context of a student completing an academic assessment? Some faculty we know have tried using cheating statistics (e.g., "Last time I taught this class, I reported ten students for cheating and all received an F in the class"). The message is simple and salient. However, Cagala and colleagues found that if a nudge gives the impression that cheating is common, it can actually increase the likelihood that a student might cheat.[31] So, statistics must be followed by an explanation of the consequences. Many faculty have also tried to use integrity pledges that are aspirational and positive, rather than negative or prohibitive (e.g., "I choose integrity because I am an honest person" versus "I will not cheat on this assignment").[32] Other research suggests that if you go this route, it's best to use the phrase "I promise" and have students make the pledge publicly, since public declarations of promises are commitments to act, which (can) effectively influence behaviors.[33]

Bryan and colleagues also reported that nudges work best when they give the recipient an opportunity to act in alignment with the nudge. So, although you should talk about integrity, and perhaps even present the nudge, at the beginning of the term, the nudge must be repeated right before students begin or submit an assessment for credit. The research on whether students should be reminded at the beginning of the assessment or the end is mixed, partly due to fraudulent data in one study.[34] If the nudge is delivered before they begin the assessment, the students have the opportunity to choose integrity throughout the process of completion. If it's delivered at the end of the assessment, students can make the choice not to submit an assessment they cheated on and accept a lower grade or to correct the aspects that constitute cheating and accept a late penalty. Making the tough choice to accept a lower grade or a late penalty is more difficult for students who are extrinsically motivated by grades and therefore less likely to be effective with them than with students motivated by mastery. The ways in which we deliver the nudge may also influence timing and the behavioral impact. Tricia and colleagues found that delivering nudges via email likely compromised their effectiveness because students may not read their emails or may not read them in time.[35] So, we recommend putting integrity messages directly on the assessments up front. Alternatively, you can split the nudge by asking students to write out their promise at the start of the assignment but sign it at the end. Although it is more complicated, this strategy has the advantage of framing students' behavior at the start of the assessment and engaging their self-image when they sign their promise.

It's also worth noting that timely reminders are not the only form of nudge. Outside of the academic integrity context, the most commonly discussed form of nudges are decision architecture defaults.[36] This is a fancy way of referring to the outcome of a decision if no choice is made. For example, since 2023, the SECURE 2.0 Act has required employers in the United States to automatically enroll new employees in the employer-sponsored retirement plan. If the change works as expected, millions of Americans will begin saving for retirement earlier. This sort of default nudge can work in your classes as well. For example, when using an online testing tool, disabling access to the course materials during quizzes won't thwart a dedicated cheater, but it might raise the barrier high enough to discourage the average student from cheating. If you have ever used the healthy-eating strategy of skipping the snack aisle at the grocery store, you've used choice architectures to your benefit already.

In summary, despite inconsistent findings of a nudge effect in the literature, nudges still seem like a possible way to encourage ethical behaviors in the classroom, just as they have been useful in eliciting other positive behaviors such as paying taxes, voting, using safety belts, and telling the truth.[37] In addition to possibly being highly effective, nudges are also a resource-light way to communicate about integrity. So, we encourage readers to try this approach, while cautioning you against fully replicating Bryan and colleagues' study by calling your students cheaters (because context matters). Use the technological options in learning management and online course delivery systems to automate nudges to be delivered at critical times (for example, twenty-four hours before an assessment is due); this can be an effective way to nudge students asynchronously. We also recommend that if you implement integrity nudges, track the effects because there is a need for more research and understanding in this area, particularly in real class settings.

Co-create Ethical Standards with Your Students

Creating ethical standards with your students is a way to communicate integrity with an us together rather than you-versus-them dynamic. Co-creating ethical standards has many benefits. Co-creation naturally opens a conversation about ethical conduct, so you don't feel like you are preaching integrity to your students. Co-creation also enables students to hear from their peers which behaviors they find acceptable and which they don't. This is effective because, as we discussed in chapter 1, cheating is powerfully influenced and shaped by what peers are doing, what peers think, and what students think their peers are doing. Co-creation can engender greater buy-in from the students because the act of co-creation creates culture, and it is culture, not the cultural artifact, that actually influences behaviors.

Ethical standards are a way to codify shared beliefs about or expectations for appropriate, or ethical, behaviors in a particular context. Accountants have ethical standards, as do engineers, doctors, pharmacists, lawyers, sociologists, teachers, and so on. Many organizations, including Samsung and Adidas, also have ethical standards.[38] Do a quick search of these ethical standards and you will see the frequent use of words that convey the fundamental values of integrity: courage, honesty, respect, responsibility, fairness, and trustworthiness.[39] Regardless of what they're called (codes of ethics, honor codes, statements of values, or something else) ethical standards, if they are widely known and discussed, help to signal ethical conduct and make community members less accepting of unethical conduct.[40] McCabe and colleagues would endorse this claim but remind us that this codification—they specifically studied honor codes—is a reflection of the underlying values and beliefs within the culture; that is, the code isn't a top-down imposition but a bottom-up consensus. Hence, co-creating the standards with, not for, your students is effective.

Codifying ethical standards helps to communicate expectations and articulate shared values. Everyone in the classroom comes to that learning space with different backgrounds, identities, and lived experiences, which can all lead to different understandings of integrity and learning. So, it is unreasonable to expect that all of your students would respond to the same assessments or class activities in the same way. What one student may consider cheating, another may consider collaboration or getting help. In fact, studies have shown that much of the unethical conduct that occurs in organizations arises not from unethical intentions but from a failure to recognize the ethical dimensions of the situation at hand.[41] Codifying ethical standards and providing concrete examples can help activate an ethical awareness in students. Ethical standards are also effective because they may reduce the misperception that unethical conduct is widespread, which may help reduce misconduct.[42] This makes sense given that that students are more likely to cheat if they believe that others are cheating.

To codify ethical standards with your students, we suggest a simple process like cowriting a statement of values or a code of ethics based on the International Center for Academic Integrity's six fundamental values.[43] For example, list the values on the left side of the page, then make a column for the students and a column for the instructional team. For each value, you and your students discuss and decide what behaviors would uphold the value. For example, in the "honesty" row, students might identify "always submit work that you did yourself, or credit the sources you used to produce the work" for their column. For the instructional team, the students might identify "always provide truthful feedback to students that will facilitate their learning and improvement." You could provide students with the statement of values table ahead of the class session, ask them to reflect on it individually, then have them spend about twenty minutes in class discussing it in small groups, with each group contributing to the statement in a shared document. This process can be done in small or large classes, although for large classes, you might have all students contribute asynchronously to the document, which you then finalize and present to the class for a short discussion and agreement. This mutual conversation and co-creation demonstrate to the students that it is everyone's responsibility to create and maintain a culture of integrity in the classroom.

You could also choose the code of ethics route. It is similar to a statement of values in that you start with the values and the behaviors that would uphold those values. A code of ethics, however, would also list behaviors that would undermine those values, as well as how the class community would hold themselves accountable to the code. For instance, when Tricia teaches using team-based learning pedagogy,[44] she presents her students with a prewritten statement of values (this is the academic integrity portion of her syllabus). Then she has her student teams create their own team code of ethics. They create this code themselves during class time, with the only parameter being that their team code of ethics cannot conflict with the class statement of values or the university's academic integrity policy. The process of creating the code provides students with a structured opportunity to do what everyone should do when starting work with a new group of people—establish shared understandings about acceptable and unacceptable behaviors. For example, for the responsibility value, a team might agree that each member will show up on time and prepared for the week's activity. They might debate what behaviors would undermine responsibility, like procrastinating on the pre-class work or repeatedly freeloading on the team. Then, when discussing accountability, they might come up with a rubric like, "First violation, warning. Second violation, conference with the professor. Third violation, dock team contributor points." This whole process of creating a code of ethics need not take more than twenty to thirty minutes of class time, especially if you preface that time with some pre-class work where individual students start thinking about what type of team environment they want.

Codifying ethical standards in statements of values or codes of ethics may be insufficient to guide fully ethical behavior. Bazerman and Tenbrunsel caution that it is also necessary to identify and remedy ethical "sinkholes," those scenarios where abstract ethical values succumb to short-term and present pressures (such as deadlines).[45] To address such scenarios, assign a self-reflection exercise for the students to complete after the class discussion. Ask students to reflect back on times when they acted in ways contrary to their own values (for example, lied to a friend, cheated on an assignment, been disrespectful to someone) and what led them to act that way (such as time, pressure or stress). Then, have them provide a short plan—with concrete strategies—for how they will resist those ethical sinkholes this term. These self-reflections do not need to be evaluated, but if time permits, it would be helpful to identify sinkhole and strategy themes in the assignments, then feed those back to the class (anonymized) so that the students can learn from one another.

This may also be a good time to speak with your students about GenAI tools, not just tools that generate a product (like ChatGPT, Dall-E, and Co-Pilot), but also those that assist with learning and research (like PowerNotes and ResearchRabbit) and those that assist with writing (like Grammarly and QuillBot). You may be surprised at how much you learn simply by asking your students, "How do you ethically use GenAI tools to assist you with your learning and academic work?" or "What are you worried about when it comes to the use of GenAI by me or other students?" Any statement of values or code of ethics that is devoid of any mention of GenAI will be incomplete. Students and teachers alike are learning about these tools and how they can be used, but also how they *should* be used. Avoiding this conversation because you are unsure of where you stand will only lead to problems (ethical or otherwise) for your students.

If you choose to co-create a statement of values or code of ethics with your students, you should still have some statement in the syllabus that will function like an anchor to the institutional policy and an introduction to the creation exercise that you'll do together. The syllabus can cover the basics of academic integrity—the behaviors you're not willing to compromise on and the values that you think are important. Then, facilitate students talking to one another about integrity. This strategy will take more class time and more facilitative effort on your part than other options. However, it's not only entirely doable, but hearing your students talking about values and how they want to uphold them in the class can be really rewarding. It will remind you that most of your students want the same thing as you do—an honest environment in which everyone can learn.

Final Thoughts

Communicating about integrity is a necessity because of the diversity of opinions and beliefs about what is (and isn't) behaving with integrity in your particular class. You cannot assume that all of your students are on the same page as you are about cheating, especially in the age of artificial intelligence. So, you need to communicate early and often. Communicating early sets the table; it allows students to understand the expectations for how they need to go about their academic work this term. Communicating often serves as a behavioral nudge, a timely reminder to students that they should act and should want to act with integrity. Communicating about academic integrity is no silver bullet. Because the reasons why students cheat are complex, unfortunately so too must your solutions be. Communicating is certainly the very least you should do. Yet, if you only communicate about integrity but don't take a good look at how you teach or design your assessments, then you'll likely still encounter more cheating than you'd prefer. So, in the next chapter, we'll turn to the course design strategies you can adopt to enhance the likelihood that integrity will prevail over cheating.

Next Steps

1. Choose one communication strategy that you will implement next term and one that you will think about in more depth for later adoption:
   a. Updating the academic integrity statement in your syllabus
   b. Using integrity nudges
   c. Co-creating ethical standards with your students
2. Think about the causes of cheating outlined in chapter 1 and plan for how you will begin to mitigate their effect with your chosen strategy. For example, how will your chosen strategy help students to see the value of learning in your course (increasing intrinsic motivation)?
3. Decide what you will say about GenAI. Will you prohibit its use throughout the course? Will you allow it but require acknowledgment? Or will you have a conversation with your students about it and draft a policy together?
4. For institutional leaders, take a look at your academic integrity policy, training opportunities for incoming students, and cheating definitions. Do they provide sufficiently clear and understandable examples? Also, hold a conversation on your campus about cheating, or survey your faculty and students, to determine points of agreement and disagreement and where more clarity is needed (especially around new technological developments such as GenAI).

3

DESIGNING COURSES FOR INTEGRITY

Our friend and colleague Professor Cath Ellis has been known to caution faculty that you can't design academic misconduct out of your classes, but you can certainly design it in. Let's look at an example. A professor at a large public university designed his class around two specific parameters: (1) his lack of grading assistance, and (2) his need to publish a book to obtain tenure (note that neither was focused on what was best for students). Given those parameters, the professor broke the grading scheme into three chunks: 20 percent for attendance, 35 percent for a five-hundred-word essay and 45 percent for a thousand-word essay. The attendance grade was easily gamed, with students using clickers to record attendance for absent students. The two essays were both high stakes yet easy to complete. Surely the students wouldn't cheat on such short essays? But, in fact, they did; the professor had to report thirty students for contract cheating that term. This is what Cath meant by designing in cheating, particularly contract cheating (or cheating by artificial intelligence). The class and assessments were perfectly structured to entice contract cheating—high-stakes assignments that were so generic and so short that they would be easy for GenAI to generate or cheap to contract out. In the era of contract cheating services and AI-based writing, students also perceive a dishonest strategy to be a low-risk, high-reward opportunity.

So we agree with Cath that although there is no way to "cheat-proof" an assessment or a class, you can do the opposite: you can design cheating *into* a class, creating assessments that motivate the average student to find a reason and a way to cheat. What the course instructor does and doesn't do matters. Generally, students are more likely to cheat when they feel that (1) an assessment is insurmountable (they lack self-efficacy); (2) succeeding is more important than learning (they are focused on performance or extrinsic goal orientation); (3) there is an easy means of rationalizing cheating; and (4) cheating is easy to do and doesn't seem risky. So, even though we can't control students' behaviors or beliefs, we can create a learning environment that mitigates these cheating factors. Yes, it will take time and energy to revamp courses and assessments, but this chapter provides the strategies that will give you the best bang for your buck—changes that will increase learning, improve student engagement, and ultimately reduce the temptation, need, and ability for students to cheat. The benefit of the strategies presented here is that, as James Lang noted in *Cheating Lessons*, changes that reduce cheating often also result in increased authentic learning.[1]

Articulate Learning Objectives

Have you ever been in a professional or personal situation in which you had no idea what others expected of you? How you were supposed to act. What you were supposed to say. Perhaps why you were even there. How did that experience make you feel? We suspect maybe lost, perhaps frustrated, even possibly desperate or angry as you tried to find some sort of guidepost or compass to help you find your way. Maybe you have felt that way every time you've joined a new academic department or started a new degree or even started a new relationship. Not knowing what people expect of you, especially people who matter, who have (real or perceived) power over your future does not usually engender good feelings or even effective behaviors. Being a student in a course without learning objectives, or with bad learning objectives, likely feels a lot like that.

In a well-designed course, learning objectives are the keystone from which instructors construct the precarious arch that is a syllabus.[2] Objectives serve as a mission statement for a course, notifying our students about the knowledge and skills we hope and expect they will gain by putting effort into the class. Learning objectives also set the stage for intentional course design, guiding our choices in pedagogy and assessments and ensuring that they are always centered on student learning.

Creating dynamic learning objectives is an excellent first pedagogical step because they help to enhance integrity and reduce cheating in four ways:

1. Foregrounding the practical, meaningful goals of the course gives students a target to aim for and the satisfaction of achieving it or at least making progress in that direction. Learning objectives downplay performance goals and focus a student's attention on mastery or achievement.
2. The focus on goals helps students to see their efforts in terms of what they have learned rather than their mistakes. Once students believe themselves capable of successful learning, self-efficacy can blossom, undermining the need for cheating.
3. Learning objectives make it possible for students to understand how their grades are being determined, increasing their perception that the course is fair. When activities and assessments align with instructors' stated objectives, students have faith in the learning process and are less prone to form neutralizing attitudes.
4. Lastly, using a taxonomy of learning like Bloom's to raise learning objectives from low levels (for example, remembering) to higher levels (for example, creating)[3] can help. Of course, in introductory courses, low-level learning objectives are necessary. However, if students are asked to create, evaluate, or analyze instead, they will be more engaged (and less likely to develop neutralizing attitudes that can lead to cheating). High-level learning objectives also require more engaging pedagogy, which is also structurally more effective at deterring cheating.

One strategy for prompting self-reflection about your learning goals is one that David initially resisted but has found immensely helpful over the years—Fink's Taxonomy of Significant Learning.[4] Any number of taxonomies might serve to help you evaluate your assessment choices, but we recommend Fink's because of its breadth. Fink presents a six-segmented taxonomy of learning goals, all of which can be applied in most situations. It's not necessary to use every goal for every assignment, but each course should seek to achieve as many types of goals as possible.

Fink's segments are foundational knowledge, application, integration (connecting material to people and ideas), the human dimension (learning about oneself and others), caring (creating an emotional connection to the material), and metacognition. Foundational knowledge is an important part of Significant Learning but it's far from the only kind of learning goal. The variety of goals and associated objectives gives instructors a plethora of ways to evaluate students' work, which helps to create authentic assessments. Instructors can use the Significant Learning taxonomy as a tool for reflecting on the criteria that connect an assessment to learning outcomes, or as a component of course or assessment design to ensure that course goals are broader than a mere collection of content knowledge. In one of the first teaching and learning workshops David attended, he was quite resistant to the notion that cognitive psychology could really have an emotional component or a human dimension. In hindsight, his attitude was pretty shortsighted, but it is also true that some courses and types of material lend themselves to certain goals more than others.

Hence, it is critical to write meaningful learning objectives. In some classes, instructors may have little control over the official learning objectives because they are predefined by others. Such objectives may be overly general, with every specific sanded away to ensure that all instructors can work with (or around) them in their own courses. This situation offers an opportunity to look within the stated objectives and bring them to life for your particular group of students. To that end, ask yourself, "What do I want students to know or be able to do by the end of this course?"

Then write each item in a way that is actionable and measurable,[5] as well as easy for your students to understand.

If you're struggling with writing good learning objectives, this may be one task for which you can turn to GenAI tools for assistance. You could, for example, ask ChatGPT what defines a meaningful learning objective. In the following extract, Tricia asked the tool, and it immediately provided the SMART rubric for creating goals:

Tricia: What defines a meaningful learning objective for a university-level course?

ChatGPT: A meaningful learning objective for a university-level course should be clear, measurable, and directly related to the course material. It should guide the course design, instruction, assessment, and ultimately, students' learning. Here are some characteristics that define a meaningful learning objective:

- **Specific.** The objective should clearly state what the students should know or be able to do by the end of the course. The more specific the learning objective, the easier it will be for students to understand what is expected of them and for the instructor to assess their performance.
- **Measurable.** Each objective should be able to be measured in some way. This could be through exams, assignments, projects, presentations, or other forms of assessment.
- **Achievable.** The objective should be realistic and achievable for students within the duration of the course, considering the resources available and the prior knowledge and skills of the students.
- **Relevant.** The objective should be directly related to the course content and skills. It should contribute to the overall goals of the program or major.
- **Time-bound.** The objective should be achievable within a specific time frame, typically the duration of the course.

Not bad.[6]

The more information you give a GenAI tool about your course, the more it might be able to provide you with fodder for consideration. For example, if your syllabus has a course description paragraph but is missing learning objectives, you could provide ChatGPT with your course description paragraph as a prompt. Of course, the more context you provide, the better. For example, you could provide ChatGPT with your complete syllabus and ask it to write learning objectives at specific taxonomic levels. Naturally, you should always review and edit GenAI output before using it. Consider GenAI tools as assistants not replacements for your disciplinary knowledge, training, and experience.

Once you have written engaging learning objectives, the next step is to align the content, activities, and assessments in your course with those objectives. For example, in a research course, as your instruction moves from a level of remembering to one of evaluating, students should practice evaluating research both in class and through formative assessments:

- **In class.** An activity that has students apply newly learned material can be an engaging way to help them practice key skills. For example, a "spot the research design flaw" game show is a fun way to engage students in evaluating particular aspects of research.
- **Formative assessment.** To reinforce a learning experience, students might be given a homework assignment asking them to reflect on their performance on a quiz or to explain one of their incorrect answers during an activity.
- **Summative assessment.** There are any number of options for a summative assessment of this goal, including an essay question on an exam, having classmates peer review each other's research, or having students critique their own research as a final project.

As another example, the learning objective of "Students will understand the scientific method as it applies to psychology" can be reified in many ways to encourage students to engage with the material. Understanding the scientific method is passive, but designing or critiquing a study, making a methodological choice, or considering the pros and cons of a particular methodological decision are active and concrete goals. The more concretely students connect activities with their own learning the better, because they are less likely to engage in misconduct-prone rote behavior. Well-designed learning objectives should not simply appear on the first page of the syllabus or be mentioned only in week 1 of the course. To maintain students' focus on mastery and learning, rather than on performance and grades, explicitly tie each class activity and assessment to learning objectives. Doing so reminds students why they are being asked to do the activity in a particular way. In Tricia's syllabus, for example, she has a table that depicts the schedule of activities and assessments by week, and in the row for each week, the relevant learning objectives are listed. You can give students these reminders orally or in your class slides for each learning module as well. For example, "As a reminder, the next learning module focuses on helping you achieve learning objective number 2, which is to X and Y. We will do this by A, B, and C."

Construct a Learner-Centered Syllabus

Early in her career as a manager of academic integrity, Tricia performed all aspects of the job, from investigating alleged integrity violations to teaching students how to avoid future violations. One day, as Tricia was processing a new case, she saw a name she recognized. Tricia was disappointed that Sam apparently had cheated again and was denying the (very obvious) evidence that cheating had occurred. Soon thereafter, Sam unexpectedly entered Tricia's office, sat down, and almost immediately started crying. She recalls him saying,

> I originally denied cheating because I was so scared. I knew I was going to be suspended. So I lied. I lied and said I didn't do it. But then I wasn't able to eat or sleep. I was stressed and worried and racked with feelings of guilt. I found myself

> just curled up in a ball, crying and alone. And that's when I decided to tell the truth. And so here I am. I did it and I'm sorry.

Tricia took a deep breath. She could feel Sam's pain, guilt, and embarrassment. After a moment, Tricia asked Sam what would have helped him avoid this second violation. It turns out that Sam's first infraction was a direct violation of the course rules, written in the syllabus. So what Sam learned from that experience was to abide by the rules. What he didn't learn was to focus on mastery and learning, rather than rules and grades. So, when the rules weren't stated or weren't clear, Sam chose whatever strategy would best accomplish his goal of passing the class. This story illustrates how critical the syllabus can be as a strategy for creating a mastery-oriented class and inspiring intrinsic motivation for learning. Sam wasn't using the syllabus in that class as a learning tool; he was using it as a rulebook for what to do and what not to do. It was transactional. It was unidirectional. And it wasn't supporting Sam in making good choices.

In contrast, a learner-centered syllabus reconnects students back to the primary focus, which is learning. It triggers the desire for learning (intrinsic motivation) that is very strongly correlated with integrity. It helps to create a sense of belonging (a strategy still to be described), enabling students to envision themselves as members of the class and in relationship with the class and the content. In fact, a learner-centered syllabus improves students' perceptions of good instruction.[7] A learner-centered syllabus is warm, friendly, even collegial (using language like "you" and "me" rather than "students" and "instructor"), and approachable (for example, inviting students to seek help). A syllabus has no power in and of itself, so if a learner-centered syllabus is not followed up with a learner-centered class, then students will likely approach the coursework in a more typical transactional and extrinsic fashion. The goal is not just about constructing the syllabus, it is about intimately tying the syllabus to class design. When you have designed a learner-centered class, the learner-centered syllabus is like wrapping paper on a carefully crafted and wrapped gift, the symbol that what is inside it will be valuable, personal, and even precious.

A learner-centered syllabus highlights positive learning actions more than the (seemingly) arbitrary rules of the road. By showcasing the learning objectives front and center and repeatedly tying them to the activities, assessments, and grading (or ungrading) decisions, you remind students that learning, not grades, is the main goal of the class. Whereas the traditional teacher-centered syllabus conveys the instructor's command of the content and of the class in a tone that is "dry/boring" or "punitive/controlling," the tone and the pedagogy expressed in a learner-centered syllabus is "positive, encouraging, inviting, [and] engaging."[8]

A learner-centered syllabus differs from a teacher-centered syllabus in three areas: community, power and control, and evaluation/assessment. According to Richmond and colleagues, there are three community factors: teachers make themselves accessible, they provide a rationale for learning, and they encourage collaboration. With regard to power and control, teachers give students some say in course policies and remind them of their agency to bring their outside knowledge and resources to bear on classroom learning. Finally, in terms of evaluation/assessment, course expectations and standards are made clear, there are both formative assessments (given to facilitate learning) and summative assessments (given to measure learning), and students are able to revise and resubmit assignments to advance their learning.[9]

Within the qualities that Richmond and colleagues outline, you might sense what Sara M. Fulmer highlights about the learner-centered syllabus: it's not written as a dictation of the rules by the teacher as authority figure over the students, but as a guideline for learning in community or in partnership.[10] For example, imagine language like this: "In this course, together we will . . ." versus "in this course, the student will . . ." This language is not meant to convey a lack of intellectual rigor—the teacher's expectations for learning can still be high. Rather, it is about saying, "We're in this together. I will do my best to design a class environment, course structure, and pedagogy that will facilitate your learning, and I hope you will join me on this journey by engaging in the course and the course content with me and your classmates." As you can see, the learner-centered syllabus is positively toned, and highlights intrinsic rather than extrinsic motivators.

Though this may seem to be stating the obvious, remember that constructing a learner-centered syllabus will not make cheating the exception and learning and integrity the norm unless it is backed up by course structures designed to place the focus on learning. Therefore, the rest of this chapter focuses on specific course design decisions that can make a big difference for learning, not just reducing cheating.

Reduce Either-Or Decisions by Implementing Flexible Deadlines

One of the most common stories we hear in academic integrity proceedings goes like this:

> I had a lot going on at home, so I wasn't able to begin this assignment [assigned two weeks ago] until the night before. I thought I would have enough time to finish, but as the deadline got closer, I realized that I wouldn't make it. My professor doesn't accept late assignments, and a 0 in this class would drop me below passing. I wouldn't normally do this, but I went online and found the answer to a similar assignment and used that as a model for my answer. It's not like me, and I regretted it the moment I did it.

First, let's be clear: this is academic misconduct and should be treated accordingly. The student is responsible for their actions and should be held accountable in a way that is appropriate and focused on helping them grow from the experience. It's also true that some students will procrastinate under any circumstances. However, a far better outcome would be achieved if this student were able to complete the assignment legitimately, even if that means turning it in a little late.

This story highlights a very important question we as educators should ask ourselves: *What are the reasons for assessment deadlines?*

This may sound absurd at first glance, but stop and think about it for a moment. There are likely many reasons for deadlines, but how many are actually connected to the learning objectives? Deadlines intended to help the student achieve the desired learning outcomes often appear in scaffolded assessments—a paper outline must be submitted in time to receive and incorporate feedback before the rough draft is due, or a data analysis plan must be reviewed before the data are collected. These deadlines are worth having. Another reason for deadlines is for students' benefit. Helping them budget their time, get more sleep, and improve learning through spreading out study time are all valid reasons to set deadlines.

Other reasons for deadlines have little connection to student learning but exist for administrative or convenience purposes. The registrar needs grades by a certain date. It takes three days to grade each paper set and there are only so many graders to do the work. These are logistical deadlines that are designed to keep the educational machine going; they exist for a reason and can't be changed. Don't worry about these. Instead, focus on those deadlines over which you have agency.

If there is no pedagogical or administrative reason for a deadline, does it need to be absolutely rigid? Deadlines might make it easier for students to rationalize cheating when the stakes become all-or-nothing, and the rules seem inflexible and arbitrary. Long before they make the decision to cheat, students may infer that their instructor cares more about their grades or the grading process than about learning. When we set deadlines mindlessly, students notice. We know many faculty who assign deadlines at 11:59 p.m. Why? To make it "fair," so all students get the same amount of time? But is it fair if the instructor is not going to start grading until the morning? Other faculty assign deadlines on Friday at 5 p.m., even though they have no plans to review the work until the next Monday. Students observe that we've set the deadlines for our convenience or for no reason at all (or, at least, no expressed reason). If students have this perception, it focuses them on performing rather than learning, which can undermine their motivation to work honestly.

A performance-oriented class cues students to consider assignments as performances and grades as rewards for good behavior, often to the detriment of their long-term learning. Another lesson students take from a deadline policy they perceive to be arbitrary or unfair is that the instructor doesn't respect their time or needs. It's the same feeling as waiting all day for the cable repair van when you were promised an 8–10 a.m. service window. Arbitrary deadlines feel rude and disrespectful and engender neutralizing attitudes: "It's so stupid that we have to submit this by midnight when they're not even going to grade it until tomorrow, so it's their fault." "This teacher sucks. They obviously care more about deadlines than how I get this done." Moreover, in most cases the consequences of a draconian late penalty mean that being caught cheating isn't much worse than not turning in the assignment at all. From a rational economic perspective, students aren't maximizing their utility by following the rules. Perverse incentives are the hallmark of a poorly thought-out policy, so if students are cheating in part because deadline policies are too rigid, it's time for a change.

We suspect that many of the deadlines you have set could be changed without any loss of learning by students or much inconvenience to the grader. Such arbitrary deadlines should be dispensed with. There are few easier ways to reduce cheating without sacrificing rigorous learning than by creating reasonably flexible deadlines whenever practical. Students' self-efficacy increases because the task seems more reasonable, they are harder pressed to rationalize cheating when they have a viable alternative, and the structure of the course now emphasizes their learning, not an arbitrary performance standard.

Instructors do not have to abandon deadlines (and we don't recommend that you do). However you can *design deadlines to minimize cheating by looking for alternatives to the traditional approach.* One of our favorite alternatives to a firm deadline is a "best by" date. While deadlines are occasionally arbitrary, they do serve to focus the mind. Providing students with a timeline for the course is a powerful organizational tool for their success. David uses flexible best by dates for some assignments in his cognitive psychology class, and students still ask for extensions. They have been trained to take these dates seriously, and for the most part they do. When a student requests an extension, it's easy to let them know that they can turn in their work when it's ready at no penalty. Best by dates work best for assignments that require time for feedback. In reality, it's actually easier to have these assignments trickle in rather than flood your inbox because it allows time for more thoughtful responses to students' work. Best by deadlines should have some structure, though. In David's class, students must make a good-faith effort to complete each weekly quiz review before the quiz, but they can make revisions later. They must submit their interim assignments for the final project in the designated order and must respond to feedback on each iteration. Those strictures make it effectively impossible to complete those assignments at the last minute, without adequate time in between.

Even when deadlines need to be firmly established, there should still be some flexibility. The goal is to keep students focused on the learning goals of the assignment rather than the (to them) arbitrary aspects. For example, a modest penalty for lateness is better than a zero-tolerance policy. This won't prevent cheating entirely, but students do weigh the consequences of their actions, and some will opt for a minor penalty rather than risk being caught in misconduct, whereas they would take that risk to avoid a zero on an assignment. It also maintains a level of fairness. Flexibility is great, but all students must be afforded the same opportunities.

Another way to be flexible is to use Cath Ellis's three-stage approach, which gives students agency over the time frame of their submissions. Students who submit by the first deadline receive "rich feedback . . . because they have ample time to feed it back into their next task." Students who submit by the second deadline receive "limited feedback . . . because they have limited time to feed it back into their next task." And students who submit by the third deadline receive no feedback because time to incorporate the feedback has run out.[11] Cath encourages students to take advantage of earlier deadlines and the value of feedback by providing them with some incentives, rather than penalizing those who are "late." The incentives are related to the final task, an oral exam. Students who meet the first deadline get the first chance to schedule their oral exam, students who meet the second deadline get to pick next, and students who met the third deadline pick last.

You can see in Cath's approach an elegant way not only to be flexible about deadlines, but to be flexible in a way that helps students develop better time-management capabilities. The problem with rigid policies or hidden flexibility is that foolish consistency (to paraphrase Ralph Waldo Emerson[12]) isn't very educational. For example, a student who suffers an unforeseen family tragedy and misses a deadline should not be treated the same way as a student who waits until the last minute to complete an assignment and discovers that the software does not work on their home computer. Equal treatment in these cases is not particularly fair, and the virtues of equality and fairness need not be mutually exclusive.

Of course, we don't want to incentivize students to be dishonest about their reasons for needing flexibility. One way to handle this is a floating "free pass" for a late assignment that students can use once and without need for explanation. Such a policy allows a student who genuinely needs a little extra time to use the pass to finish a project and a student who is experiencing a crisis to complete their work and maximize their learning opportunities. Flexible deadlines can also be harnessed to teach students the skills to make strategic decisions about their use of time. A free pass also serves as a prompt for a discussion of time-management strategies, institutional resources for learning time management, and, if appropriate to the course material, the psychology of why people miss deadlines. This strategy cedes some control to students, gives them a chance to develop time-management skills, and provides an alternative to either cheating or earning a zero on a big assignment. Especially for students who struggle with organization—like those with attention-deficit/hyperactivity disorder (ADHD)—having a deadline structure with some flexibility can provide them the tools to be successful.[13]

Thus, making deadlines flexible both aligns assessments with learning goals and prepares students for the "real world." As any scholar who has missed a review deadline or waited months for paperwork knows, deadlines in the real world are often suggestions rather than absolutes. Even the Internal Revenue Service allows extensions and a grace period for filing! It's simply fairer to be flexible, as long as that flexibility is afforded to all students equally. We all know colleagues (or are those colleagues) who talk tough about deadlines and rules in the abstract, but when a student asks for an extension or exception, we are reasonably accommodating. This might be an attempt to be nice, but it is definitely not fair. Of course, every rule can have exceptions, but when there is a hidden rulebook accessible only to those who ask for it, we create inequity. Those students who don't know to ask, who do not feel entitled to exceptions, or who are simply too shy to ask are disadvantaged relative to their entitled, bold, and informed peers. Whatever the rules are, flexible or rigid, they must always apply to everyone and should be clear and transparent.

Reduce Cheating by Focusing Away from Grades and Grading

Many readers of this series will be aware of the critiques of traditional grading and of exciting alternatives like mastery grading, specification grading, and ungrading.[14] While we strongly encourage consideration of these strategies and discuss them in depth later in this chapter, switching your grading scheme certainly isn't an entry strategy for reducing cheating, and it may not even be an option for some faculty in some institutions. The good news is that it is still possible to improve the integrity culture of a class by modifying the structure of a traditional grading scheme and the way you talk about grades.

The way in which you talk about grades creates either a performance-oriented or mastery-oriented class, thereby either encouraging or discouraging cheating. Picture yourself as a student in a class with a professor who says this: "The point of grades is to weed out the weak and identify the strong. About 10 percent of you will flunk out, so if you don't want to be one of them, make sure you figure out now how you're going to land in the 90 percent." Are you thinking about how to learn and master the material at that moment, or have you gone into survival mode, ready to do whatever it takes not to flunk out? When the professor foregrounds grades, the students will do so as well, and extrinsically motivated students are more likely to use any strategy to get that grade, including cheating.

Many readers won't remember the bad old days when grades were posted outside the professor's office after an exam, often with names or initials as identifiers. It was a horrifying experience for most students; even the ones who did well had "survivor's guilt" and felt the stress of hiding their successes or their happiness from their peers. We think (hope!) this practice is defunct thanks to privacy standards, but we still hear about faculty who continue to spotlight grades unnecessarily in their written or oral rhetoric. Examples include faculty who berate students (even as a group) when their grades are low or report class averages or grade distributions after every assessment. Among the most powerful performance goals are negative performance goals, in which people strive to avoid negative comparisons, which are often publicly embarrassing.[15] If students believe they will be made to feel bad about their grades in public, even if they're not named, that becomes a strong motivation to avoid getting a low grade by any means necessary, including cheating.

The purpose of talking about grades and grading differently is to create a class motivational structure that emphasizes learning goals first and performance (that is, competitive) goals secondarily. This doesn't mean that you need to avoid talking about grades entirely, but discussing grades in a healthy way is important. After all, grades are supposed to be proxies, merely representatives of something else—learning. Instead of talking about grades as the end goal, talk about learning and explain the connections between learning and the grading system. After an assessment, instead of focusing on the class average or grade distribution, focus on the content and learning objectives—which key concepts do students need to improve their mastery, and what strategies could they implement to improve that mastery?

When discussing grades with students, direct their attention toward the connection between learning outcomes and grading rubrics so that they see the goal as demonstrating excellence (or competence) rather than earning points. Don't do this all at once; do it in a timely way as you introduce each assessment. Students want to know that their time is being used wisely, that there is a specific learning-based purpose for everything they are asked to do, and that their grades will reflect their learning. They also want to direct their efforts toward the most important aspects of an assignment but don't always have the context to intuit the purpose of an exercise without guidance. For example, when given a seemingly repetitive set of equations to solve, students appreciate knowing that those equations are the building blocks of a later lesson and may strive to master the process of solving them for that reason. This helps them understand why part of their grade is based on something as mundane as homework problems. Incorporate the learning objectives and key aspects of the grading rubric into each assignment so that the relationship between goals, class activities, and assessment remains transparent.

Our grading schemes speak as loudly as our words. Many faculty determine course grades based on a percentage of points earned, which emphasizes the gap between a student's performance and perfection, creating a performance rather than mastery orientation. Also, in such a schema, when students receive a graded assessment, they look for points they lost, asking, "Why did I not get 100 percent?" When people are faced with a potential loss rather than a potential gain, they tend to act in risky ways to avoid that feeling of loss.[16] To test this hypothesis, consider gas stations where cash customers pay a little less to offset credit card fees. This difference can be described as either a cash discount or a credit card surcharge. The frame of reference changes, but in either description the price difference remains the same. Since nobody likes paying a surcharge and most folks like a discount, it's more palatable to offer a discount from a baseline price (leaving those paying the baseline feeling neutral) than to alienate credit card purchasers with a surcharge. From the armchair perspective, it's obvious that these options make no difference to the price, but in the moment, people's intuitions are to avoid a loss. Consider the way you frame your communication about grades in this light. If an assessment is worth 20 points, compare the psychological impact of earning 18 points as compared to 90 percent. While the grades are functionally equivalent, the focus on the points earned rather than the 10 percent lost can help motivate students toward learning rather than avoiding the loss of points. Because, like all humans, students dislike losses more than they like gains, this framing can lower the emotional stakes of assessment and help them learn authentically, even though they may not perform perfectly. Encourage students to view grades as reflections of a set of accomplishments rather than as penalties for insufficient or incorrect answers.

Changing how you communicate about grades might be a particularly appealing strategy because it doesn't require any change in content, use of class time, or academic rigor. Conveying to students that you value learning through your words and the structure of your classes can really focus their motivation on learning and, in turn, their desire to complete their work authentically. When you discuss extrinsic goals such as earning good grades, satisfying others, or getting high-paying jobs, you remind students that they are seeking a *degree* rather than an *education*. In that goal frame, cheating becomes a much more appealing option.

Avoid All-or-Nothing Grades for Large Assignments

When students believe they've worked hard on an assignment, earning a zero on it feels unfair and undermines motivation. Because a zero is so detrimental to a running average and has such a powerful psychological effect, it's best to avoid giving zeroes on any work that is submitted.[17] We've seen computer science syllabi, for example, in which students are given a zero if their program doesn't run without errors. Imagine a hardworking, honest student who tries their best on a programming assignment, has learned all the concepts and applied them properly, but has misplaced a parenthesis. Does a zero reflect their effort, learning, or progress on this assignment? Would there be a similar all-or-nothing consequence in the real world? Of course not! In the workplace, a colleague would likely spot the stray parenthesis and help fix the error. Yet in school, the same mistake tanks a student's entire grade. The arbitrariness of such an inflexible rule, which was likely implemented to make grading easier, is not lost on students and serves to undermine their self-efficacy and mastery motivations, while increasing their willingness to rationalize cheating. From an economic perspective, cheating on coding assignments is very easy to do (especially now with GenAI) and is often undetected, so it becomes the logical strategy to avoid getting a guaranteed zero.

Don't Give Points for Attendance

It seems logical that if we want our students to engage in a positive behavior like coming to class, whether online or in person, then we should reward that behavior. Grades seem like the obvious reward in a class setting, so many course syllabi include points for "class participation" as a thinly veiled proxy for attendance and good behavior. This route is tempting, and it does make it easier to penalize those students who don't engage in the course or even disrupt class sessions. Unfortunately, there is a downside to directly incentivizing attendance: it can undermine intrinsic motivation, leading to the *overjustification effect*. Students who attend class only to earn points may actually enjoy the course less, engage less, and be more prone to cheating, or at least feeling resentful.[18]

In Festinger's famous studies on cognitive dissonance, participants rated a miserable task (turning a bolt with a wrench for no reason) as less aversive when they were *paid less*! Paying them twenty dollars to say nice things about the task gave them implicit permission to dislike it, whereas paying only one dollar led participants to think the task was more worthwhile. In the context of grades, giving students points for attendance implicitly signals that the only reason to come to class is for the points.

The alternative to attendance or participation points is to give students the opportunities to earn points through meaningful in-class activities. These can be as simple as exit tickets, in which students submit a question or comment at the end of the class, homework assignments that are presented and explained in class, or fully in-class activities (such as in flipped classrooms where little to no lecturing takes place during the synchronous time together). Regardless of the form the activity takes, the goals are to give students an affirmative reason to come to class that relates to their learning and to award grades based on activities that have clear intrinsic value. Consequently, grades are associated with learning experiences, not just showing up and keeping a chair warm.

Design Courses to Engender Metacognition

Metacognition literally means thinking about thinking. How often do you suppose your students think about their own thinking? What about contemplating their learning processes—such as how they write or how they study—and how effective those processes are for helping them learn and master the material? Probably seldom to never. Cheating often seems to arise from a lack of consciousness or mindfulness about the act of learning, which can lead to faulty estimates of how long an assignment will take to complete or how much studying will be needed to learn the material. These underestimates lead to cheating as a strategy to get an activity done after the opportunity to get it done without cheating was missed. As we discussed in chapter 1, students struggle with time management, and much of that struggle is related to poor metacognitive skills.

Metacognition has two dimensions: knowledge and regulation. *Knowledge of metacognition* is what a person knows about how they think. *Regulation* refers to the processes a person engages in that facilitate learning and memory.[19] Knowledge might include Tricia's understanding of her own abilities (such as knowing that she has difficulty remembering facts that aren't anchored to meaning or relevancy), her assessment of a particular task (for example, that memorizing the names of the bones in a human skeleton will be challenging), or the strategies that are available to help her with a task (for example, if she connects the bone names through song—the knee bone's connected to the thigh bone, the thigh bone's connected to the hip bone—she's more likely to learn them). Regulation, on the other hand, is about her observing the success of her learning and memory strategies and adapting or continuing those strategies as appropriate. So, Tricia expects that she can learn the body parts using a song, but she does not persist with that strategy if it proves to be ineffective. Instead, she regroups and tries a new strategy.

Students who have a good understanding of their own cognitive processes, and of the activities that facilitate their learning and memory, have the tools necessary to help themselves and therefore have less need to cheat. Therefore, teaching students metacognitive skills and giving them practice with those skills help them to develop their own internal learning soundtrack. When students feel comfortable with their learning soundtrack, they develop self-efficacy for mastering the coursework. That belief in their own effectiveness is a powerful antidote for the temptation to cheat. Furthermore, students who can evaluate their own learning are more likely to have successes (both in terms of mastering the material and in their performance), which in turn, reinforce their efforts at authentic learning.

We can start to engender metacognition in our students by dispelling some of the myths that students hold about studying and learning.

Myth 1: The Power of Mnemonic Clues

Although we used the skeleton song as an example earlier, neither of us could actually remember the lyrics. Yet mnemonic clues—usually in the form of acronyms—are ubiquitous. Just typing PEMDAS sends shivers down the spines of the mathematically disinclined, even now. Although creating a strong and easy-to-retrieve mnemonic cue that represents a large chunk of information is a very effective way to encode information, it is very brittle.[20] If one forgets the acronym in whole or in part (Tricia, for example, cannot recall what PEMDAS stands for), the strategy loses effectiveness.

What is the antidote to this myth? It's really helpful for students to understand that any encoding strategy must include effective chunks, like mnemonics, but also meaningful connections between information. Long-term memorization requires an understanding of the material to be remembered and how it connects to the overall topic of the course,[21] so helping students to derive meaning from the material they study is a very effective way to help them learn. Giving students a set of orienting questions to guide their studying can help them to develop meaningful connections. These questions can be general, such as, "Do you think that the evidence in our readings is persuasive? Why or why not?" A more specific question might ask students to contrast two theories, so that information they learn about one theory can serve as a cue for remembering information about the other, creating more paths for retrieval. It also benefits students if you purposefully scaffold their studying during early assessments, then remove these training wheels to allow the students to try these techniques on their own as the course progresses.

Myth 2: Study, Study, Study!

Students seem to believe that the more they study, the more they'll learn (and ace the assessment). You undoubtedly have several stories of students who arrive in your office halfway through the semester lamenting that they've been studying hard but their grades are still poor. Many of those students really are studying hard but are not learning as they need to. Unfortunately, these students don't know how to study effectively and don't have the metacognitive regulation to realize that what they are doing isn't working. If we teachers had a dollar for every student who studied by "going over their notes and highlighting important passages in the book," we could all buy ourselves a sandwich, if not a car.

What is the antidote to this myth?

The testing effect.[22] In many academic traditions, testing is conducted sporadically, often once or twice a year. It is also common in the United States to structure classes around two long exams (a midterm and a final) or some variation on that theme.

A high-stakes exam given infrequently incentivizes short-term learning and dishonest techniques to perform well rather than learn the material. This is particularly true of exams that are not-cumulative. In these cases, students have no incentive to learn the material for the long term, but only for a short period (measured in hours). On the other hand, more frequent lower-stakes assessments—either formative or summative—like frequent quizzes or interactive activities have many benefits for authentic learning.

The testing effect shows that after an initial study session, testing leads to more learning than studying does, so learners should study by self-testing not more studying. This technique is startlingly easy to adopt. The idea is simple. In a class that is currently structured with two or three exams, simply break up the material into weekly chunks, setting aside a portion of class time to administer the assessment each week. For example, an exam with fifty multiple-choice questions and four short-answer questions could become ten quizzes, each with five multiple-choice questions and one (or no) short answer question. The assessments in the new version of the course need not differ in content from the older version, just be scheduled differently. Having early and frequent feedback also gives students the opportunity to experience early success or to rebound from a slow start. The assessments seem more manageable, which results in increased self-efficacy and less dishonesty. At the same time, students must study each week to prepare for the quiz, distributing study time more effectively. More frequent assessment also allows for the repetition of questions or concepts that are essential to the course or that are particularly challenging. This structure mirrors the testing effect research, providing students with multiple opportunities to practice the retrieval of key concepts.

Myth 3: Cramming before the Test Is Better than Getting Some Rest

Students are known to brag about how they stayed up all night to cram for a test. Yet, when exam time comes, they remember only a portion of the information that they thought they knew so well when they put their materials away. What happened? Simply put, forgetting happened. When material is learned perfectly (that is, 100 percent retrieval), one's ability to retrieve it begins to decline within hours, dropping up to 40 percent within three or four days.[23] Evidence from research studies found the same effect—little memory decline in the short term but just four days later, a 30 percent reduction in retention of material that was crammed.[24] In other words, cramming is efficient for short-term memory but not efficient for learning. The metacognitive challenge for students is that right at the end of the study session, they feel like they learned as well or even better by cramming than by using multiple study sessions. Only later do they realize that little long-term learning has taken place. Yet they often continue to study in this way (because they're focused on short-term performance).

"Study smarter, not harder," the saying goes. To break students of their cramming habit, show them that they must continue learning information until they have overlearned it. *Overlearning* means learning the material, then continuing to study it even after one has achieved initial proficiency (usually through self-testing), and then learning it again. A critical feature of overlearning is *distributed study*. In place of mass studying (that is, cramming) where one reviews a set of material over and over again without a break, distributed study inserts a break between each relearning of the material.[25] If you want students to practice distributed study, asking nicely might work, but changing your assessment structure to require it is more likely to change behavior. One simple strategy is, again, frequent lower-stakes testing, which requires students to pace out their studying.

Another strategy for encouraging distributed study is creating weekly schedules. The idea behind weekly schedules stems from the asynchronous online learning environment, which lacks the natural rhythm of weekly course meetings to keep students on track. However, even students enrolled in synchronous classes can benefit from an explicit weekly routine. When you build a weekly routine for coursework, provide students with frequent deadlines for small assignments that are the same each week. For example, quiz preparations are due every Sunday at midnight, quizzes themselves are due on Tuesday, a formative assessment or activity is due on Thursday, and the pattern repeats. A consistent schedule serves to lift some cognitive load from students, because it's predictable and naturally leads to distributed studying. This structured-schedule approach breaks down tasks that were previously lumped together as "studying for a test" into manageable chunks appropriate for students who are just developing their metacognitive skills.

A caution about frequent quizzes. Now might be a good time to address how more frequent assessments can backfire as both a teaching and a learning strategy. First, with distributed studying and assessment also comes distributed grading. If you can't keep up with all of that grading, students don't receive timely or regular feedback, negating the positive effects of frequent testing. This may be a good use of technology; if students complete the assessments on computers and you have the right tools in place, you can provide students with instant feedback without significant human investment.[26]

Next, keeping quizzes short may mean that there is little time each week for questions that require longer and more thoughtful responses. Frequent testing works best when used to measure learning on the lower levels of Bloom's taxonomy, such as remembering, applying, and understanding new concepts. So, if you currently use high-stakes tests for assessment at the lower taxonomy levels, you may want to switch to more frequent low-stakes tests for that content. Retain the activities that encourage students to create, analyze, or critique as a high-stakes assessment at a time that makes sense in your course. Third, since most students think of themselves as fundamentally honest,[27] even honest students may be more likely to cheat on a quiz, since it's "just a small assignment." Addressing this challenge requires use of other strategies in this book to "raise the cost" of cheating for students.

Lastly, if you implement frequent testing without redesigning your class to a mastery orientation, this can cause additional stress for students. We saw this dynamic during the COVID-19 pandemic. Faculty had to shift immediately to emergency remote teaching and were worried about cheating, so they replaced high-stakes assessments with more frequent low-stakes assessments but didn't change the performance orientation of their classes or their pedagogy. As a result, students experienced burnout and cheated regardless. It is important to maintain a learning-first attitude toward frequent assessments through course communication as well as structurally. Allowing students to earn partial credit for post-quiz correction exercises or for retaking frequent mastery-based assessments can both reduce stress and encourage a growth and learning approach to errors.[28]

How do these myths and antidotes lead to a teaching strategy for integrity? The bottom line is that we as instructors should develop assignments for which the path of least resistance (the default strategy) is to complete them in a cognitively efficient way. Use these assignments as opportunities for students to practice new ways of doing their work, then highlight for them the positive results of using these new strategies.

We started out this section with the metaphor of a study soundtrack, so let's think about metacognition this way—without it, students' soundtrack will be something in a minor key like the theme from *Jaws*. It will signal impending doom, but the students won't realize that they are working harder, not smarter. Their ineffective efforts can lead to disappointing results, which in turn lowers their self-efficacy, creates neutralizing attitudes, and focuses them on their comparative failures. All of these outcomes are bad on their own, but they also encourage more cheating. When students begin to use metacognitive strategies to inform their learning, their study time will be more productive, more engaging, and yes, more challenging. Imagine if all studying were like the training montage from *Rocky* (the one that ends on the steps of the Philadelphia Museum of Art). While learning could still be a struggle, there would be a reward at the end of that struggle—achievement and progress.

Use Scaffolding to Break Down Big Projects

When you learned to ride a bike, you likely started with a tricycle. The tricycle allowed you to learn how to pedal and steer, without the worry about or need to balance or even brake (because you could just put your feet down to stop your forward momentum). With less risk of injury on a tricycle, you were much more likely to be successful and want to continue learning how to ride a "real bike." Once you mastered riding a tricycle, you were likely gifted a bicycle with training wheels. Although less stable than the tricycle, the training wheels still provided some assistance with balancing, so you were able to learn how to balance with less risk of injury than you would face without the extra support. Once you gained confidence in balancing, braking, and steering, the training wheels could come off and you could continue your mastery on a bike you already knew and were comfortable with. This is what education researchers call *scaffolding.*[29]

Scaffolding takes large concepts or tasks and divides them into smaller components, each with its own lesson plan to move students from novice to master. Scaffolding is so common in course design that you probably often use it without realizing that you are doing so. That's great, but it's also helpful to consider scaffolding explicitly as you consider the big goals of your course and design assessments to evaluate learning outcomes. Scaffolding isn't necessary for all assignments in all courses. In general, scaffolding is most critical for large, important assessments or projects. When trying to decide when to use scaffolding, Caruana suggests that a "good rule of thumb is the higher the stakes, the more scaffolding you need to include. In other words, the heavier the weight, the stronger the support."[30] Particularly in courses where developing writing and research skills are explicit learning objectives, we prefer the time-tested approach of breaking larger projects into smaller ones and providing different instruction for each chunk.

Scaffolding should work to reduce cheating by chunking projects into smaller, achievable tasks. When David teaches psychology research methods, he asks students early on to self-disclose whether they're apprehensive about the large research project that's due at the end of the term. Almost all are willing to acknowledge their concerns. When he interrogates those concerns, a common theme emerges—they're not sure that they can do what's asked of them. David then asks his students to reflect on their most cherished accomplishment and what it was like to embark on the journey that ended with that success. Most students will recognize that they didn't know how to do the thing they're most proud of when they started, but that they grew into the accomplishment over time.

David's students may realize that this conversation is about self-efficacy (because they're good psychology students), but they usually don't know that it's really about reducing the likelihood of cheating. Such a conversation helps the students to establish that "can-do" spirit (that is, a growth mindset),[31] and the scaffolded course structure backs up the talk with action. By communicating the goals of scaffolding to his students through the construction of interim assessments and learning outcomes, David reorients them away from grades and other performance goals and back toward the learning or mastery outcomes that he wishes them to aim for. Students are able to review the course schedule and envision their path through the various subgoals until they achieve the final outcome (in this case, an American Psychological Association style research paper based on original research). In combination with some of the other strategies in this chapter, like flexible scheduling and specifications grading (discussed later in the chapter), it's possible to turn down the temperature on difficult assignments and foster students' self-efficacy as well. Because scaffolding is built right into the course structure, this strategy works equally well for in-person and asynchronous online settings. When the assignments are inherently manageable, you don't need to be present in person to help students feel capable of doing them.

Once you determine that scaffolding would be useful in your course, where do you begin? Caruana's formula for scaffolding suggests that, whether you have an existing large project in mind or are starting from scratch, first articulate the learning objectives. Use plain language and be as specific as possible. "Able to design a good experiment" is a fine starting point, but then zoom in on some specific aspects of experimental design that you really care about. Examples could be "create an effective control group" or "correctly describe factorial designs" (again, GenAI may be able to help you develop your learning objectives). Once you've established the specific learning objectives, connect them to the skills and knowledge that your students will need to achieve those objectives. Next, categorize the skills (or knowledge) into three categories: prerequisite (you expect students to already know them), developing (students have been exposed to them but need reinforcement), and novel (students will be learning them for the first time).[32]

Once you have prepared the goals and skills list, conduct a task analysis of the project you have in mind to identify the subtasks that need to occur. In the case of a psychology research project, finding a research question, learning about relevant theories, generating hypotheses, and grounding those hypotheses in theory represent just the first few subtasks. The task analysis can be time-consuming since this is, after all, a big project.

After creating the list of subtasks, organize them in roughly chronological order and clusters of tasks that can be completed simultaneously. For example, finding a research question and the first articles for a literature review is a natural combination. Once you have clustered all the tasks appropriately, you can create the course structure. Determine how best to teach students each set of skills or knowledge with lessons, formative assessments, and a summative assessment for each. Make sure that the summative assessment is as similar to a component of the final project as possible. For example, don't ask students to summarize an article that they won't use for their final project; instead, make sure that their article-reading activity builds on their annotated bibliography, which in turn builds on their chosen research question.

Annotated bibliographies are a useful learning activity, but they are also easily created by GenAI tools. This creates a challenge for you as the instructor. You must either embrace the use of those tools for research or focus more on the process than the outcome in your assessments. If it is practical to embrace GenAI, then be sure to address the proper use of it when describing the bibliography assignment. Ask students to submit their prompts and note their contribution to the final submitted work beyond what the AI generated. Have them reflect on the process and the benefits and limitations of the AI tool for research.

If you prefer that students focus on their own annotation skills, then you must plan the assignment accordingly. You can do so by requiring students to use analog resources and to submit highlighted paper copies of their articles, annotated PDFs, or other documents that show their work. The process can also be illuminated by conducting a bibliography-building activity during class time and observing students' work firsthand.

Finally, there are digital tools like Perusall,[33] designed to facilitate student reading and note-taking. Perusall is an online tool into which you can load readings in PDF format and track reading times. More importantly, it allows users to collaboratively or individually annotate those readings with comments, questions, and media. Though it really shines as a group research tool, you can use it to view a student's individual reading and research process as well.

You've now created a set of learning goals, lessons, and assessments for each subpart of the project. Perhaps the most underrated aspect of scaffolding is communication. As you create your syllabus, place the subparts in a logical order and fit them in with other aspects of the class, being sure to include connections between the subparts and with the final project in each assignment description. The goal is to cue students to see the final project and the subparts as a whole in order to help them track their own learning path. Metacognition can then occur as students reflect on their skill development. Encourage them to think ahead to future tasks when completing the early ones. For instance, as students prepare annotated bibliographies, orient them toward using the annotations as notes later when they write their literature review. That way, they can self-evaluate their work for that purpose. Showing students that there is a purpose for each step in a process that will benefit them as learners is a great way to support mastery motivations at the expense of performance goals.

Remember, big projects like these are not "cheat-proof," no matter how well designed they are. Students can always copy a previous student's assignments wholesale, pay someone to complete them all, or cut and paste from other sources as needed. GenAI is able to base outputs on previous inputs as well, mimicking the development process of a human writer. However, by creating a series of activities that build upon one another and requiring students to respond to feedback throughout, some forms of cheating become more difficult, or at least more expensive, and the cost-benefit analysis tilts toward authentic learning. As a bonus, each draft of an iterative assignment gives you more opportunities to help students use GenAI tools appropriately and more chances to spot dishonest use because you gain more insight into their work process.

Rethink Grading

David used to claim that he could end cheating overnight . . . just stop grading. Tricia was never buying it, but she humored him. As it turns out, this simple proposal is wrong, but it highlights a naive belief that once the burden of performance motivation imposed by grading is lifted, students will uniformly shift to a mastery mindset. In this view, students are eager learners whose motivation is hijacked by conformity to an arbitrary grading scheme. Unfortunately, recent events don't bear out this hypothesis. Colleagues teaching large noncredit massive online open courses (MOOCs) report rampant cheating on assessments, even when there are no stakes at all.[34] We've witnessed cheating in video games,[35] chess,[36] and schoolwork designed as a learning opportunity or concept check. To be fair, there are rewards for cheating other than grades. For professional gamers and chess players, there can be big financial and reputational rewards for winning. So, while one might conclude that external rewards (like grades) do create motivations to cheat, it would be a mistake to assume that eliminating those external rewards would eliminate cheating because students are human beings and cheating, to quote our friend Jason Stephens, is normal and expected, but also evitable.[37]

And let's be frank—instructors need to evaluate student learning, and these evaluations need to be shared because they accumulate toward the end goal of awarding a degree. The traditional version of learning evaluation, in which assignments lead to accrual of points or the loss of percentage grades, can engender extrinsic motivations and neutralizing attitudes. However, if these evaluations actually represent learning and meaningful mastery experiences, they can actually be a useful tool for motivating student learning and reducing misconduct. We now review three alternatives to the traditional grade point system that may achieve these goals: mastery grading, specifications grading, and ungrading.

Mastery Grading

Mastery grading is tied to the students' level of mastery of course concepts. Given the amount we've talked about mastery versus performance thus far, you're probably not surprised by the suggestion to consider mastery grading. In a traditional points-based grading system, a student's grade can refer to many learning stages ranging from mastery of all concepts to some concepts or even none, if partial credit isn't used wisely. In mastery grading, the expectations for each level of mastery are clearly articulated, and student work is assessed for what level of mastery it demonstrates.[38] Thus, in a mastery grading system, students who master all concepts will earn the highest grades, and those who master fewer will earn somewhat lower grades. Grading in a mastery structure is generally binary (credit/no credit), but students are allowed multiple attempts at demonstrating mastery and are given extensive feedback on each attempt. Crucially, formative assessments (mastery checks) are given frequently to provide feedback to both students and the teacher about where the mastery gaps lie. It may seem obvious that in order to effectively implement mastery grading, you must also adjust your pedagogy in the ways we've already discussed, like incorporating scaffolding, multiple low-stakes assessments, and distributed studying. It also means that you will likely have to accept an iterative feedback loop that is at different stages for different students; you may be giving feedback to one student on mastery goal 1 while simultaneously giving feedback to another student who is working on mastery goal 2.

The effect of mastery grading can be profound for students. While there is some debate about the extent of learning benefits, there appears to be good evidence that students' attitudes toward both their instructors and the course material are more positive in mastery structured classes.[39] Plus, as we will explore more in chapter 5, when students perceive that their professor cares about their learning, they are likely to cheat less. Furthermore, the focus on concept mastery using formative assessment sends students the message that learning is valued over "box-checking" production of work. As we discussed in chapter 1, students who are focused on mastering the material rather than on performance or extrinsic rewards are less likely to resort to cheating as a strategy. Mastery grading can also have a salutary effect on students' self-efficacy. Because students have the option to continue to work on material until they achieve mastery, no particular assessment seems insurmountable.

However, mastery grading is not without its challenges when it comes to cheating. Consider the student who has difficulty with a concept and requires repeated attempts to demonstrate mastery. They may develop frustration, learned helplessness,[40] or a preoccupation with a negative performance goal like not feeling they are falling behind or less capable than their peers. If this happens, the student's risk of making a bad decision like cheating increases dramatically.

Specifications Grading

Specifications (specs) grading still emphasizes mastery of particular concepts but might overcome some of the challenges of mastery grading because it gives students greater control over their grades by giving them choices in assessment.[41] At the heart of specs grading is assessment bundling. Multiple assessments are bundled into groups that reflect proficiency at a certain level. Students may choose the bundles they wish to complete based on the mastery level they wish to achieve. For example, a specs-graded course in marketing might have ten bundles.[42] Students who complete five bundles would successfully submit weekly homework assignments and quizzes that demonstrate a fundamental knowledge of the terminology and concepts in the course material (roughly corresponding to learning objectives at the remember and understand levels of Bloom's taxonomy). A student who stops at five bundles passes the class with a D. A student who completes the five bundles plus a sixth bundle that includes an assignment assessing understanding of key concepts such as the analysis of a marketing campaign for a consumer product, would earn a C. Additional bundles leading to B and A grades would have learning objectives such as analysis of a marketing plan, creation of an original marketing plan, or critique of an existing one. From an assessment perspective, grades now align with a recognized set of learning outcomes that is associated with depth of understanding. Unlike mastery grading, specs grading does not offer unlimited attempts at each assignment, which reduces the grading load on faculty, but it does require very well-specified rubrics for demonstrating competence on each assessment.

Specs grading has many advantages. First, unlike traditional grading schemes, students can opt for whichever bundles (and grades) they are able or willing to attempt. Student control is a powerful force for combating rationalization of cheating through moral disengagement or neutralizing attitudes. Traditional grading schemes can seem arbitrary and confrontational to students. Specs grading provides students with the ability to "steer their own ship," which shifts their beliefs about who controls their destiny toward themselves and away from the condemn the condemners view that leads to neutralizing attitudes and ultimately to misconduct.[43] Specs grading creates a token economy that allows students a limited number of rewrites, extensions, and other types of flexibility. Students feel empowered to take risks and work with integrity, knowing that they have a safety net of rewrites and retakes.

Ungrading

Are grades really a good idea at all from an academic integrity perspective? After all, they tend to focus students on competitive performance and extrinsic rewards rather than on the intrinsic value of learning itself. They serve as reminders of students' failings and make faculty into opponents rather than allies. Grades do all of this harm without actually serving as a valid metric of learning a lot of the time. So, why are we still giving them?

We are not the first to ask this question. *Ungrading* is both a book and a movement that advocates for a shift away from grading.[44] Ungrading is not a single system or even one as prescriptive as mastery or specification grading (which are themselves pretty large tents); rather, it is a philosophy that centers student self-evaluation over faculty judgment. In the most commonly practiced version of ungrading, students are assigned both assessments on the material and also self-reflections on those assessments. The self-reflections serve as both opportunities for growth and the basis on which grades are assigned—by the students themselves. Depending on the instructor and course, these self-reflections may occur for each assignment, at the end of the class, or at some frequency in between. The goals of ungrading include many that we endorse in this book: generating mastery motivation, reducing the stakes of each assignment, and focusing on learning rather than performance. Ungrading is often coupled with the learning- and student-focused strategies that we recommend as well.

Unfortunately, as the MOOC example highlights, anecdotal and systematic evidence shows that people do cheat a lot even when there are no incentives or grades.[45] We anticipate that ungrading will reduce but not eliminate cheating, since cheating appears to be ubiquitous and because a radically student-first approach assumes so much goodwill on the part of the students that it's easy to miss signs of misconduct. As we've discussed, students cheat for multiple reasons, many but not all of which ungrading can address. Having said that, given that so many of the recommendations of the ungrading movement align with best practices for reducing misconduct, we felt it was important to mention ungrading. Interested readers can consult Blum's *Ungrading* for more details and ideas.

Final Thoughts

We realize that there are still faculty out there who believe that their job is to weed out the students who are not performing at the highest levels. For them, any mention of alternative pedagogies or alternate grading schemes (let alone ungrading!) is ridiculous at best and a dereliction of duty at worst. Some faculty might claim that all these strategies only serve to lower standards, but evidence does not support that argument. On the other hand, there is not a lot of concrete evidence that these strategies have a direct positive effect on cheating. So, our recommendations are based on a logical argument rather than direct data. In most cases, there aren't a lot of good experimental studies measuring the impact of these learning structures on academic misconduct. There is evidence that improvements in teaching—such as changes in the grading scheme, flexible deadlines, and other structures—improve learning outcomes and are associated with reduced neutralizing and misconduct.[46] Given the consistent and overwhelming evidence that these variables are negatively associated with cheating, we can reasonably infer that engaging in these pedagogies can serve to reduce cheating, and enhance equity and inclusion, in our classes. Finally, we will need to implement these principles in all aspects of our courses, starting with our choice and design of assessments. This topic forms the basis of the next chapter.

Next Steps

1. Reflect on these strategies. Based on the classes you teach and your discipline, which might have the greatest impact on mitigating the causes of student cheating?

Choose one course design strategy that you will implement next term and one that you will think more about for later adoption:

a. Design or redesign learning objectives
b. Craft a learner-centered syllabus
c. Implement flexible deadlines
d. Switch the focus away from grades
e. Engender metacognition
f. Scaffold big projects
g. Rethink grading

2. Consider how GenAI impacts your course design choices. How might you use GenAI to help you redesign your courses?
3. Talk to your department chair about your thoughts around course design. Fill them in on what you've learned and why you're thinking about making these changes. Ensure they're on board with your efforts.
4. For department chairs, consider what training, support, and funding you have in place to enable faculty to research, rethink, and implement these course designs.
5. For administrators, give some thought to the emphasis on grading at your institution. Convene a task force to consider alternative approaches, including the merits of suspending students with low grade point averages. Make sure that your teaching and learning professionals are well supported as they work with faculty to create innovative alternatives to traditional assessments.
6. Finally, for institutional leaders, consider establishing a computer-based testing facility to allow frequent, mastery-based assessments that, when executed properly, not only promote learning but reduce cheating opportunities.[47]

4

DESIGNING ASSESSMENTS FOR INTEGRITY

Imagine working hard to create a learner-centered syllabus, one that engenders metacognition, focuses on learning rather than grades, and engages students in regular formative assessments. Then also imagine ending such a class with a two-hundred-question multiple-choice exam or a structured twenty-five-page research paper. It seems incongruous, even absurd. Why? Because designing for integrity and authentic learning must include changes at every level: course design, assessment design, and instructional design (covered in the following chapter).

We can think about course design as a fractal—the same principles apply at every level of analysis. Just as we can design entire courses with authentic learning and academic integrity in mind, we can design individual activities and assessments that way, too. The same principles apply at the smaller levels as at the larger one: consider how each activity in the class will influence some of the key variables that we have discussed: self-efficacy; mastery, performance, and extrinsic motivation; students' value for the material; their ability to rationalize cheating; and their (perceived) chances of being caught.

In reviewing the research on why students cheat on particular assessments, two themes emerge:

1. First, students' motivation to learn is undermined when they don't value the work they are asked to do. A few

features especially devalue assignments in students' eyes: they don't know why they're doing the assignment or how it contributes to their learning.

2. Students cheat when they are afraid to fail. We define *fear of failure* as a combination of low self-efficacy ("I can't do this assignment") and a perceived need to complete the assignment regardless ("If I get a B, I'll never get into medical school"). Failure in this context doesn't mean literal failure. It includes students who can't complete an assignment because they don't have time or other circumstances arise. Students' goals also come into play. As the medical school example illustrates, passing isn't enough for many students with high performance or extrinsic goals. One of us had an extended conversation with a first-year student who was earning an A– in an introductory course and not handling the grade well. The student (and their parents) had unwavering ambitions of becoming a doctor and perceived the A– as derailing that goal. As you can imagine, all options, including dishonest ones, were on the table for this student.

Instructors can address these two reasons for dishonesty through a variety of strategies that focus on making integrity more explicit throughout the course, making your expectations clear through rubrics, enabling collaboration, giving students more control over the assessment (through student choice and opportunities for revision), and making assessments more like real-life learning (including oral evaluations and team-based learning).

Infuse Integrity into Lessons and Assessments

When building assignments to promote academic integrity, the most obvious strategy is to explicitly include academic integrity as a learning outcome of those assignments. You can purposefully and intentionally incorporate lessons on integrity and ethics throughout the term, no matter what subject you teach.

Teach AI Ethics

If you have decided that you are going to allow students to use GenAI in your class, even if on only one assessment, it is very important to incorporate an AI ethics lesson. There are many ethical concerns about GenAI, from how the companies procured the data on which the systems were trained to the significant environmental impacts of the technology, their inability to discern fact from fiction, AI companies' exploitation of human labor, and issues of privacy. Talking with the students about the obvious and not-so-obvious ethical challenges of GenAI technology provides a convenient entry point to segue into whether and how the technology can be used ethically in the class. Leon Furze provides some ideas for how an instructor in any discipline might infuse an AI ethics lesson into the curriculum.[1] You could, for example, have students engage in a conversational exchange with a chatbot about one of the ethical issues (such as privacy, truthfulness, or environmental consequences), then have them reflect on what they learned and how that knowledge will affect their use of the tools for completing academic assessments. You could ask the students to review the chatbot's use policy, and critique it on dimensions of privacy, copyright, and transparency. One more idea: You could provide students with some output from a chatbot and have them critique it according to ICAI's fundamental values; that is, how honest, fair, trustworthy, respectful, and responsible it is. The lesson you incorporate might be shaped according to your discipline and how much time you have, but there are many entry points you can choose to take.

Add an Integrity Lesson

In writing about infusing integrity and ethics into organizations, Bazerman and Tenbrunsel suggest that routinely asking one question when decisions are being made can stimulate more ethical behavior: "What are the ethical implications of/for (this situation, context, person, decision)?"[2] Raising the question reminds decision makers that ethics matters as much as the other aspects (e.g., economic, engineering) of a decision. You could use this strategy with your students by creating simple lesson plans to incorporate ethics into existing assignments or class discussions. To illustrate, let's look at some examples from different subject areas.

- An engineering faculty member teaching a capstone design course could ask students to analyze the NSPE Code of Ethics for Engineers as a guiding force for professional engineering practice.[3] Students would use the NSPE Code of Ethics as the basis for a code of ethics for their own design team and later reflect on how the implementation of their design upholds (or fails to uphold) the NSPE guidance.
- A chemistry professor teaching the process of producing bioethanol could add a lesson in which the students explore the ethical concerns of bioethanol (for example, use of food crops) then reflect on chemists' responsibilities to consider the ethics of their inventions.
- A history professor teaching about the founding of the United States could ask the students to analyze an ethical dilemma from that historical period (preferably one that is not well known to the general populace) according to a teacher-provided ethical decision-making framework.[4] Individually or in groups, students could determine what would be the most ethical action in that situation according to the framework. Once they have done that, they could discover the actual historical decision made or action taken, leading into a rich and interesting discussion.

If they occur often throughout the course, even brief opportunities for students to critically consider matters of ethics and integrity can influence their own decision making.

Look for Teachable Moments

Tricia once had a student, let's call her Violet, who had failed to submit one of her assessments. Violet explained that she had finished the assignment and uploaded it to the learning management system (LMS) but had forgotten to hit "submit" because she was preoccupied with returning to India to be with her family after her grandfather had died. She said didn't realize her assignment wasn't submitted until she didn't receive a grade. "Professor, could you please grade my assignment now?" Violet asked. Violet was an engaged student in the class and she seemed sincere. Yet, that didn't change the fact that Violet was now asking Tricia for a favor or an exception. So Tricia gave Violet an assignment: "Write me a paragraph or two about this situation in which you and I find ourselves: what led to it, what the ethical dimensions of the situation are, and what all of the possible resolution options are. That will help me decide what I should do." Violet wrote that piece and in doing so, demonstrated that she had a firm understanding of the situation, a mastery of course concepts, and a history of engagement in the class. So, Tricia agreed to grade her late assignment.

The moral of this story is that you can use almost any moment to infuse integrity into your teaching. While you may not be teaching ethics, you are teaching human beings who will present and create ethical dilemmas for you to address: Can I submit this assignment late? I didn't realize this was due, can I do it now? Whenever a student presents you with a dilemma that pits an honorable value against another honorable value (such as honesty against fairness, respect against trustworthiness, privacy versus equity), you can leverage that moment to discuss integrity with your student rather than just responding with a yes or no. Of course, if you are not teaching ethics, your student may not have the intellectual background to engage as Tricia's student did. But you could simplify the exercise by giving the students a guide and asking them to reflect on their request according to this guide.[5] Agree that if they can express to you why granting their request would be the ethical course of action for you to take, then you will grant it. Doing this positions students to critically consider what integrity values like fairness, for example, mean in the context of grading. They might persuade you that the most ethical course of action is for you to grant their request, or they might discover that granting their request would cause harm to another fundamental value (such as trustworthiness) that they had not considered. This practice also serves the purpose of slowing students down and making sure they are being thoughtful about their requests. Of course, if you plan on incorporating this strategy into your teaching, in the interests of fairness and consistency, we recommend that you mention it to students at the beginning of the course in some way, so they all know it is an option.

Align Expectations with Assessment Rubrics

In chapter 3, we proposed alternative grading strategies. If you're not yet ready to take that step—and that's okay—an entry strategy for facilitating more authentic learning and integrity is effective use of rubrics. By connecting evaluation criteria with learning outcomes, rubrics serve to *communicate the purpose* of the assessment and help students identify what they will learn through completing it.

Rubrics are a simple way to communicate to students your expectations—the learning outcomes—for every single assessment. Rubrics make your learning expectations transparent, so students understand up front what they ought to be focusing on. It reduces the mystery of assessment. A rubric generally takes the form of a table or grid that lists a set of criteria by which a particular assignment will be evaluated and describes how a student would demonstrate the level of learning they mastered (for example, needs work, competent, sophisticated). There are many different types of rubrics, and the best one to use likely depends on your preferences, your class, and the nature of the assignment.[6]

We are strong advocates for using rubrics as often as possible because they support integrity. Rubrics are useful for identifying your learning objectives, for communicating them to your students, and for making your assessment of their mastery transparent to them. When students don't feel confident that they understand what they can do to master the material (or achieve their external goals), they focus on the unknown and use strategies designed to increase their grade rather than their learning.

Students who believe that evaluations are unfair or that their teacher is focused on grades rather than their learning will use those beliefs to neutralize their understanding that cheating on an assignment is wrong. Having a well-developed and clearly communicated rubric can increase student self-efficacy by focusing them on learning objectives and away from grades and reducing their neutralizing attitudes. As an added bonus, having an effective rubric also makes evaluation easier, because once the criteria for meeting learning expectations are established, feedback becomes inherent in the rubric and you need to write fewer individualized notes.

Rubrics are a fairly standard pedagogical technique, but unfortunately many of us have no training in making or using them. First, as with creating course-level learning outcomes, give some explicit consideration to your motivations for that assignment. Once you have developed your goals for it, the next step in rubric design is to determine what behaviors will demonstrate mastery, partial mastery, and need for further development (or whatever benchmarks you choose). In other words, what does a good submission look like especially given that a chatbot might be able to produce something that meets the criteria of the rubric. In fact, the downside of rubrics is that a student can give the assignment prompt and the rubric to the chatbot, and have it produce the corresponding output at the mastery level they desire to fake. So, we advise to run your assignment prompts through some chatbots to see what they might produce, then adjust your rubric accordingly. If, for example, the chatbot can produce what used to be C-level work, perhaps now you decide to expect more at that level.

Many rubrics assign a grade or point value to each level of achievement. Doing so is acceptable but not ideal, because it focuses students back on points and away from learning. Creating a full rubric can and should take time and effort, because you will need to specify and describe all the levels of performance for each learning goal and determine how and whether to add more weight to particular goals. For example, you may determine that mastery of key concepts is more important for a particular task than developing connections or making applications.

An example rubric for a short assignment taken from the website of the Eberly Center at Carnegie Mellon University does an excellent job of achieving these objectives.[7] It uses the broad categories of Sophisticated, Competent, and Needs Work to evaluate student work on each criterion and mentions points only secondarily. Note that the terminology is positive and is still growth oriented even when few points are awarded. The evaluation criteria connect with the assignment description and goals. This particular rubric is designed to assess students' level of mastery of the skill of making an argument from research, so the criteria are Introduction (which is evaluated based on the clarity, specificity, and appropriateness of the position articulated), Research (which is evaluated on relevance, clarity, appropriateness of theory, and connection to the argument), Conclusions (evaluates overall logic, and connection to research), and Writing (which connects the rubric to a course goal of improving written communication).

Once you have designed the rubric and ensured it's connected to your overall goals, it's useful to back-test it against some previous submissions for the assignment and against chatbot output (preferably ask a colleague to produce this output, so you don't know which submissions are from humans and which are from machines). Pay particular attention to whether your intuitions about the quality of the work correlate with the rubric outcomes or whether you would have felt an urge to fudge the scores in some categories for a better fit. In the latter case, consider whether the mismatch represents a misalignment of particular goals, or whether a goal or behavior is missing from the rubric. Your work on this step will be important for students because they must perceive the results from the rubric as fair and consistent. Fudging in back-testing is a sign that the rubric isn't working the way you expected it would. If you find yourself changing rubric scores to make the grades fit your intuitions, then the rubric becomes window dressing. Students can detect that your grades don't match the rubric, which in turn will trigger neutralizing attitudes that may lead them to rationalize cheating.

Although creating a grading rubric for every assessment isn't an easy task, it's a good place to start your teaching-for-integrity journey, since many institutions require them anyway. Also, you can divide the workload by collaborating with your colleagues to develop common rubrics for shared courses, share language for common learning objectives across courses, and create a library of rubrics for common activities that can be modified for each course context. Some LMS platforms have features that make sharing rubrics easy, so before reinventing the wheel, conduct a search there or online more generally for rubrics that share your goals and are available for public use. Or use a chatbot to help you generate rubrics for your assignments. You can easily do this using Dan Fitzpatrick and colleagues' PREP model: Prompt (give the AI tool a task), Role (give it a role or voice), Explicit (be detailed and clear in your instructions), and Parameters (give it the scope and boundaries for the task).[8] The following is an example of applying the PREP model to a genetics assignment:

Prompt	Create a grading rubric for a genetics assignment.
Role	You are a university professor teaching an introductory course in genetics.
Explicit	I will give you an assignment that I have designed and the learning goals associated with that assignment. You will create a grading rubric for that assignment. The rubric needs to include the assessment criteria, five levels for each criterion, and marks for each level.
Parameter	Write the rubric in a style and level appropriate for undergraduate students in their first or second year of study.

This is the input we provided to ChatGPT4 for this example:

Create a grading rubric for a genetics assignment.
You are a university professor teaching an introductory course in genetics.
I will give you an assignment designed by Teach Genetics at University of Utah and the associated learning goals. You

will create a grading rubric for that assignment. The rubric needs to include the assessment criteria, five levels for each criterion, and marks for each level.

Write the rubric in a style and level appropriate for undergraduate students in their first or second year of study.

Assignment: Students take an inventory of their own easily observable genetic traits. Working in small groups, they observe how their trait inventories differ from those of others. Students record their observations in a data table and make a bar graph to show the most and least common traits in the group. Learning Objectives: Traits are observable characteristics that are passed down from parent to child. An individual will have many traits they share in common with others. An individual's overall combination of traits makes them unique. Some traits are more common in a population than others.[9]

The output we received is presented in table 2. Though it's not perfect, the output at least gets you started and does the low-level work (such as formatting) for you.

Providing rubrics is only helpful if students know how to use them to shape their self-directed learning. Therefore, foreground the rubric when introducing the assignment to help students better understand the purpose of the assignment and how it is connected to the overall learning goals for the course. This will help stimulate their intrinsic motivation because they'll see the benefits of mastering the skills and knowledge required to complete the assignment. They will also be able to assess their current competence and create a mental map of the path to achievement at a given level of the rubric. David often encourages students by reminding them that the point of the activity is to help them learn and do something they couldn't do before taking the class. He follows up by highlighting the course structures that will support them in building the competencies they need to succeed at the goals that the rubric outlines. Remember, the explicit goal is to help students succeed, but the implicit goal is to help them believe that they *can* succeed.

TABLE 2. Rubric for an introductory genetics assignment as generated by ChatGPT-4

Criterion	*Excellent (5)*	*Good (4)*	*Satisfactory (3)*	*Needs improvement (2)*	*Unsatisfactory (1)*	*Marks*
Trait inventory accuracy and completeness	Inventory is complete with all observable traits accurately listed; descriptions are detailed.	Inventory is nearly complete with minor inaccuracies; descriptions are mostly detailed.	Inventory includes most observable traits with some inaccuracies; descriptions lack some detail.	Inventory is incomplete with several inaccuracies; descriptions are vague or missing.	Inventory is largely incomplete or inaccurate; little to no effort in descriptions.	20
Data table clarity and organization	Data table is exceptionally organized and clear, with accurate recording of all group members' traits.	Data table is well-organized and clear, with minor errors in recording traits.	Data table is organized but with some confusion or errors in recording traits.	Data table is poorly organized, making interpretation difficult; several errors in recording traits.	Data table is extremely disorganized or incomplete; fails to accurately record traits.	20
Bar graph presentation and accuracy	Bar graph is well-constructed with accurate representation of the most and least common traits; highly legible.	Bar graph accurately represents most traits with minor inaccuracies; legible.	Bar graph represents traits with some inaccuracies; somewhat difficult to interpret.	Bar graph has significant inaccuracies; difficult to interpret.	Bar graph is inaccurately constructed or missing; fails to represent traits appropriately.	20

Analysis and interpretation of data	Provides a thorough analysis and insightful interpretation of the data; clearly relates findings to learning objectives.	Provides a solid analysis with good interpretation of the data; relates findings to learning objectives with minor omissions.	Provides a basic analysis and interpretation of the data; somewhat relates findings to learning objectives.	Analysis and interpretation are minimal or flawed; poorly relates findings to learning objectives.	Lacks analysis or interpretation; fails to relate findings to learning objectives.	20
Group collaboration and participation	Actively engages with group members; contributes significantly to the task.	Participates well with group members; contributes to most parts of the task.	Participates in the group; contributions are adequate but not extensive.	Limited participation in group activities; minimal contribution.	Does not participate in group activities; no contribution.	20

Source: Text generated by ChatGPT, OpenAI, February 3, 2024, https://chat.openai.com.

Allow and Co-opt Collaboration

Students frequently report working together on assignments that are intended to be individual work. This is actually the most commonly self-reported kind of academic dishonesty.[10] And, it's not difficult to imagine that working with a chatbot on an assignment intended to be individually completed unaided will soon become the most common behavior. Collaboration with other humans or machines is very difficult to prevent, so it's worth asking yourself whether you need to prevent it. Clearly copying homework is not helpful for learning, but genuine collaboration can be among the most effective ways to promote deep understanding of difficult material. It's not always possible to allow students to collaborate with each other or with chatbots on assessments, but when it's appropriate for facilitating the achievement of learning objectives, consider permitting it. When collaboration is not appropriate because, for example, you need to assure that individual students have a competency to build on for later activities, then (as we discuss in chapter 2), make sure the expectation and rationale for requiring individual work are clearly articulated.

The first reason to allow students to collaborate is a practical one. If they are likely to collaborate anyway, why spend the time and effort to punish them for what they feel is a natural response to difficult work? Of course, if collaboration undermines learning goals, that is a different matter, but collaboration often enhances rather than undermines learning. This is particularly true when genuine collaboration occurs. When each student is required to think deeply about the material, practice necessary skills, and engage with the work of their peers or a chatbot, collaboration can be even more productive for learning than solo work.

Unfortunately, collaboration can also lead to disengagement, social loafing, and less learning than individual work. When students do collaborate on assignments, be sure to create a collaborative structure that fosters, and even requires, all students to play an active role in the learning activity. To this end, it's useful to require them to report on the collaborative process. Ask them to submit a short reflection on which aspects of the assignment they and their (human or machine) partner(s) contributed and what they gained from the process. If they collaborated with a chatbot, have them submit their exchange and ask them to reflect on what they might do differently next time. If they collaborated with peers, this exercise could reduce social loafing, since students know that their team members will be commenting on each other's contributions. In human-chatbot collaborations, it can mitigate an overreliance on the chatbot's output. Reflection may also aid the development of metacognition and allow students to get help from their peers (or chatbots) without fear of punishment. Be sure to frame the purpose of the entire assignment as learning and practice for higher-stakes assessments, to give students the space to try new things without fear of failure. Thereby, students may develop a more growth-oriented perspective toward their coursework.

For complex assessments, or when introducing collaborative work, it can be useful either to highlight or assign key roles that students must play so you can make sure that each task is completed collaboratively and in accordance with your learning goals. For example, almost any task has managerial, organizational, research, logistical, and other aspects that must be completed. Students can be given the task of creating a work plan that incorporates these categories or particular steps involved in completing a task. Collaborative assignments can be structured in advance to ensure that each student participates in those tasks that are essential for learning outcomes (such as doing research) and that the logistical work is distributed fairly or offloaded to the chatbot.

You can combine collaboration with rubric design by giving students a worksheet for evaluating their own and their peers' (or chatbot's) contributions to the learning process. Such a worksheet would list the various kinds of contributions an individual might make to the collaborative assignment and ask each student to estimate the percentage of each contribution made by each (human or chatbot) team member. This gives students a structure to conceive of collaborative work and a way to formally evaluate their collaborator(s). The worksheet is useful for grading too, of course, but when you present it ahead of the collaborative assignment, it also gives each student a way to envision their own contributions, even those who are not traditional leaders or who do not see themselves as having as much to contribute.

Almost any assessment can be made collaborative, but not every assessment should be. In particular, we recommend using collaborative activities only when the course structure will allow you to devote time and attention to the collaborative process so that it is intentionally designed and purposefully evaluated. A friend of David's who worked in the nonprofit sector described collaboration as "an unnatural process engaged in by unwilling participants." We think this description is unnecessarily cynical, but it does highlight the difficulties of collaborative assignments, especially when students are asked to collaborate with other humans outside of the shared class time. Many of our students have complained about group work, not necessarily because they don't want to work with others, but because it adds logistical complexity to their already busy lives. So, it's important for you to spend the time to plan collaborations properly or allow students to collaborate with chatbots instead of other students. Make sure that the task is amenable to sharing, that the assessment requires all students to achieve key learning goals, and that students have a clear strategy for sharing the workload with one another or the chatbot while holding themselves and their human collaborators accountable in a positive way. Also, if you can build the course to enable collaborations to occur within class time, do so.

Give Opportunities for Revision

When Tricia was in the second year of her undergraduate psychology degree, she enrolled in a psychology of learning course. That course had the reputation of being extremely challenging, partly due to the professor, whom a lot of students didn't like. He was smart but rather insensitive. He was challenging but rather brusque. He was available but terse. Tricia remembers one class in which he actually made a student cry. In this course, the final grade was based on multiple-choice tests (designed to encourage students to learn the underlying course concepts) and one big project designed to enable the students to demonstrate their ability to apply the course concepts. The big project? Teach a rat to do a task. At the end of the semester, the students had to present their project in two forms: (1) the rat had to perform its task, and (2) the student had to write and submit a research paper about the experiment. Tricia absolutely loved this class. The professor was very clear about his expectations, and the project was interesting and meaningful. As a result, Tricia approached the class with gusto, trained her rat to raise a Canadian flag on cue, and submitted her research paper on time. To her dismay, the professor extended the paper deadline (yes, the "mean" professor used flexible deadlines) at the request of other students. Tricia (don't judge her here) complained to the professor that it wasn't fair that other students had more time. The professor offered to review Tricia's paper and provide feedback so she could revise and resubmit it. By the time the final paper deadline (extended twice) arrived, Tricia had revised her paper extensively, subsequently earning an A+ on the assignment. In this story, the opportunity for revisions not only created a sense of fairness (and therefore enhanced integrity), but motivated Tricia to keep learning and improving her research writing skills.

Tricia's story illustrates the power of flexible deadlines for reducing cheating and increasing students' intrinsic motivations (as covered in chapter 3), as well as the power of giving students opportunities to revise their work whenever possible. This suggestion is rooted in three beliefs:

1. Opportunities for revision reduce the stakes even on major assignments, so that students focus on learning rather than grades.
2. Opportunities for revision signal to students that your assessment goal is learning, not just sorting them into grade categories. Once that belief is established, neutralizing attitudes become harder to form and cheating will decrease.
3. Providing opportunities for revision gives students a sense of control over their own destiny and a road

> map for success. In addition to lowering the stakes, ceding assignment control also increases students' self-efficacy. In particular, students who experience evaluation anxiety can benefit from having a second chance to show what they know rather than resorting to cheating to alleviate their fear of failure.[11]

Revision can take many forms, depending on the structure of the initial assessment. For tests, particularly ones containing multiple-choice questions, you could have teams of students take the test again, allowing them to compare their answers and revisit the material to determine the correct answer.[12] A more common strategy is to allow students to complete a post-test assignment. Such an assignment typically requires students to reflect on their incorrect answers, select the correct answer, and explain their original reasoning and their current understanding of the concepts involved. Although this kind of assignment is sometimes created ad-hoc after a poor test performance, we advocate building it into the syllabus as an option for all students.

You might be thinking, "But in the last chapter, you advised us to assess more often. Surely you don't expect us to allow revisions if we incorporate frequent testing and assignments!" But, alas, yes, we do. The purpose of allowing revisions on low-stakes assessments is to engender metacognitive knowledge and self-regulation, both of which we know can reduce cheating, as discussed in chapter 3. So, for small weekly homework assignments, we recommend grading on a credit/no credit basis using mastery criteria. In David's classes, the weekly homework assignments are called "Quiz Prep" and are explicitly designed to elicit responses that require good study techniques. In particular, students are asked to determine the key points in the weekly material, summarize them in plain language, and generate a follow-up question for class discussion. The active nature of this assignment encourages deeper processing of class material than simply reviewing one's notes, which is passive and therefore the kiss of death in studying.

David's students also generate a multiple-choice question for each of their key points, so that they learn to think about the topic like a psychologist (or at least an instructor). With respect to revision, these homework assignments are graded as satisfactory or needs revision. Students must submit a good-faith effort before the quiz, and revisions must be turned in before the next assignment is due. Students generally report that the homework activity forces them to study more effectively (this sometimes takes the form of complaining, but that's OK), and most of them even like the structure.

Unfortunately, this task can be performed dishonestly using a chatbot, but that doesn't render it useless. It's a structured study technique, so if students can use a chatbot to complete the assignment and still do well on in-class quizzes, so be it. But that's unlikely. If the quizzes are well designed, then authentic study will benefit them, and "cheating the grind" will be reflected in quiz scores. In fact, the Quiz Prep assignments can be managed like an entry ticket for the quizzes rather than separate assessments. Students who mindlessly use a chatbot for their entry ticket gain no point benefit from that behavior and lose the opportunity to learn from the activity. On the other hand, if a student is able to use the chatbot thoughtfully as a collaborator to improve their mastery of the material, then that's great too!

For large projects and papers, revision is best combined with a scaffolded assignment structure. For each scaffolded piece of the assignment, students are given feedback and suggestions for revision (not grades or grades based on process), which they can then incorporate into their final draft. This back-and-forth process of writing and revising teaches students that a one-shot-and-done approach isn't the best way to learn or write.

Pedagogically, revisions like we've described so far provide students the opportunity for extra study time on concepts they found to be particularly difficult, for practicing self-regulated learning practices, and for developing metacognitive skills that will help them be more successful on future exams. From an academic cheating perspective, we remind students that their learning, rather than their performance, is the ultimate goal and allowing students who need additional help the opportunity to receive it reduces the stakes of the assessment. On a technical note, we don't recommend allowing rewrites for extra credit but only for learning and improving. Extrinsic incentives no longer support good study habits but instead motivate the students to do as little as possible because they know they'll have a chance to redo their work.

Revisions also give instructors openings to address inadvertent or ignorance-based plagiarism without resorting to a nuclear option. When a student plagiarizes (or you suspect they did) on a draft, this creates a teachable moment. If you design draft assignments effectively, it's possible to manage plagiarism (including submitting chatbot material as their own) as a fixable error rather than a moral failing. We suggest adding an originality component to the requirements for all drafts and incorporating feedback on originality into the draft, to give students a chance to learn and to correct any errors. With detailed feedback about paraphrasing and referencing, or even a stern warning about dishonesty, students may learn from their mistakes without focusing on facing or avoiding punishment. By creating an opportunity for understanding, learning, and growth, we encourage students to change their future behavior rather than shaming them for being caught plagiarizing. Revision is an excellent way to create these opportunities.

Give Students Choice and Control

Team-Based Learning (TBL) is a superb example of a pedagogy that incorporates student choice and control.[13] The class begins with the students being given the decision about what percentage of their grade will come from individual effort versus team effort. This is not an individual choice. Rather, teams of students come to a decision, then a representative from each team negotiates with the other representatives to come to a decision for the entire class. Students also have choice and control over their test scores. The students take their weekly quizzes first individually, then as a team. After the team test has concluded, they have choice and control over whether they appeal any of the questions they got wrong. Tricia also incorporated more choice and control within individual assignments—students could choose which organizational code of ethics to analyze, and students (in teams) could choose the topic for their final project. Tricia has taught for a number of years using TBL. The students love having choices and a sense of control. It animates them, it motivates them, and it reduces cheating. As a result, Tricia found teaching with this pedagogy a joy.[14]

The purpose of giving students more control over assessment is to avoid extrinsic or performance goal structures, in which students complete assignments only because they need (or want) points. It's not always possible to redesign an entire course assessment structure, but it is still possible to increase students' sense of control over their class experience by creating flexibility within each assessment. Giving students flexibility may spark their interest in the material, making learning more appealing than plagiarism. Students also feel more capable when they have some control over their environment. In a famous study by Ellen Langer, participants valued a lottery ticket more when they could choose it themselves than when it was assigned to them.[15] The illusion of control powerfully influences human behavior and can be harnessed to encourage student learning. In addition, when students have selected their own topic and chosen their own deliverable, they are much less likely to blame the instructor for any challenges that arise. From a more positive perspective, when students are required to complete a project in a format with which they are uncomfortable, they experience performance anxiety. Student choice mitigates this anxiety and thus reduces the temptation to avoid it by outsourcing or plagiarizing the assignment.

In David's content-focused courses, he has tried many different creative deliverables, including a Wikipedia article for his History of Psychology course, blog posts in Cognitive Psychology, and a paper outlining a practical application in Judgment and Decision Making. All these assignments provided more interesting, engaging, and authentic options than yet another research paper. Of course, such assignments can also become routine if students don't have a choice. The comment, "Oh, God, not another blog!" came up altogether too frequently for David's liking. Allowing students to choose a deliverable for demonstrating their learning is definitely easier in courses where the learning objectives are focused on content (for example, understand the structures and properties of organic and biomolecular species) rather than on skills (for example, learn how to write a research paper), but doing so is also possible in some skills-based courses. For example, in a public speaking course, students could choose to deliver their public talk live in an academic style similar to a TED video or live via video in a political-rally style. Even in a lab class, students could choose to demonstrate their mastery via a traditional lab report or an oral presentation or a PowerPoint with recorded narration. If the particular form of the deliverable is not part of the learning objectives, then choice and control is possible.

Remember that choice and control reduce cheating by engaging students' desire to work authentically, not by making the assignments inherently more secure. Some forms of alternative assignments can be generated as deepfakes today and many more will be coming online soon. We will discuss ways of securing assignments against technological spoofing in chapter 6, but *spoiler alert*, even those solutions are far from foolproof.

Students, especially undergraduates, are not used to being given choice and control. So, phasing in the degree of choice is a good idea to ease them into the process. You can begin with an exploratory activity. In David's classes, the first project activity occurs within the first two weeks of a term and requires students to skim ahead in the course materials to find three to five topics that seem interesting. Students then explain why those topics interest them and how the topics connect to the readings and their own lives. Following this exploratory activity, students submit a proposal for their final project based on one of the topics they previously selected, incorporating any feedback they've received. This process then cycles through an outline, sample use of evidence, a rough draft, and a final project. If detailed feedback is provided at each stage, then the entire process might be considered to be a scaffolded activity, but even with little feedback, a phased assignment can motivate students who appreciate being asked to share their own perspectives. Because so many students are unused to having control over their own work, providing interim, low-stakes feedback can make the process somewhat less daunting for them.

The results of student choice can be mundane, but also glorious. On the mundane end of the spectrum, students who are risk-averse will choose a typical and familiar deliverable and express gratitude for not having to step out of their comfort zone. This is an opportunity lost, to be sure, but if the goal is to give students the chance to make connections to the material, the distraction of a "creative" deliverable might not benefit everyone. For students with diverse interests or an adventurous streak, these projects give them permission to move up Bloom's taxonomy and create authentic learning experiences for themselves. Although David has yet to receive an annotated interpretive dance for a psychology course, he does live in hope. In the meantime, visual artists among his students have created artworks on paper and electronically annotated them to show connections between their creative work and the course material. Practical application projects are very popular as well. In one memorable example, a student who was also a peer tutor created new cognitively derived training materials for tutors who teach study-skills workshops.

Unfortunately, flexibility on large assignments does have downsides. First, grading rubrics must become much more generic to apply to a variety of deliverables. It's difficult to anticipate the ways in which very different deliverables (like an oral presentation on AI in the workplace and a painting with an artist's statement about neural networks) would both show excellence. To avoid creating a moving target for students, instructors should stick to the initial rubric. Therefore, it's necessary to be sure that the rubric is as flexible as the assignment. Second, allowing flexibility in content makes the process of outsourcing the assignment to another human or a chatbot much easier. An assignment that allows for a range of submissions also allows students to purchase one of many preexisting documents to submit. By contrast, a highly specified assignment is more expensive to outsource because less existing material is available (a human contractor will charge more and a subscription version of a chatbot might be needed), and it is more labor intensive to complete. How, then, do you reconcile the benefit of flexibility with the ease of outsourcing? Fundamentally, outsourcing can never be entirely prevented by assessment design, so we recommend you focus on creating excellent learning opportunities for your students and rely on the many other cheating mitigation strategies we've recommended throughout the book. In particular, requiring flexible assignments to include content that is specific to the course and that chatbots or ghostwriters can't easily access (as we discuss in chapter 6) is a good way to make outsourcing more difficult.

Make Your Assessments Authentic

> During the Cuban Missile Crisis, President Kennedy was being advised to order a targeted military strike to eliminate Russia's nuclear missiles, but he chose a different strategy. Briefly describe the strategies Kennedy considered, including the one he ultimately chose, and explain why he thought his chosen strategy was the best one.

As you might have guessed, the preceding excerpt is an exam essay question. How easy do you think it would be to cheat on this question if the exam were online or take-home? When we typed, "What strategy did Kennedy choose during the Cuban Missile Crisis and why" into a web browser, we got 721,000 hits, the first one being a full explanation from the JFK Library website. Easy to copy and paste. When we gave the prompt to ChatGPT4, we got a pretty solid five-paragraph response with an opening paragraph, one paragraph each covering the strike and naval blockade options, one paragraph briefly describing the other options, and a final paragraph explaining why Kennedy ultimately chose the blockade.

That leads us to ask, What is the point of asking such a question in the age of the internet, let alone in the age of GenAI and contract cheating? It falls low on any taxonomy of learning. It requires no deep insight or knowledge that could be achieved only by attending an institution of higher learning. It has no application to today's world (at least, the question doesn't ask for that). It has been asked and answered over and over again—likely on millions of (at least American) assessments since 1962. Yet it continues to be asked. Why? As Tricia implied back in 2008 in "Academic Integrity in the Twenty-First Century: A Teaching and Learning Imperative,"[16] educators are still teaching and assessing as if it were the twentieth century and the internet didn't exist! Now, in the second decade of the twenty-first century, we are teaching and assessing as if artificial intelligence and contract cheating didn't exist. It is certainly time now, if it wasn't before, to change assessments to be more authentic and, therefore, more meaningful.

The movement toward rethinking assessment has focused on the concept of *authentic assessment* as a way of describing activities that forge meaningful connections between academia and real-world experiences.[17] Faculty often have two thoughts on hearing the phrase "authentic assessment." The first is, "Oh, great! Another fad coming out from the teaching and learning folks. I'll just put my head down, bide my time, and the fad will be over soon enough." But that attitude is not realistic. The reason you are hearing about authentic assessments is because teaching and assessing in the twenty-first century has to be different than it was in the twentieth century. There is no way around it if we have any desire to make higher education meaningful and our degrees conferred with integrity.

The second response usually is, "Sure, it's easy for faculty in engineering or art to do authentic assessments. But I can't in my discipline, which requires basic knowledge and is theoretical." If you are one of those faculty, we hope to open your mind to the idea that any discipline, at any level of education, can employ more authentic assessments.

Grant Wiggins, who is credited with coining the term *authentic assessments,* would distinguish them from purely academic (or unrealistic) assessments and performance (e.g., doing a task) assessments.[18] According to Wiggins, authentic assessments differ from other types in their structure and logistics (e.g., they involve an audience or public output), intellectual design (e.g., they are representative challenges from the discipline or field), grading/scoring (e.g., they include self-assessment), and fairness (e.g., they don't involve comparison between students). Wiggins's list of characteristics is long, and he originally constructed it as a critique of K–12 testing practices. In higher education, we might turn to the definition used by our colleague Phill Dawson, which positions authentic assessment as composed of activities or tasks that match the skills, knowledge, and attitudes that students will need to have as professionals.[19] (We would add "and citizens" to the end of that definition.) For higher education, it is possible to sum up authentic assessments as follows: challenging, as similar as possible to a meaningful task, and involving performing a task or completing a project many times in a collaborative fashion.[20] The principles of authentic assessment dovetail with other recommendations we make in this book, including scaffolding, iterative feedback, promotion of metacognition, transparent expectations, and flexible deadlines. At their core, authentic assessments are more interesting, fun, relevant, and, therefore, more meaningful to students as compared to traditional assessments.

To explore how you might make your assessments more authentic, start small, at the level of questions or prompts in traditional assessments. Can you make a question/prompt more authentic by adding metacognitive subprompts, requiring the application of knowledge learned in the class or in the students' own lives, or updating it to be relevant to the contemporary context? For example, asking students to reflect on what surprised them about a topic can lead to unique and thoughtful responses. In the age of GenAI, creating a text that is correct on the surface and meets assignment criteria is relatively easy, but to create one that is consistent with the learning context requires more work by the user. Any time we can make it more difficult for students to offload their thinking and learning to a machine, we raise the bar on the temptation to use the machine to cheat. For example, asking for strong connections to class discussions, concepts, and readings would require the student to feed that information into the chatbot to make any output it produces useful. So, strong connections to the class experience are a good example of a low-effort intervention that can both yield positive learning outcomes and make misconduct harder.[21]

If you're ready to replace some of the traditional types of assessments, revisit your learning objectives and consider how you might assess those objectives with alternative deliverables, flexible time lines, student choice and control, and public deliverables in a way that has relevancy to the field or the real world.

For example, a professor of marketing we know partnered with the local tourism commission to have the students create marketing ideas to attract international travelers to their small city (meaningful). These were collaborative projects that received iterative feedback throughout the process. Ultimately, the city used the students' work as part of its overall marketing strategy (audience). In a history course in the same city, students were asked to create interpretive signs for a local historic site. In the process of doing so, students researched nearby events to understand the importance of that place and its people (meaningful). They then created actual materials that visitors see today (audience). In History of Psychology, David asked students to choose an important but underrepresented figure in psychology then write (or expand) Wikipedia articles on them. Students learned to conduct basic historical research, to evaluate that research both for accuracy and as a tool for communication, and to write factually accurate short prose.

A more systematic, cross-disciplinary example can be found in Passion-Driven Statistics, an introductory curriculum created by a team based at Wesleyan University.[22] Students are given learning opportunities in biology, business, education, and other disciplines with the express goal of using actual datasets as learning sandboxes. The result is a set of authentic exercises designed to foster the skills required to use statistics in disciplinary research. Assessments take the form of typical research statistics tasks used across disciplines, such as data visualization, determining causality, and using data to justify claims. For many STEM students, the opportunity to use their knowledge immediately on real-world data rather than practice exercises will be quite compelling.

In the preceding examples, students understand that their audience is not merely a single grader but a group of people with various backgrounds who will evaluate their work for its usefulness rather than to assign a grade. In all cases, the work is challenging and, being a real-world activity, is applicable beyond the classroom and meaningfully connected to course material. Authentic projects involve extensive feedback and encourage metacognition. In particular, because students are creating content for an audience with different backgrounds and interests than theirs, they are required to consider the needs of that audience and create content that fits those needs. This emphasizes to students that communicating about what they have learned is an important part of getting an education. It makes the link between academic learning and real-life applications explicit.

As we have mentioned, motivation is powerful force in shaping students' behavior. While there is certainly no guarantee that motivation alone will eliminate misconduct, authentic assessments are more difficult to plagiarize than a typical essay because the information is not easily found on the internet or constructed by artificial intelligence. Let's take the example at the start of this section—the Cuban Missile Crisis and Kennedy's actions. One could make that question somewhat more meaningful by asking the students to compare Kennedy's decision to a time in their own life when they were being pressured to make a decision and how the pressure influenced their decision and subsequent action. The answer could still be fabricated but perhaps the student will be less motivated to do so. Lastly, because many authentic assessments are either done collaboratively or presented publicly, more of the work process is transparent. That makes it more difficult for a student to outsource or cheat on the work, and it makes identifying any cheating easier. We know that ease of detection reduces the likelihood that students will cheat. Again, while they aren't cheat-proof, assessments that students *want* to do authentically will have a direct positive impact on academic integrity and learning outcomes.

Instead of Banning Technology, Plan for Cognitive Offloading

One way to make your assessments more authentic and generally more engaging is to incorporate what Phill Dawson (and others before him) calls "cognitive offloading."[23] This is something that we do every single day. *Cognitive offloading* involves using external technology to reduce the cognitive load created by a task. It can take multiple forms:

- Writing something down so you don't have to remember it.
- Using a calculator so you don't have to add a series of numbers in your head.
- Using spelling or grammar checkers when composing emails, essays, or books.
- Using twenty-first-century artificial intelligence tools like large language models (e.g., ChatGPT) and image generators (e.g., MidJourney) to produce content, gather information, and translate languages.

As Phill points out, students will cognitively offload, whether or not you want them to. Also, with advanced technology being integrated into our daily tools (e.g., GPT integration into Google Workspace and Microsoft 365), prohibition is not a viable option. The GenAI writing assistant Grammarly has more than thirty million users each day.[24] The horses have left the barn. Can you imagine banning ballpoint pens? Our parents (David's anyway) were forbidden to use the newfangled ballpoint technology for fear that their handwriting would be forever ruined when writing with (then mainstream) fountain pens. The same vignette could be written about calculators or spell checkers in the 1970s and 1990s, respectively. Authors of future books like this one will no doubt be writing about the epochal changes brought about by GenAI in the 2020s.

So, rather than retaining your existing assessments and adding artificial intelligence to your list of prohibited aids (thereby defining the cognitive offloading as cheating), we concur with Phill and others that assessments will need to be redesigned to engage students more authentically with the tools that are available to them. While every course will require different approaches and guidelines for using cognitive offloading tools, a good first step is to reexamine the course learning objectives to decide three things:

1. Should any of the learning objectives change given advancements in technology? For example, most higher education instructors have removed spelling and grammar from their rubrics because those tasks are completed by machines not by students. These skills may still be assessed for beginning writers (or in language classes), but perhaps they can be offloaded in discipline-based writing. What other skills no longer need to be assessed in your courses because they are not necessary building blocks for the discipline? Consider a chemistry lab course, for example. Should it retain "learn how to write a scientific report in the format of an American Chemical Society journal" as a learning objective? After all, not only can artificial intelligence do the heavy lifting on that assignment, but most undergraduates will not be writing academic journal articles after they graduate (and therefore will not find the assessment meaningful or authentic). Such a learning objective, combined with a prohibition on artificial intelligence tools, is more likely to design in cheating than help students develop relevant skills. Perhaps the learning objective could instead be "create a presentation to relay your findings, conclusions, and implications to an audience of your choice." The presentation format could be the students' choice (e.g., lab report, journal article, talk with PowerPoint slides, poster, web page, or blog), as could the intended audience (e.g., the owner of a company, academic colleagues, a group of schoolchildren). For those students with designs on a graduate degree in chemistry, the laboratory report option would seem more authentic, but for those aspiring to teach, a lesson plan may be more relevant.
2. Which, if any, of the learning objectives must students first accomplish without the aid of a tool? In deciding this, consider whether there are fundamental skills or knowledge—building blocks—that students have

to develop in order to master higher-order skills. For example, in a statistics class, perhaps students still need to learn how to calculate chi-squares and ANOVAs on their own so that when they analyze output from a statistical tool, they can evaluate it for correctness and understand the implications. In that case, a proctored assessment will likely be needed to ensure that the students do not resort to the aid of a tool.

3. Can you assess students' performance on learning objectives in alternate ways that take into account the existence of artificial intelligence and contract cheating? For example, if the learning objective is to analyze voice, audience, and the clarity of writing in a text, students could do this with output generated from a chatbot. Imagine asking students to use a chatbot to write a paragraph using only passive voice, then to comment on the feel and readability of the result. Or, if the goal is to learn the techniques of outlining an essay, perhaps the students could use a chatbot to reverse-outline an essay and analyze the output for insight.

Tools are inherently value neutral, but they can quickly become a negative influence if our pedagogy fails to account for their availability. Many of the techniques we describe in the book can be modified to account for cognitive offloading, and we encourage this practice throughout the course and instructional design process.

Include Oral Assessments

Why do we require doctoral students to orally defend their dissertations? Why do we gather (virtually or in person) at conferences to hear each other speak about our research? Why, at work, do we have meetings or conversations about important topics or decisions to be made? Because talking and listening aids understanding. Because asking questions helps humans to probe and learn. Real-time communication with another person in any form is a distinctive experience. It allows for answering questions, expanding knowledge, clarifying misunderstandings, and effectively speculating past the point of current knowledge. Yet, it is not common practice in either physical or virtual classes to give students a chance to say what they know in real time.

Many of us are familiar with oral exams, which can range from highly controlled and predictable to interactive and exploratory. They are the final step to complete a doctorate ("the defense") worldwide. Oral exams are typical in language classes, as you might expect, but in Europe and the United Kingdom, they are also commonplace in graduate and undergraduate courses in all disciplines, and their use is growing in the United States. Molly Worthen, in a December 2022 *New York Times* op-ed on the topic, described a few key successes in disciplines ranging from biology and chemistry to philosophy. Overall, students reported being more stressed by the oral exams, but also learning better because they had to study more to prepare. The project we mentioned earlier, conducted by UC San Diego engineering faculty during the COVID-19 lockdown, found similar results: even though students were initially worried about the oral exam, they learned more and appreciated the opportunity to speak directly with the course instructor or a teaching assistant about their knowledge and understandings.[25] Worthen also highlighted a project by Doug Luckie and colleagues at Michigan State University in which they added an oral final exam as an option for their undergraduate biology students.[26] Students generally liked having the choice, and follow-up research indicated that those who opted for the oral exam retained knowledge better and showed more evidence of transfer across domains. It's hard to know whether these differences reflect a selection bias or genuine differences in learning, but the evidence suggests that oral exams are good for learning.

One form of oral assessment with which many of us are familiar is the typical academic presentation. A student presents—usually with some visual (e.g., a slide deck)—their knowledge of an academic subject and answers a few questions. Other oral assessments might be more like informal conversations with students to delve into what they know or don't know about a particular topic. Such informal assessments can be used either to diagnose where a student is struggling or to allow them to share what they know beyond what they've written on a typical assessment.

To begin thinking about how you might incorporate oral assessments into your classes, we recommend an article by Gordon Joughin. In this article, he highlights the key distinctive variables to consider and provides options for constructing the best oral assessment given your situational context.[27] The first decision is whether the oral assessment itself should be included in the learning goals (i.e., students will learn how to orally communicate their research findings), or whether the sole purpose is to develop and assess the students' content mastery. Second, will students work in groups, collaborate with a chatbot, or work on their own? Third, will the assignment itself be authentic, as in the example of a medical student presenting a case to an attending physician, or will it be more academic, like a typical thesis defense. You must also decide who will be evaluating the students and whether the evaluators are the intended audience. Even if instructors or instructional assistants are the graders, students' presentations may be pitched to novices, experts, or any other relevant audience. Finally, you must decide how interactive the assessment is to be. A recorded presentation has little to no interaction, whereas a live assessment can include conversation and questioning. Let's examine this vast landscape of choices with a few examples.

Oral exams can be as formal or informal as you like. In the UC San Diego example, the faculty initiated a National Science Foundation–funded project to examine the effectiveness of oral exams.[28] The teachers-researchers scheduled students for fifteen- to twenty-minute virtual sessions to ask them about their content knowledge. While the interactions were somewhat formal, the researchers structured the assessment to feel more like a conversation than a thesis defense. You could make your assessment even more informal. Picture a conversation over coffee with a student about what they've learned in the course. The topics for discussion would be very similar to the essay questions that you might present in a written final, but in the oral version you would ask clarifying and follow-up questions on each topic. Follow-up questions give students a chance to show what they have learned, to experiment with using terminology or key concepts, and to be assessed at whatever level of Bloom's taxonomy they are capable of. At Johns Hopkins University, math professor Richard Brown found oral exams to be an indispensable method for giving him a comprehensive view of what a student actually knew. He would ask a question and if the student didn't quite answer it or couldn't answer it, he could give a hint or probe to help them articulate their knowledge.[29] Will Styler, at UC San Diego, posts his oral exam policy and procedures online, making his expectations transparent and the rules of the road clear to the students.[30]

Other kinds of oral assessment can provide some of the benefits of an exam with less pressure and more authenticity. One type of nonwritten assessment that most educators are familiar with is an oral presentation. As compared to an oral exam, presentations are more authentic because public speaking is a practical skill. At the same time, presentations retain much of the control that oral exams have because they are structured, timed, and amenable to the use of rubrics. However, presentations are typically less interactive than oral exams, with only a few minutes being allowed at the end for questions, so they may not as be as effective for assessing what the student actually knows versus what they are parroting from a text or a chatbot. Oral presentations can be conducted in groups or individually and can be used to assess only learning objectives relating to the content, or those along with objectives pertaining to the presentation process.

To ensure that we are making the best choices for our students in terms of authentic and equitable learning, we recommend starting with hybrid assessments that include written and oral components. This is what the UC San Diego researchers are doing with great success. Make the oral component a follow-up, even an optional follow-up, to the written component. In undergraduate education, we most commonly see this hybrid approach in research-based classes, where a written report is followed by an oral presentation. However, a written report followed by an oral presentation that repeats the same content can easily be undermined by cheating and plagiarism. So, instead require the students to give an oral presentation about their thought processes, their choices, their process for completing the project, the application of course principles, and/or the skills they used to complete the written report. This framework has proven successful for assessing medical students' clinical reasoning and is frequently recommended as a means of deterring misconduct.[31]

Oral assessments are effective for enhancing academic integrity because students who know that they will be expected to orally explain their written work must prepare accordingly. Many will choose to complete the written work themselves, but for those who don't, their lack of familiarity with the material is a strong indicator that they committed academic misconduct. Overall, oral assessments are much harder to cheat on than written exams or assessments completed outside of the classroom. We say that there is nowhere to hide in an oral assessment, because it is more difficult to engage in the most common types of misconduct in that context. Copying from other humans or machines, using unauthorized resources (spy technology notwithstanding), contract cheating, and even getting material from those who have already completed the assessment are much less effective. Faking verbal fluency about a topic that one doesn't understand is much harder than faking written fluency. This is particularly true for oral assessments, which are relatively less structured and more spontaneous than their written counterparts. A student who has not prepared authentically will present their knowledge much differently than one who has done so. Also, it is much easier for a potential cheater to change the font and headings of a purchased or downloaded paper than to find a complete presentation online or construct one with a chatbot, reuse the visual materials, and learn their lines from a script. GenAI can certainly help a student prepare the script for a presentation and can even create the voiceover for a recorded video, but at least for now, it can't deliver an in-person presentation.[32] As with any assignment, there is no way to design out cheating entirely, but oral, in-person assessments raise the cost of cheating in time and effort.

Of course, oral assessments are not perfect, and many faculty have concerns about using them. Foremost is a concern about the stress they may cause to students who have a fear of public speaking. Jerry Seinfeld is quoted as saying, "According to most studies, people's number-one fear is public speaking. Number two is death. Death is number two. Does that sound right? This means to the average person, if you go to a funeral, you're better off in the casket than doing the eulogy." While this is probably not psychologically accurate, it does have a certain ring of truth to it. However, it doesn't make sense to avoid oral assessments simply because they might cause stress. Lots of things cause stress for our students. Some students are more stressed at the thought of a written exam than an oral one. Other students are stressed by the thought of writing a research paper. Stress is not a bad thing but a fact of life, and it is important that our students learn how to speak about their knowledge despite feeling stress. Picture your student later in life attempting to convince the boss that there is a flaw in a new product that must be remedied before it goes to market. Stressful? Yes. Imperative that they communicate effectively? Absolutely!

The stress of an oral assessment can be minimized by using the same techniques used to scaffold written assessments: lowering stakes and giving students practice runs. Or, instead of one lengthy oral assessment, break it into more frequent but shorter oral assessments, which give students more opportunities to practice, more success experiences, and a chance to habituate to the experience. Also, having teaching assistants conduct oral assessments, as Baghdadchi and colleagues do at UC San Diego, might reduce stress because of the student-to-student, rather than student-to-teacher, interaction. However, some students experience severe anxiety when orally presenting their knowledge. For those students, and others with documented accommodations (e.g., students who are nonverbal or stutter severely) you might have to have alternatives in place. We recommend working with your local disability resource office to decide what types of accommodations would be appropriate.

Faculty are usually also concerned that oral assessments might unfairly penalize students who are not fluent speakers of the language of instruction. These students also need practice at communicating their knowledge in the language of instruction (something that is, for now, expected when they graduate). Giving students plenty of time to orally communicate what they know, asking follow-up questions, and making the assessment low stakes and relatively informal can mitigate this concern.

One way to use oral assessments to the benefit of students in need of support comes from Curt Schurgers, one of the professors involved in the oral exam project at UC San Diego. Schurgers transitioned from using oral assessments as an academic integrity check after a written exam to using them as an early intervention for at-risk students. Students who appear at risk of performing poorly in the course are contacted and offered an oral assessment for extra credit. Curt says that this offer encourages students to come in and connect with a teaching assistant or the instructor, who can either identify the cause of the struggle or sometimes even help the student realize they are struggling. The latter case is almost a metacognitive assessment—an intervention that will raise the student's awareness of the need to rethink strategies that are not working well. This type of oral assessment would be suitable for both native and nonnative speakers.

When considering oral assessments, faculty are usually also worried about the grading piece. Is grading harder? Is it too subjective or time-consuming? When compared to machine-graded (i.e., multiple-choice) exams, this concern is certainly valid, but in comparison with grading a research paper or written exam, oral assessment grading can be much quicker. For example, if each research paper takes fifteen minutes to grade, a ten-minute oral assessment will take about the same amount of time when you factor in five minutes for notes, feedback, and recording a grade. A thirty-minute oral assessment might replace a longer exam with essay and short-answer questions.

Finally, some research has shown that the inter-rater reliability of oral assessments tends to be lower than the reliability for written assessments (which is not great to begin with).[33] This means that, even with the same rubrics and instructions in front of them, two different graders might evaluate the same presentation differently. More concerning is the likelihood that a single grader might not even evaluate the same assessment equally twice. This should give us instructors pause about using oral assessments without the proper planning, training, and structures in place. However, we would argue that the reliability problem likely exists for many written assessments as well (unless you are one of the rare instructors who has delved into and fixed this issue), so this is an issue that should be considered but not used as an excuse for not trying oral assessments (especially if they aren't graded but used to supplement the assessment of written work).

Final Thoughts

We hope that you will use your current concern about academic integrity as an opportunity to be bold and creative in your teaching. The moment demands it and gives us all a rationale for making radical change, even if it doesn't always turn out the way we anticipate. Move slowly, then quickly, then slowly. Plan your course changes carefully, seeking support from your department chair and guidance from your local teaching experts, supportive teaching communities within and outside your school, and scholarly research. Once you make your plans, be bold and execute them quickly. Higher education is changing by the moment and there is no time to waste in contemplation. Once you have made changes, slow down again and evaluate their effect. Consider your learning goals, the demands placed on you and your students, and the levels of authenticity and misconduct in your courses. Even check in on your students' attitudes toward your class and others. Be data driven in your changes and, like a writer, don't be afraid to "murder your darlings" when a good idea doesn't survive contact with the classroom. Not all of the suggestions in this chapter (or book) will work for you. Some of the mismatches will be obvious, but others will only be uncovered by trying them out. We owe it to our students to figure out which changes to our courses will help them to learn authentically. We owe it to ourselves to make changes that will reduce the stress of dealing with cheating. And we owe it to higher education and society to make those changes happen.

Next Steps

1. Reflect on the following strategies. Based on the classes you teach and your discipline, choose one strategy you can implement next term and another you'll spend more time learning about:
   a. Infuse integrity into lessons and assessments
   b. Align expectations with assessment rubrics
   c. Allow and co-opt collaboration
   d. Give opportunities for revision
   e. Give students choice and control
   f. Make your assessments authentic
   g. Plan for cognitive offloading
   h. Include oral assessments
2. If you have already read the course design and communicating integrity chapters, consider how your chosen strategy connects to the ones you chose from them.
3. Play with some GenAI tools to plan how they might help you deploy your chosen strategy.
4. For administrators, provide professional development opportunities for faculty interested in creating grading rubrics. Provide the infrastructure to enable faculty to share rubrics, assignments, and other assessment tools.
5. Also for administrators, consider making instructional designers available to help instructors design or redesign in-person, hybrid, and online courses.

5

STRATEGIES THAT PROMOTE SUCCESS WITH INTEGRITY

Mariah was a good student. She always came to class, did her work on time and well, and once or twice during the semester asked engaging questions. More often than not, though, she kept quiet and to herself. David inferred that Mariah was a quiet and serious person on the basis of his interactions with her in class. Then Mariah joined the Honor Council. In council meetings, David observed her to be a force of nature. She was a natural leader who commanded attention and respect from her peers and professors alike. She spoke her mind consistently and firmly, but always respectfully. It was as if Mariah had a twin sister, so different were her two personae. What accounts for the difference? In short, Mariah, like all of us, was profoundly influenced by the demands and expectations of her physical and social environment. She was acutely aware that classrooms and council meetings demanded different things of her and adjusted her behavior accordingly.

The point of this story is that students, as a rule, are sensitive to the demands that they perceive in their environment rather than being inherently cheaters or good people or whatever. The nature-versus-nurture debate long held within psychology has never been resolved unless you consider the answer "both" as a resolution. Decades of studies with identical twins have revealed that physical differences (e.g., propensity for diseases) and personality and behavioral differences are a result of a complex interplay of genetics and environment.[1] The environment—specifically the behaviors of those within your circle of friends and family—has been shown to shape many interesting phenomena typically thought of as individualistic, like divorce, obesity, and smoking.[2] Social contagion theory suggests that behaviors, attitudes, and ideas spread from one person to another, especially when the people are connected through a social network.[3] Students in higher education are not immune to the strength of environmental forces on their behaviors. For example, first-year college students are more likely to drink heavily if they perceive that their friends drink heavily and approve of drinking.[4] Students can also "catch" bad behaviors from their instructors: if an instructor does not perform as expected or acts with a lack of integrity, students may use that behavior to justify their own cheating.[5]

This chapter builds on the previous chapters; we move from course and assessment design to the nuts and bolts of instructors' behavior and instructional delivery and how these can create environments that either encourage or discourage integrity.

Modeling the Behaviors You Want to See

> I'm not a role model. I'm not paid to be a role model.
> —Charles Barkley, 1993

Even Sir Charles's views on role modeling have matured. In 2023, in the face of discrimination against the LGBTQ+ community, he stood up in a bar and announced to the crowd, "If you're gay, God bless you. If you're trans, God bless you. And if you have a problem with them—(expletive) you."[6] Clearly over the course of thirty years, Barkley's understanding of the importance of role-modeling has changed quite dramatically.

A student, let's name her Alice, was reported for plagiarizing because the text in her paper matched the text in a book, and not a book that was an assigned reading. Alice denied ever having read the source text and instead produced her sources: her own notes from a high school class and her high school teacher's lecture slides. It turns out that Alice's high school teacher plagiarized from the identified book without citation. Alice then plagiarized from the teacher without citation. The actions of Alice's teacher implicitly taught her that using other people's words and ideas without citation was acceptable. Alice learned what she was taught. Did the teacher intend to model such behavior? Probably not. Just like Charles Barkley didn't intend to model an athletic dream unrealistic for most of the young kids who looked up to him. But when we have authority and expertise, and we exist in someone's social network or environment, we can infect them like a social contagion.

This story brings us to our first classroom strategy for promoting success with integrity—role modeling. Professors are modeling when they send written communication, when teaching in front of the class, during office hours, and even when walking across campus. As educators, we influence students through what we say, but more so by what we do, the examples we set.[7] If I say, for example, that I value hearing student feedback on my teaching, but I never ask for feedback, students won't believe me. If I say that I value honesty and trust in the classroom, yet students see me fail to intervene during a cheating incident, they will infer that I value something else entirely (e.g., avoiding conflict). Quite simply, if we expect our students to act with academic integrity, then we need to model that behavior. If we want them to cite their sources, we should cite our sources. If we expect students to show up on time, we must show up on time. If we expect students to submit assignments by a deadline, we should honor deadlines for returning feedback and graded assessments. In social contagion language, students will "catch" behaviors from their teachers, as we saw in Alice's case. Students can also "catch" stress, motivation, and emotions from their teachers,[8] so it's imperative we model those appropriately as well.

It is a tremendous responsibility to realize that students are always looking to us as their instructors for guidance on how they should act. But they are, whether we acknowledge that or not. It is better to be aware and consciously choose to be a role model (even knowing that we're not perfect) than to be unaware and unintentionally model behaviors of which we would be ashamed. This awareness can also serve as a reminder that we can communicate directly with students as well. In Alice's case, it could lead to a discussion about when it's acceptable to use standard material and when citations are required. Helping students to understand why we do as we do can turn even mundane class activities such as showing slide decks into teachable moments.

At this point, let's make a brief digression to talk about reinforcement. *Reinforcement learning* is the idea that all creatures are more likely to behave a certain way if they are reinforced for it, meaning that something pleasant or good comes after the behavior. For example, a child is more likely to clean their room if they receive praise afterward. Reinforcement is usually understood to be a direct form of learning, but it can also happen secondhand through vicarious reinforcement, observation learning, or incrementally in small steps through *shaping*.[9]

The power of changing behavior through modeling has been researched and understood for decades, and has been purposefully applied in many fields, including machine learning and medical education.[10] The recognition of the power of modeling in shaping behaviors is largely attributed to social learning theorist Albert Bandura, who sought to uncover and understand how people learn through others.[11] Specifically, Bandura theorized that people learn how to behave in a certain situation by observing how others behave and shifting their behavior to match, if necessary.

However, the process is obviously not that simple. For Person A to shape Person B's behavior through modeling, Person B must notice Person A's behavior, retain the observation, internally treat it as a guide, see themselves as capable of repeating the behavior on their own (self-efficacy), and then be motivated, and perhaps even reinforced, to do so.[12] Let's return to the act of citation as an illustration. If a professor wanted to model this behavior, it would probably be insufficient to just use citations and hope students learn the lesson implicitly. Instead, the professor would need to first draw the students' attention to the citation by, for example, explicitly narrating what they were doing and why:

> You'll notice that my data on this slide comes from X, Y, and Z. I tell you this because it is important for you to know that what I am conveying are not my own ideas but the ideas of others. This helps you verify what I am sharing and gives you sources to which you could go for more information. Citation is important in this way—it is a way for the writer (or presenter in this case) to implicitly converse with the reader (or listener). It's like saying, "These are the readings I found helpful for enhancing my knowledge, and you might find them helpful, too."

Then, to help students retain the lesson and see themselves as capable of the behavior, the professor may have to give them a risk-free opportunity to practice citing their sources. Finally, to help students develop an intrinsic motivation to continue the behavior, the professor may want to talk about the values that undergird citation, such as honesty (being clear when I am using others' words or ideas) and respect (paying homage to those who came before us).[13]

One way to motivate students to emulate your behavior, rather than their peers' (who may be engaging in cheating behaviors) is to make yourself relevant or relatable.[14] You can do this in many different ways, but one place to start is by putting students' accomplishments into perspective in an effort to enhance their self-efficacy. Share the hardships and challenges that you had to overcome as a student. Highlight that your successes came from effort, dedication, and persistence, not just innate ability. Share your past experiences or interests, ones that help students see you as a human rather than strictly as an instructor. Also keep in mind that you can reach students who are different from you as well—those who may not see themselves in you—by relaying stories of people more like them. For instance, if you are a male math professor, talk about successful female mathematicians to remind the women in the class that women are capable of math, thereby alleviating the "detrimental effects of women's mathematics stereotypes."[15] Subtle versions of this technique work well. In the social sciences, it's a common habit to cite research by the authors' last names, but David makes a point of using their full names as a way of both humanizing the scholars who conduct research and pointing out the diverse identities of the scientists who have contributed to our disciplines. While one professor can't be a complete role model for all students, they can intentionally provide an inclusive view of their field as an entry point to welcome all students.

Modeling should work to reduce cheating and enhance learning for at least two reasons:

- First, and likely most obvious, if you role-model the skills that are necessary for integrity (e.g., citation), students will also learn and practice those skills.
- Second, intentional modeling can help to create a sense of belonging for students who might otherwise not see themselves in you, in the discipline, or in the classroom, and evidence shows that belonging can reduce the likelihood of cheating (as discussed later in this chapter).[16] Also, role modeling can enhance self-efficacy among the students,[17] and, as we've already addressed, self-efficacy is linked to reduced cheating and enhanced learning.

Let's return to the International Center for Academic Integrity's Fundamental Values for inspiration on how we can model our values as educators. We can model honesty, responsibility, and trustworthiness by citing our sources in our lecture materials (so we're not implying that other people's words and ideas are our own). We can model responsibility and trustworthiness by providing students with feedback according to the promised time frame. We can model responsibility by being prepared and organized for class. We can model fairness by creating fair assessments and grading them according to the established and transparent rubric. We can model respect when challenging students to think more deeply and critically even as we express respect and appreciation for how they arrived at their perspective. We can model courage by responding to cheating when it occurs.

You get the picture. To figure out what modeling integrity looks like for you in your particular context, we suggest that you

TABLE 3. Planning how to model integrity values for your students

Fundamental values of integrity	*Instructional behaviors that uphold these values*
Courage	
Fairness	
Honesty	
Respect	
Responsibility	
Trustworthiness	

take a blank page (digital or otherwise), create a two-column table, and write down the six fundamental values of integrity (courage, honesty, respect, responsibility, fairness, and trustworthiness) in the left-hand column. Then, in the right-hand column, articulate the behaviors that you (and your instructional team) would need to follow through on in order to uphold those values (see table 3).

Share and discuss these with your instructional team, and make clear that everyone is expected to model these behaviors. Share them with your students (refer to communication tips in chapter 2), and model them as best as you can. Then, when you make a mistake, be transparent about how you are holding yourself accountable for that mistake and how you plan to do better going forward.

Be Engaging and Intentional

When Tricia first started as an academic integrity professional, she was asked to present to a first-year bioengineering class focused on "being a bioengineer." Tricia was worried because she would be one of the few speakers who would not be talking about bioengineering research or careers. Pushing through her fears, Tricia thoroughly prepared and arrived on time so that she could sit at the back of the very large, tiered lecture hall to watch the first speaker. As she settled in, Tricia noticed that the majority of students had their laptops open on their desks. She also noticed that they weren't taking notes, but instead were checking social media, playing games, or surfing the web. They were not paying attention.

To determine why, Tricia turned her attention to the bioengineering professor whom the students were ignoring. After a few minutes of observation, Tricia realized the professor was, well, boring. She was quiet. She was tentative. She was, dare we say, robotic. Picture the late painter Bob Ross from the Public Broadcasting Service at the front of a two-hundred-plus-person lecture hall, trying to give a lecture. Although he might have been charismatic and mesmerizing right in front of the camera, his persona wouldn't have translated and his voice wouldn't have carried to every student in such a large space. As the first speaker wrapped up, Tricia wondered how she would ever get the students to close their laptops and pay attention. But as Tricia started speaking, she saw the laptops close one by one and the students become engaged. The conversation Tricia had with the students that day was dynamic and energetic.

Instructor Engagement

What was the secret to Tricia's success? Two simple words: good instruction. First, Tricia was enthusiastic about the topic. You don't have to be Ginger Rogers doing everything better, backwards, and in high heels. You do have to show some engagement with the content you are teaching. If you don't demonstrate care for and interest in the content, why should your students care or be interested? The speaker before Tricia might have been enthusiastic about her research, but she didn't show it in a way that projected to a large lecture hall. Second, Tricia looked students in the eye as she spoke, rather than focusing her eyes mostly on the screen or the PowerPoint on her laptop. Third, Tricia moved around. She engaged students not just in the front of the room, but in the middle and the back. Fourth, Tricia used stories, examples, and lived experiences to which the students could relate to illustrate her points. The combination of these features caused more students to perceive good instruction, see Tricia as engaged with them, and therefore become present with her. Just wait, you're thinking. This sounds like you're telling all of us that to give good instruction, you have to be an extrovert like Tricia.

David explored this very idea with his research students: as an instructor, is your personality your destiny? The students mentioned a colleague of David's as an example of extraversion. This colleague is dynamic, enthusiastic, and a brilliant leader of class discussions. David knew that colleague's other side, though, since outside the classroom she is quiet, shy, and most definitely an introvert. That colleague is a world-class instructor not by sheer force of personality, but because she is a master of her craft and dedicated to her students' success. Those students went on to research the relationship between instructor variables and cheating. They found that the most important aspect of an instructor's behavior was preparation. Being organized, knowing the material, and having a structured class period (with space for fun and spontaneity, of course) were all associated with a reduced intention to cheat. Surprisingly, charisma and likability were not associated (in their study) with reduced cheating.[18] The important lesson is that while charismatic presentations can be engaging in the short run, in the long run anyone can be a good instructor through preparation and dedication to their craft. Students notice the quality of instruction, and it really does affect their learning in subtle ways.

On the other hand, as Tricia's earlier story illustrates, students perceive instruction to be poor when the instructor appears to be disinterested in the content, the class, or the students. Students also perceive instruction to be poor when the professor is disorganized, unresponsive to students, and unclear in their communication. You've likely had a teacher like this at some point in your academic career. Perhaps you can even picture them right now. The disorganized instructor is the one who exhibits a pattern of behaviors such as showing up to class late, mismanaging class time, frantically searching for notes or slides at the beginning of class, and not returning assessment feedback on the promised date. The instructor who does not communicate clearly likely finds themselves having to announce corrections throughout the term or having to respond to dozens of emails from confused students. Both of these suck up time, often leading to further disorganization and lack of responsiveness to students.

Let's be honest. We've all had bad teaching days. Even bad teaching weeks. We won't even talk about March 2020. In this section, however, we're not talking about short-term mistakes or blips. We're talking about a pattern—behavior that is evident throughout the whole term and in term after term. When you have occasional bad days or weeks, students can still perceive good instruction as long as you acknowledge that you're having a bad day, apologize, and promise to show up better next time. If you have a forgiveness policy for their mistakes, they will likely have one for you, too.

Perceived poor instruction can lead to cheating for many reasons, but a particularly powerful one is its impact on the students' motivation. As Anderman and colleagues note, students have three needs that drive their behavior: autonomy, competence, and relatedness. *Autonomy* is the need to have "control over one's own learning." If the instructor is unclear or unresponsive, students are more likely to feel helpless to control their own fate. *Competence* (synonymous with self-efficacy) is students' perception that they can accomplish or achieve in any particular course. If the instructor appears disinterested in the content or disorganized, students are more likely to feel that it is impossible (or maybe not even worthwhile) to achieve mastery. Interestingly, even simply being transparent about intentional course design can enhance not just students' self-efficacy but their sense of belonging, both of which can reduce the motivation to cheat. Finally, *relatedness* is students' perception that someone (instructor or peers) cares about them and their learning; if the instructor is unresponsive, students are less likely to feel a sense of connection and belonging. An unresponsive professor might also raise the amount of effort that a student would need to expend in order to be successful. So after weighing "their expectancy for success on a task with/without cheating,"[19] a student might decide that the cost of not cheating is higher than the costs associated with cheating. A decreased motivation for learning results in cheating as the best or only mechanism to reach the desired course grade.

In this discussion on creating an engaging and interesting class, you may assume that we are talking about in-person classes. As many of us learned in emergency remote teaching, the tools and structures that make for engagement in person often fall flat or may even be counterproductive online. Still, many of the aforementioned features of a competently designed course are relevant in all contexts. Students appreciate organization, follow-through on plans, and consistency between elements of the course no matter the teaching context, and the benefits of these virtues are not dependent on in-person relationships. On the other hand, we acknowledge that there are unique and important challenges to online courses, such as maintaining a presence in students' lives when we're distant from them in both time and space.

Aspects of Presence

The relationships between students and their teacher, as well as among classmates, can be framed by the idea of presence. This concept has received more attention in online courses than in the classroom environment. In the early days of online learning, many of the courses were designed to be asynchronous, which required a more conscious and intentional focus on presence because the environment lacked organic opportunities to observe presence.[20] We would argue that in the large physical lecture halls common in many universities around the world, students can feel and be equally as anonymous as they would be in online classrooms, so it would behoove all instructors to be intentional about presence.

Presence helps to form a *community of inquiry* (COI), a Deweyan tradition of constructivist learning in which students and teachers co-construct learning and knowledge—the "guide-by-the-side" rather than "sage-on-the-stage" model of education. There are three types of presence essential for facilitating learning in a COI: social, cognitive, and teacher.[21]

Social presence is about presenting oneself as a human being—warm, caring, and empathetic.[22] This requires extra thought in a remote classroom. However, we would argue that it is necessary to pay attention to your social presence in all classroom contexts because your authority can inhibit students from seeing you as a human being who cares about them and their learning, rather than only as the person who has power over their fate. It is important not only that you be socially present, but also that you cultivate an environment in which the students can feel socially present. When students feel socially present, they feel connected to their peers and experience a sense of belonging, which invites them to bring their whole selves to the learning experience and facilitates the creation of personal and purposeful relationships.[23]

We invite you to reflect back on the emergency remote teaching environment of the COVID-19 pandemic. Students who were formerly enrolled in in-person classes and programs found themselves stuck in remote learning environments that they didn't want or expect to be in, and found ways through technology like Discord channels to stay connected and socially present with their peers. While sometimes students used these channels for cheating on assignments and tests, most were not set up with that intent; they were set up to create community. Humans are social creatures, and this social need is intimately tied to the cognitive development we aim to cultivate in higher education.[24] Social presence is critical for enhancing integrity and reducing the likelihood of cheating because social presence is linked to higher self-efficacy and intrinsic motivation.[25] This feeling of being socially present with other humans will become increasingly important for higher education institutions as we learn to differentiate ourselves from artificial intelligence–based learning platforms. Students do not need to come to us to learn; they need to come to us to learn with and from other humans (and to be certified, of course).

Social presence is not just about being nice, though. Social presence requires that faculty inhabit our roles as three-dimensional humans. If you're a warm person, be warm in class. If you're stern, be stern. Authenticity is much more important than portraying any particular social presence. It is not necessary to be students' friend or confidant. Social presence does not require the obliteration of healthy boundaries, and it can be harmed by too few boundaries just as much as by too many. The key goal for creating social presence is to bring as much of yourself to the classroom as you are comfortable with and not to bring anything that isn't authentic. Make your boundary expectations clear to students and be consistent; they will appreciate the transparency.

Cultivating a social presence in and of itself is insufficient. Social presence provides the foundation upon which the structure of cognitive presence is built, and the two intersect to create a shared community around the purpose of learning and inquiry. *Cognitive presence* enables students to explore course concepts, integrate them into their ways of knowing, then apply them in new situations.[26] Readers might recognize notes of Deweyan constructivism or Kolb's experiential learning theory. Learners create knowledge through action, experience, and interaction, not simply through reading, studying, and writing on their own, for example.

If social presence is the foundation for cognitive presence, then *teaching presence* is the climate or environment that supports the growth of cognitive presence. Teaching presence is grounded in two functions: design and facilitation. *Design* involves the choice and presentation of course content as well as activity and assessment design. The teacher and students can both facilitate learning, but the teacher's constant presence in the facilitation of learning has been found to be critical, especially in online environments.[27] In summary, teaching presence is more than being physically or virtually present, likable, and kind. While these things are worthwhile, a likable and kind professor cannot make up for bad course design or facilitation; students may like you but not enjoy the class and not want to take a class with you again because you are not really present in the learning with them.[28]

Presence should reduce cheating and enhance integrity by helping to create or maintain intrinsic motivation to learn. Self-determination theory would predict that students have a need for relatedness, or a "perception of care and belonging," in the class, and if that need is frustrated or unmet, students will lose intrinsic motivation and cheating will be more likely.[29] A strong presence in the classroom might also reduce cheating by enhancing learner engagement.[30] Presence creates connections between learners and the instructor and among learners, which in turn fosters trust and encourages social norms of reciprocity and fairness, and undermines students' ability to generate neutralizing attitudes. Finally, social presence seems to influence *expectancy*[31]—a belief that one is capable of doing a task or learning (i.e., self-efficacy)—which is directly related to cheating behaviors.[32]

To explore how you might establish presence in the classroom, let's return to the story at the beginning of this section. The students were physically present in that bioengineering lecture hall, but many of them were not socially or cognitively present. They were on their computers, doing anything other than something related to the class. Why was this? The teacher wasn't present, at least she wasn't present beyond being physically present. So, let's agree now to end the myth that presence is "natural" for in-person teaching and therefore doesn't require concerted attention. Instead, let's agree that whether teaching online or in person, presence is something worthy of our attention and our intentional construction.

To engender social presence, you can create opportunities for the students to purposefully interact with each other and with you.[33] So, whether a course is online or in person, social presence will not develop within a banking model of education, where students show up every class simply to be lectured to. Classes that are interactive, like active learning (e.g., Team-Based Learning, problem-based learning) or even lectures with some peer instruction, are going to be better at creating social presence. Flipping your classroom to be more active takes a lot of work and time up front, but that workload levels off after a few iterations. Still, for an easier entrée into cultivating social presence, try incorporating an eight-minute routine at the beginning of every class (or at least the first class of each week) to enable student-to-student interaction and discourse. This routine can work in any size or modality of instruction. It can take the form of a quick check-in, like think-pair-share: Ask the students a question, give them a minute to reflect, have them share with a classmate, then have the pair contribute to a digital whiteboard or polling tool. Finally, you share your thoughts and their thoughts with the entire class. The check-in question can differ every time but should always have a theme that ideally is not related to class content. So, the theme could be about learning process (e.g., What is one study strategy you used this week that you found successful? Or, What's one thing you do to become present and ready to listen in class?). Alternatively, the theme could be more personal (e.g., What is one thing about you that most people don't know? Or, What is your favorite activity to stay healthy?).

David had a class in which students were required to bring in three course-related clarification questions each session on paper (this was a while ago). At the beginning of each class, students paired up and tried to answer at least one question each. If, after discussion, the pair was unable to clearly answer the question, then they shared the question with the group. The students tried to address each unanswered question, and only if the group was unable to come to agreement on an answer did David respond. This process worked for factual questions, follow-up questions, and conceptual or philosophical ponderings, and students felt cognitively present throughout it. In the digital era, this strategy is easily supported by most LMS platforms and could be a nice way to develop presence within an online course.

Cognitive presence also needs to be intentionally designed into any course. Discussions, activities, and tasks need to move students up a taxonomy of learning from application to synthesis, and you need to actively facilitate this movement. Many of the techniques outlined in chapter 3 would facilitate cognitive presence. Active learning pedagogies are particularly good for this purpose. Take Team-Based Learning (TBL), for example.[34] In TBL, cognitive presence is cultivated by having an explicit and direct connection between individual work and in-class work in teams leading to a final project or result. Students individually do pre-class work to establish some knowledge of a problem or concept. They then bring that knowledge to the class. where they work with their team to solve a problem or respond to the concept in an intentionally designed activity. Together and individually, the students work to construct and synthesize meaning from various discourses, critical reflections, and activities. The student teams then reach a resolution of the problem, which the students then present as their summation of what they learned. In such an active learning pedagogy, there is little space for a student to hide or not be cognitively—or socially—present.

Teaching presence is cultivated through instructional management, active facilitation, and direct instruction. *Instructional management* is more or less what it sounds like—it involves determining the curriculum, designing assessments, establishing parameters, and leveraging the provided classroom space (online or physical) in the best possible way.[35] *Active facilitation* is the exact opposite of passive lecturing, or the banking model of education. Active facilitation might take the shape of the Socratic method, where you engage in actively questioning the students to build understanding, establish and share meaning, and explore ideas to debate and challenge. Active facilitation is a natural part of flipped classrooms that use active learning techniques such as problem-based learning, TBL, or POGIL (process oriented guided inquiry learning),[36] all of which are advanced strategies for cultivating teaching presence. Finally, direct instruction acknowledges that, as the teacher, you are the content expert responsible for presenting content, providing feedback to students on their paths toward mastery of the learning outcomes, and redirecting them if they are heading down the wrong path or are blocked;[37] in these ways, you are scaffolding learning.

In summary, to cultivate presence, be intentional about your pedagogical choices, be explicit about what students will learn and how they will learn it, show up prepared and with enthusiasm, and incorporate ways for students to engage with you and with each other as fellow humans and learners. To be clear, you can cultivate presence even if you're not ready to flip your classroom; just make sure you fold in those eight-minute opportunities to connect, speak actively and enthusiastically on the topic, articulate the meaning behind what you're doing and why, and give students frequent and timely feedback. And again, because we can't say this too often, students need colleges and universities to provide this kind of substantive human-to-human interaction designed around developing durable human skills like communication, critical thinking, empathy, and collaboration. This is how we differentiate ourselves—whether in person or online—from the artificial world.

Create a Sense of Belonging

Most of us have at one time or another felt out of place or out of step. One of David's formative learning experiences was walking into the University of Michigan's Nikki Giovanni Lounge (a space designated for informal learning on multicultural issues) to work with a friend on a class project. David's was the only white face in the room, and he felt as if everyone there was already judging him merely for his presence. This one-time event punctuated the privileged cluelessness with which David, a white man, had traveled through university life. Many of our students experience this disconnect on a daily basis due to race, status as a first-generation university student, disability, or myriad other reasons.

Our students walk into our classrooms or log in to online courses with their entire life behind them—usually at least seventeen years of it. Their life experiences shaped them; created their cognitive structures about whether they can learn, what they can learn, and how they can learn; formed their beliefs about what they are good at and not good at; taught them that the predominant systems or structures are either designed to benefit or harm them; and developed what they know and don't know in terms of content or disciplinary knowledge. And yet, many educators teach as if all the students in their classes (in person or virtual) are the same and can learn the same way (as other students and as instructors do). If they can't, then it's their problem to solve, not the professor's.

Creating a sense of belonging should reduce cheating because students feel less like a number or object, and more like a human whom the professor (and other students) cares about.[38] Again, the root causes are intrinsic motivation to learn, social norms of trust and reciprocity, moral engagement rather than disengagement, and self-efficacy. If I don't feel like I belong, I'm less likely to see myself as able to succeed or learn.

We are using "create a sense of belonging" as a catch-all category for many classroom strategies that serve this function. Popular strategies discussed in the literature include pedagogy of kindness (POK), equity pedagogy, and culturally responsive teaching (CRT).[39] All three pedagogical approaches have the same purpose and offer many of the same suggestions. All three seek to acknowledge that our classrooms are diverse, our students have different educational (and personal) experiences, some students have been more advantaged than others, and each student has valuable and unique contributions to make to the shared learning experience. Based on these premises, we can create a sense of belonging by using the following strategies to help individuals feel valued, welcomed, and empowered to contribute, co-create, and learn, no matter their background or their identity:

See the Human in Your Students

- Pay attention to signals that a student is at risk of falling behind or disengaging, such as late submissions, missing submissions, lower levels of mastery, and absences. Reach out to the student to express care and concern, ask questions, and co-create a re-engagement strategy.
- If a student is struggling or "being difficult," see the student as a human who needs assistance, rather than a challenge to be tolerated.[40]

Recognize the Potential in Your Students

- Have a growth mindset that all students are capable, rather than a fixed mindset that closes off opportunities for some students

Teach to All Students

- Choose readings that reflect the diversity of thought on the topic of instruction and the diversity in your classroom (e.g., Are you choosing mostly male authors? European authors?). Offer students the opportunity to add readings that interest them to projects or class discussions.
- Create assessments and activities that are meaningful for every student in your class, which usually means allowing them to have some choice and control over who they read or learn from and how they present their learning and knowledge.

One caveat—creating a sense of belonging doesn't mean that you have to ignore human nature or overlook cheating because to respond wouldn't be kind. In the OneHE course on pedagogy of kindness, the presenter tells the story of how the academic integrity statement in her syllabus communicated a lack of trust—that she expected her students to cheat. So, she revised her statement to "I believe that everyone in my course is fundamentally honest."[41] The statement that everyone is "fundamentally honest" is not factually true.[42] So, instead, we suggest a more honest and research-informed approach for creating a sense of belonging. For example, you could say, "I believe that everyone in my course wants to learn and wants to be honest. I also understand that we are all human beings who can make mistakes or bad decisions under pressure. So let's have an honest conversation about when we might make those mistakes and how we can prevent them from happening."

David's version of this is to make the affirmative choice to trust his students while acknowledging that some of them, some of the time, will take advantage of that trust. It's a worthwhile trade-off for him to foster a trust-based relationship with them. Having said that, though, David highlights for his students the fact that honesty fosters positive relationships, increases learning, and creates a sense of fairness for all concerned. It's not fair to honest students to pretend that everyone is honest. After all, being kind is about being honest. And, creating a sense of belonging invites the whole student, flaws and all, into the learning community, rather than pretending that the student can rise above normal human nature.

Make Your Class More Accessible

Another fundamental change over the last twenty years has been the remarkable increase in the diversity of our students, not just in terms of physical disabilities and neurodiversities, but diversity in all its forms. Unfortunately, even as the demographics of our student populations have changed, our pedagogies, assessments, and policies have not, at least not to the same degree. The lecture, two midterms, and one final assessment model; deadline inflexibility; and other teacher-centered practices continue to dominate. And we understand why. Educators continue to lecture because it was the way we were taught, and it worked for us. The majority of us also were not taught how to teach during our doctoral programs, so it's difficult to change our practices without sufficient knowledge or training (or time to learn). Some professors continue to assess with two midterms and a final because these are the easiest and quickest assessments to manage with large classes (which enables faculty to get on with what is rewarded by the institution—grants and publications).

The problem with this scenario is that the pedagogical and assessment choices are not based on the learners' needs, but the professor's needs; it is teacher-centric course design. To be sure, some students—likely those traditional, neurotypical students who come from strong college preparatory secondary schools, have been trained in test-taking strategies, taught by tutors, and mentored by educated parents—will find such a classroom environment to be easily navigated, straightforward, predictable, and therefore comfortable. They may not learn much (since struggle rather than comfort typically leads to more learning), but they'll likely perform well (i.e., get a high grade) in the course. Other students, however, may not perform or learn well in a class like this because such traditional strategies and policies are not accessible for them. In such environments, those students may feel motivated to achieve their goals in other, counterproductive ways.

Making your class more accessible does not mean watering it down, making it easier, or catering to student satisfaction. It's about improving the learning experience for all students while simultaneously removing (or at least reducing) the logistical hurdles that interfere with learning. As a side benefit, it also reduces your need to make accommodations in ways that are less consistent and more time-consuming and labor-intensive. The dominant current system of making education accessible is deficit-based: these students don't have the abilities to adapt to the way I've set up the classroom, so I need to accommodate them. The accessible approach is more positive and proactive, asking how can I make learning more accessible to all students?

Universal design for learning, pioneered by Sheryl Burgstahler and Rebecca Cory, is one approach to making learning more accessible for all students "without the need for adaptation or specialized design."[43] Their main emphasis, with which we strongly concur, is the creation of flexibility in all aspects of course planning. You'll recognize these flexibility suggestions from elsewhere in this book. Make your syllabus more inviting and learner-centered, while encouraging students to discuss their learning needs with you. Offer students "multiple means of perceiving, comprehending, and expressing their learning."[44] This could look like providing choice and control in how the students learn (e.g., reading, watching videos, discussing, attending lectures) and demonstrate their learning (e.g., research paper, presentation, blog post, poster presentation). Ensure class materials (notes, lectures, readings) are in accessible formats. Build in flexible deadlines with scaffolding, opportunities for feedback, and a "free pass" for missing a deadline.

Making learning more accessible will reduce the motivation to cheat because an accessible environment is less likely to paint students into the cheat-or-fail corner. In addition, it can increase self-efficacy, particularly among those students whose needs have been neglected in other contexts. They will see opportunities to showcase their abilities instead of experiencing obstacles to overcome, which will reduce the temptation to cheat. Furthermore, all students will recognize the attention to inclusivity and presence. This orientation can dampen neutralizing attitudes, because when students believe that their instructor cares about authentic learning, they are more likely to strive for that themselves.

Develop Teacher Metacognition

A teacher does not enter their career as a tabula rasa but rather, like their students, as a complex human who has been shaped by their experiences, experiences that formed beliefs and ideas about teaching, about teachers, about learning, and about students. When Tricia started teaching at the University of San Diego during her PhD program, her ideas and beliefs had been formed by years of experience in experiential learning settings (e.g., cooperative education), her study of adult learning theory in her master's program, her work as a supervisor of student volunteers, and her own doctoral course of study. Because of this background, Tricia had formed beliefs that the best teachers facilitate, coach, and mentor students to construct their own knowledge through immersive and active learning experiences. She already believed in the power of designing meaningful learning around Kolb's experiential learning cycle,[45] giving students choice and control over their own learning, and challenging them to engage in new ways that would create struggle because through struggle can come deep learning. Tricia had also experienced very active and engaged classes as a student, so she knew she wanted to teach as she was taught. This means that Tricia has never taught a straight-up lecture class; all her classes have been designed with active pedagogies, from quite obscure ones (like the Harvard Kennedy School's case-in-point method[46]) to those that have been widely documented, researched, and implemented (like TBL).

Tricia's journey illustrates that teacher metacognition—the way we think about teaching, teachers, learning, and students—absolutely dictates how we design our courses and assessments, the pedagogy we choose, and how we present ourselves in the classroom.[47] That's why it is so unfortunate that people with terminal degrees (EdDs, PhDs, JDs, MDs, etc.), those who eventually go on to become the professoriate in colleges and universities, are generally not taught how to teach (at least not in the United States). These are failures of the US education system and of our preparation of graduate students, who will become educational leaders and facilitators of student learning without any teaching qualifications. Because of this, we professors often simply teach how we were taught, or teach in the way that we like to learn.

Teacher cognition will directly impact how you attempt to enhance academic integrity and reduce cheating in your classes. If you believe that students have fixed mindsets about integrity or ethics, you're not going to choose the strategy of communicating integrity or infusing integrity lessons into your curriculum. If you believe that teachers are not police officers, and that preventing and detecting cheating are law enforcement–like activities, then you won't adopt the strategies discussed in chapter 6 on ensuring integrity in assessments. If you believe that learning is best achieved when students come to class to hear you lecture, you'll likely never try a different pedagogy. Or, if you believe that it's up to the students to figure everything out on their own, you're not likely to try very hard to create a sense of belonging. In other words, your mindset dictates your choices, so if your mindset is not aligned with what we have proposed in this book, it is unlikely that you will put in the effort to create a classroom where integrity is the norm and cheating is the exception.

Your teacher cognition is a strong influence over your choices and behaviors, and you are likely to filter the data you receive from executing your choices to continue to support your beliefs. For example, let's pretend that you believe (despite our pleas to the contrary) that students can only be motivated to come to class if you entice them with attendance points. But, you decide to experiment with methods for increasing students' intrinsic motivations to come to class. So, you replace the attendance grades with peer instruction. But when the first student doesn't come to class, you use that one piece of data to support what you believe: "See! I told you. If you don't give them points for coming to class, they won't! They're inherently uninterested in doing the work and in learning!" Of course, possible alternative explanations are that the student is sick or working two jobs while going to school, or that you still haven't done the work necessary to make your class a place where students experience intrinsic value from attending. Teachers, because they are human, use limited data points to confirm their existing biases and beliefs. So, to improve your teacher cognition—your knowledge of your beliefs about teaching, teachers, students, and learning—you need to be intentional. Here are some suggestions to do that.

Reflect on your experiences as a learner. What types of learning experiences and teachers did you respond to best or enjoy most? What types of learning experiences and teachers did you hate, or when did you find yourself tuning out of a class? Tricia, for example, loved learning in environments where she could verbalize or do something. Those situations could be as simple as her senior psychology seminar, which required her to come to class having read assigned articles so that she could engage in a discussion with her teacher and classmates about them. Alternatively, it could look like her psychology of learning class in which she trained a rat to raise a Canadian flag. On the other hand, Tricia hated lectures in which the professor not only didn't ask any questions of the students, but if the students asked questions (as Tricia was prone to do), the teacher would shoot them down. This leads us to the second reflection question you could ask yourself to develop your teacher cognition.

Which of the things you loved or hated as a learner are showing up in your teaching? Even better than reflecting on this, ask a peer or a teaching consultant to observe your teaching. Can they help you see if your practices match what you believe in and what you believe you're doing? For example, you might believe that you are being inclusive in the classroom by asking students from all different backgrounds to contribute, but your observer may notice that you actually usually call on students that look or sound like you. This would be a difficult observation to notice yourself, which is why it is so critical to have that third, unbiased eye to help you really raise your teacher cognition.

Take a class on pedagogy or learning or take a teacher training course. It's important to attend with an open mind and respect for the course instructor. Don't go just to check a box. It's really helpful to engage in some self-reflection first. If you are not aware of your existing cognitive structures and beliefs, then training will not help you form new cognitions about teachers, teaching, students, or learning. It's also possible to engage in self-reflection after a course, but if you do so, mentally prepare yourself for your own resistance to change, which can sneak up on even the most open-minded teacher.

For each pedagogical, assessment or content choice you've made for a class, write out your rationale. Why did you make the choice you did? Was it influenced by context (e.g., it's a large class so I chose two midterms and a final because of grading time pressures), by personal belief, or by research on teaching and learning? Then, study how your choices are influencing your students. Ask the students about your choices. Look at measures of success, like their mastery of the material. If writing isn't your style, try finding a teaching "workout partner," with whom you can discuss your ideas and whose feedback can be invaluable to your change-making process.

Write out your beliefs about your students. Do you ascribe a growth or deficit mindset to them? Have you unconsciously applied any stereotypes (e.g., girls aren't good at math) that will threaten their potential or limit your pedagogical and assessment choices? Do you think about students as people who want to learn or as grifters who are just trying to play the game?

Final Thoughts

In *Deep Listening: Impact beyond Words,* author and podcast host Oscar Trimboli discusses the five levels of listening:[48]

Level 1 is to listen to yourself. So, before beginning a conversation, take a moment to become aware of what's going on in your head so that you can limit what might otherwise distract you.

Level 2 is to listen to content. Content is not just what is being said but how it's being said (e.g., facial expressions, body language, tone, pauses).

Level 3 is to listen for context. Context is the backstory of you (the listener), the speaker, and the conversation.

Level 4 is to listen for what is not being said because, according to Trimboli, there is often a disconnect between what someone is saying and what they're thinking.

Level 5 is to listen for the meaning that's being created during the conversation and, together, work to make sense of that meaning.

Teachers might think of themselves as predominantly speakers, not listeners. However, we are suggesting that teachers should think of themselves as deep listeners. Before entering a class, take a moment to become present and be present with the students who are in the room. Listen not just to students' words, but their actions and inactions, their tone, their pauses. Take time to understand the context of your class, the backstories that may be shaping the interactions and conversations that are occurring. Definitely pay attention to what is *not* being said. Who is missing? Who isn't talking? What questions aren't being asked? And, of course, co-create meaning with your students. When you see yourself as the listener rather than the speaker, you can center the experience on the students rather than yourself. This is deep teaching with and for integrity.

Next Steps

1. Reflect on these strategies. Based on the classes you teach and your discipline, choose one strategy you can implement next term and another you'll spend more time learning about:
   a. Model the behaviors you want to see
   b. Be engaging and intentional
   c. Be present as an instructor
   d. Create a sense of belonging
   e. Engage in universal learning design to make your class more accessible
   f. Develop teacher metacognition
2. If you have already read the assessment design, course design, and communicating integrity chapters, consider how your chosen strategy connects to strategies you selected in those chapters.
3. Make a presence worksheet for one of your classes. Observe how and whether you are present, either in person or through class structures, and make changes to create a more vibrant community of learners.
4. For institutional leaders, ask yourself how you are modeling integrity on a daily basis and in front of your instructors and students. Is your institution creating a

sense of belonging for all students, and if so, how are the institutional efforts helping (or not helping) class cultures? Finally, do instructors have sufficient support to make their classes more accessible, or are you unintentionally creating an accommodation-dependent culture?

6

PROTECTING ASSESSMENT INTEGRITY

Many years ago, one of us had an experience that stuck with us. A student described a class he was taking in another department as unnecessarily difficult, requiring unreasonable, "impossible" amounts of memorization. As the student told it, in order to get good grades, all the other students in the class were cheating. As a result of the good grades, the professor didn't realize just how unreasonable the expectations were. The student then relayed that he was dropping the class because he wasn't willing to cheat in order to keep up.

This story illuminates a failure of both academic integrity and assessment security. In fact, it describes failure on many levels—of the professor failing to connect assessment with content and meaningful learning, of the institution failing to give students a voice in academic integrity, and even of the student failing to take a more direct approach with his peers and the instructor. In this chapter we aim to offer strategies to help instructors of courses like these secure the integrity of their assessments. While course design is important, the execution of that design still matters. Instructors must actively manage academic integrity throughout their courses to avoid this sort of outcome, which led to the loss of learning opportunities for both the students who stayed in the class and those who dropped or never registered for it because of its reputation for cheating. It is absolutely critical that we protect the integrity and learning of those students who make the difficult choice to complete their work honestly. Throughout this book we've taken a positive and proactive approach to academic integrity. We've argued that it's critical we respect our students as learners and people of integrity by providing them with excellent learning experiences.

However, we have also pointed out that students are humans who will still be tempted to cheat for a variety of reasons, even when they may be motivated to learn. We have also described some people enrolled in our institutions as not really students at all, but "enrolled persons" posing as students but cheating their way through to a degree. We have a responsibility to our authentic students and to society to ensure that those enrolled persons do not graduate with degrees. So, while we advocate for the practice of trusting our students, that trust must also have boundaries. We trust our neighbors, but we still lock our doors. So too must we take commonsense approaches to securing assessments. As our colleague Phill Dawson argues, "Assessment security starts where academic integrity finishes." Assessment security, which are "measures taken to harden assessment against attempts to cheat,"[1] is necessary because cheating undermines the validity of our assessments and the degrees we confer. While we try in this chapter to address the particular security concerns inherent in online-only assessments, we also discuss common solutions to assessment security regardless of context. Note that many of the approaches are considered to be quite controversial. In fact, for some security strategies, the cure may be worse than the disease. Therefore, we won't always make firm recommendations, recognizing that the best option is both subjective and context dependent.

As educators, we have a difficult balance to strike: trusting our students yet putting mechanisms in place to ensure the assessments we've designed were completed by the enrolled student and in the expected fashion. If we do not do that, then we risk our postsecondary institutions awarding degrees that do not represent what they are supposed to. We owe it to civil society to make sure that higher education is as free from grade-based corruption as possible. Moreover, we know that if we leave the doors open to cheating, it will only encourage more cheating. Recall our conversation in chapter 1 about neutralization or moral disengagement, whereby an individual is able to rationalize a behavior that otherwise would violate their moral code. Students are easily able to justify their cheating by blaming the professor who failed to adequately protect the integrity of the assessment. Skeptics may question whether we should cater to such dishonest students, but we must remember that most students will violate the rules in certain circumstances. We are not catering to cheaters but creating an environment where vulnerable students are nudged toward upholding rather than neutralizing their values.[2] On the assumption that most students are mostly honest most of the time, we should strive to set up our assessments so that academic dishonesty is just a bit harder, especially when it doesn't significantly add to our workload or create an atmosphere of distrust.

We argue that most students are at least willing to consider academic misconduct if they find themselves in the right (wrong?) circumstances. Take, for example, a student we'll refer to as Mayra. Mayra was reported for cheating during an online exam because one of her answers looked like it was generated by a chatbot. Sure enough, Mayra admitted to falling victim to the temptations at her fingertips. It was very easy for Mayra just to open another browser, ask ChatGPT for help, then copy and paste that answer into the LMS. In fact, some GenAI tools have created browser extensions so students do not even need to leave their LMS window to get that "help." Mayra recognized that it was very difficult for her to resist cheating in an unproctored setting, so she asked if she could take the rest of her tests in the testing center. While it may be reasonable to expect students to develop the ability to do the right thing when no one is watching—which will serve them well as professionals and citizens—perhaps expecting that of a seventeen- to twenty-one-year-old during a high-stakes situation within the context of a bonanza of cheating options is not reasonable.

It is therefore instructors' responsibility to create the circumstances that guide students toward making good academic choices. In Jewish tradition, the Torah prohibits *lifnei iver*, which translates loosely as "don't make it possible (easier) for another person to transgress."[3] In this context, the rabbinical commentaries would say that a good instructor should not create circumstances where the temptation toward cheating is great because access to unauthorized materials is so easy.

Ellis and Murdoch have followed up on Dawson's call for assessment security with a "framework for challenging and responding to student cheating."[4] In it, they explicitly place student behavior on a continuum from honest but in need of training to criminally dishonest. In response, they propose that helping students to avoid cheating through self-regulation can be seen as fundamental to the work of academic integrity, but it must be paired with institutional efforts at "command regulation" (investigation, punishment, etc.) to ensure assessment security. Their paper should be required reading for all administrators with responsibility for assessment or academic affairs. If you are in a position to do so, please pass it along to your friendly neighborhood vice-provost.

No More Recycling Assessment Material

"But my test and assignment questions are so good and the core concepts of my field are eternal, so why shouldn't I recycle materials?" you may ask. The most common forms of cheating in our own research are unauthorized collaboration and use of unauthorized resources on homework assignments.[5] In practice, students often work together when they are asked not to, they share homework answers, and they search online (or go to a GenAI tool) for questions and answers to homework and test questions. With the advent of online "homework help" websites, it's safe to assume that any assessment materials that you create or that are packaged with a textbook are compromised as soon as they become available. Simply put, when you use predesigned assessment items or reuse assessments, it makes cheating very easy. It's so easy that we'd compare it to leaving one's wallet on a restaurant table while washing one's hands in the restroom. Of course, we hope that we can trust our fellow diners, but why create temptation? If there is one single biggest threat to assessment security, it is the recycling of assignment and test questions. Changing assessments frequently can make a major upgrade to security.

However, writing and rewriting good assessments, especially tests, can be extremely time-consuming, so we are loath to recommend something so difficult without providing ways of managing the additional workload. In keeping with the assessment design principles we proposed in chapter 4, we recommend the practice of asking students to generate assessment questions as part of their study process. As we mentioned, there are powerful learning and motivational benefits to this practice, but here we focus on the assessment security benefits. If each student in a class of twenty-five generates three questions, that provides a set of seventy-five questions from which a test designer can choose. David has found that with a little instruction or help from a chatbot, undergraduate students can create effective questions at various levels of Bloom's taxonomy that require only a little bit of editing before inclusion in a real quiz. These questions will be representative of students' understanding of the material and will also provide you with clues about which material the students found to be most central to their overall mental map. Treat test construction as an exercise in curation and editing rather than creation. With a little practice, this task becomes a very quick way of ensuring unique questions for each assessment. Of course, it's possible for students to use test banks and other unauthorized resources when generating their questions, so care must be taken to screen for questions that are already available online. This strategy works equally well for online and in-person assessments.

Other time-saving strategies are to use GenAI tools to help you generate many new questions, or to use published test banks as inspiration for your own assessments but change the stem of the question sufficiently so that an online search won't easily find the original question. It's also important to change the question so that the correct answer is different (at least sometimes); that way, even if a test-taker finds the original answer online, they are not able to benefit from that information. It's very easy to give test bank questions to a GenAI tool for paraphrasing. As ever, check the output for accuracy!

There is increasing hope that GenAI tools will become useful for generating a nearly infinite number of exam and practice problems. This is an exciting possibility for the future, but one that has two significant limitations for the near term. First, since GenAI creates content on the basis of frequency matching of content from the training materials, this will bias assessment questions toward the most frequently available material. Teachers design assessments to focus on the most important and trickiest material, and the content that provides a foundation for future work, goals that a Gen AI tool will not necessarily achieve. Second, GenAI tools are only as good as their training sets. It comes as no surprise that not everything on the internet is factually correct, so tools trained on publicly available content often generate incorrect questions as well as hallucinated answers. The good news is that more finely tuned GenAI tools are being created on a daily basis, so one specifically trained to generate exam and assessment questions will likely be accessible tomorrow (or perhaps already is, depending on when you're reading this book).

Of course, it is even easier for students to cheat on recycled or published materials when the assessments are completed unproctored. The easiest form of cheating we've ever seen is the unauthorized use of answer keys that are provided at the end of textbooks! When instructors ask students to solve a problem knowing that the answer is already provided to them, it's no wonder that students are tempted to "check their work" before the work is really done. Clearly, providing answers to assignments can be valuable for enabling students to check their work and self-regulate their learning, but timing the release of the answers can remove this temptation and foster authentic learning. Most LMS platforms can do this automatically, and we encourage instructors to enforce good learning practices by creating a consistent schedule of assignments and feedback through timing the release of answer keys.

Randomization Techniques

At an in-person institution we know, students take final exams in a large room that's different from their usual classroom. Multiple classes are intermixed with a fixed seating arrangement so that no two students taking the same exam are seated within five feet of each other. There is a bag check and an electronics ban (including smart watches and phones); even wearing a baseball cap with the brim facing forward is banned to minimize the likelihood of unauthorized materials being sneaked into the room. These measures may seem somewhat extreme, but unquestionably each of these precautions can make a certain type of misconduct more difficult. On the other hand, it is also true that some of these measures are extremely intrusive and may engender a neutralizing perspective. When we say that the cure may be worse than the disease, we mean instructors must measure the preventive value of a measure against the possibility that more students will decide cheating is acceptable in this instance because the heightened security must mean that cheating is a common strategy among their peers. The punchline to this story is that students did, in fact, still cheat by hiding course materials in the restrooms and checking them throughout the exam. Even draconian measures can't completely secure an exam from a determined cheater, but they can undermine motivation for all students.

The good news is there are alternatives that increase security without alienating students; one is the randomization technique. Randomization techniques can raise the price of cheating with much less burden on honest students. They can occur at the macro, meso, and micro levels. At the macro level (in physical rather than virtual environments), students can be randomly assigned to seats when they are completing summative assessments (like midterms and finals), so they cannot arrange to sit next to a confederate or know whether the exams around them are worth copying from. If you are not sure how to do this easily, we recommend checking out a tremendously helpful video tutorial from UC San Diego lecturer Glenn Tesler.[6] In this video, Tesler walks you step-by-step through the process of installing necessary add-ons to CANVAS, using your class roster to make a spreadsheet of seat and student assignments (with sample Excel sheet provided), uploading the spreadsheet to CANVAS, and viewing the seat assignments. In other videos, Tesler also offers ideas for randomly assigning seats, handling special seat requests (like left-handed seats), and logistics for the day of the exam. Although specific to CANVAS and UC San Diego, Tesler does offer advice for instructors at other institutions, and the tutorial may help you figure out how to do something similar at your institution and for other LMS platforms as well.

At the meso level, in either physical or virtual classes, the test given to students could have multiple versions, with the questions in different orders or even with different questions designed at the same taxonomy level and testing the same concept. Computer-based testing tools like those found in your school's LMS or other third-party software have a setting for randomizing the order of test questions. Even better, use artificial intelligence to create large question sets quickly and easily, then set your LMS testing software to randomly select a subset for each student. To ensure equitable test construction, use question groups in your LMS to create a precise distribution of questions on each topic. Alternatively, a third-party platform like PrairieLearn can easily accomplish this.[7] PrairieLearn enables instructors to write the assessment questions in code, then the program generates infinite variants of the questions, meaning not only will each student receive a different question variant, but if a student completes the assessment multiple times (as in mastery-based learning) they will receive different questions each time (and, as a bonus, immediate feedback). If these assessments are completed in a computer-based testing facility, then assessment security is strong, even while the students are able to complete the assessment on the day and time of their choosing.

In addition to randomization, most test software will also allow changes to formatting so that only one question is presented at a time. Even if two students get similar test questions in the same order, the chances that they will have them on the screen at the same time is very low. Students have reported to us that they prefer having the option to change their answers throughout the exam. Since it is possible to present one question at a time but allow forward and backward paging through the exam, it is worth considering whether the security risk of allowing students to change their answers is offset by the additional stress that forward-only formats create.

At the micro level, in either physical or virtual assessments, individual questions can easily be randomized in the testing software so that each individual student receives unique questions, or at least a unique order of questions. Perhaps the most intriguing use of randomization is to create questions containing values that are randomly varied (within fixed parameters) for each student. This is easy to implement using most test software, and for questions that require calculations it is much more difficult to share answers without detection. When a student copies from another test, the answer will be wrong for their exam and the source easy to detect. Furthermore, if a student submits an exam question to a "homework help" site, even if they use an anonymous account, it is clear to whom the question can be attributed. Thus, this technique can even be effective in preventing and detecting some forms of contract cheating. While we've seen finance and chemistry professors use this strategy, it can be altered for items that do not require calculation by using the question group feature discussed earlier. For example, in a literature course, an instructor can create a question group of passages to be analyzed along with a set of analysis prompts. Each student can then be randomly assigned a passage-prompt combination (or more than one on a longer assessment). In this manner, ten passages and ten prompts can yield one hundred unique combinations. Even a large class will have few replications of each pair, making direct copying very difficult. Using AI paraphrasing tools, it may even be possible to create a uniquely phrased exam for each student in a large class, so that peer-to-peer sharing and contract cheating become easier to detect when searching for online traces of contract cheating. We are not asserting that these changes will eliminate cheating, but at the margins, when a student is faced with a difficult assessment item or is not sure of the correct response, randomizing seats, test delivery, and assessment questions can make completing the assessment with integrity easier than cheating.

Taken as a whole, variations at the meso and micro levels will be invisible to the students but will make it harder for them to look to another student for answers or engage a contract cheater undetected. Moreover, with the exception of making only one question at a time visible, these randomization techniques are completely nonintrusive to the exam experience. Of course, randomization doesn't make a test cheat-proof, particularly in online environments. Students are still able to search the internet for answers to unique questions, ask a chatbot to generate an answer, text friends for help, or rely on a contract cheating website.

These cheating techniques do take time, so establishing a time limit for each question or for the assessment as a whole can reduce students' ability to bypass the randomization strategies. Unfortunately, time limits also serve to reduce the time honest students have to complete the test. Students with test anxiety report that strict timing policies can exacerbate their condition. This creates a conundrum for instructors. Not only does a strict time limit make testing uncomfortable for many students, but it can also create neutralizing attitudes as a result. A possible compromise is the use of shorter, more frequent assessments, as discussed in earlier chapters. With fewer questions, time limits feel less onerous to students but still provide a measure of security. If the assessments are short enough, even bathroom breaks become unnecessary.

"Anti-cheating" Technology

With the rapid move to online learning during the COVID-19 pandemic, students and faculty familiar with in-person learning environments were thrust into novel remote learning situations without much preparation or reflection. As a result, there was an increase in cheating and an increase in concern about the prevention and detection of cheating.[8] Because so many technological solutions like LMSs, video conferencing, and video recording were brought to bear on remote teaching, many instructors turned to technology to secure assessments as well. We implemented lockdown browsers, remote exam proctoring by third-party companies, and similarity/plagiarism detection tools in an attempt to secure in-person assessments that were moved online with little modification. As with so many changes during the pandemic, speed was the primary concern; only later did we have opportunities to reflect on the consequences of our choices for learning, student and faculty well-being, and long-term sustainability. There are a variety of technological tools that are designed to reduce the temptation or opportunity to cheat, but each has its limitations.

Lockdown browsers are designed to prevent the user from using other applications on the host computer while an exam window is open. This functionality became very popular during the move to remote learning in 2020–21.[9] Naturally, it's difficult to proctor exams at a distance, so software that prevents internet-search-based misconduct was seen as useful. It is true that lockdown browsers can make it more difficult for students to access the internet during exams, but only if those students don't have access to a second device or sufficient technical knowledge to circumvent the lockdown browser in other ways. Thus, we describe lockdown browsers as equivalent to building a two-foot-high wall to protect a home. It looks nice from a distance, but it's expensive and doesn't provide much protection from anyone who can avoid simple obstacles. A particularly problematic factor is that those students who are best able to circumvent such limited security are those with structural advantages such as wealth, social capital, and technological capabilities.

However, just like a two-foot wall, lockdown browsers signal boundaries, which can help some students self-regulate. Returning to our story about Mayra, she suggested that a lockdown browser would have helped her, even in a remote setting. Why? It would have required her to reach for another device to access the chatbot, which she saw as a step more indicative of being a "cheater," something that would have caused her to pause. Also, having to get the answer off of a second device and onto the exam already open on her computer would take more work and time; she couldn't, in other words, just copy and paste. So, these lockdown browsers could help students resist cheating temptations in an online setting, and certainly would in the in-person setting where the measures to circumvent a lockdown browser are more obvious. Therefore, using a lockdown browser for remote and in-person online exams might deter some forms of exam cheating.

Lockdown browsers are sometimes packaged with remote proctoring software. These tools are sometimes likened to student surveillance systems designed to observe test takers. They require students to maintain a video connection during testing and often require a "video tour" of the testing environment. The videos are monitored by human proctors, artificial intelligence, or both, which flag suspicious behavior for further review by the course instructor. Remote proctoring requires that students' exam videos be recorded and stored, creating a durable record of the process.

Products that detect similarities between documents were created to address the plagiarism concern long before the pandemic. Similarity detection tools for narrative assignments compare student-submitted texts to a variety of sources on the internet, in databases of published material, and (as an optional feature) to submissions for other courses. Specialized tools have also been created to detect plagiarism in computer programming code. Now, with the introduction of chatbots that produce text which students could submit as their own work, there are tools that claim to detect when text has been machine—rather than human—generated.

Remote proctoring received particular criticism during the COVID-19 pandemic and emergency remote teaching era. Students reported, for example, that being viewed remotely could be very stressful for several reasons.[10] Having to share their background with strangers caused a lack of privacy. They feared the risk of being flagged as "suspicious" because of background noise or activities of other household members. Finally, the system has challenges interpreting the movements of students who have disabilities or a dark skin tone, so these students risked being falsely accused of cheating.[11] As a result of these fears, students reported sitting particularly still in uncomfortable positions to avoid possible flags for dishonesty. These factors can conspire to make online remote tests more difficult for students than in-person ones. Disturbingly, the challenges of online proctoring compound the disadvantages certain students may already face. Students of color, those with limited financial resources, and those with preexisting anxiety may be targets of discrimination in all aspects of their lives, and online proctoring can exacerbate this issue. Remote proctoring has been challenged for other reasons as well. An Ohio court ruled that arbitrary and capricious decision making about whether or not to use online proctoring is problematic because the technology is a potential violation of privacy.[12]

Remote proctoring tools have been shown to reduce exam scores.[13] This effect has been attributed to reductions in cheating, but another possible cause is the increased cognitive load created by the online proctoring itself. So, whether online proctoring actually reduces cheating remains an open question. Furthermore, the burden that online testing places on students, especially those who are already disadvantaged in online education, presents a challenge to faculty seeking equity in higher education. Some economics faculty at UC San Diego designed a proctoring approach intended to address the privacy and equity concerns inherent with third-party proctoring services. They had each student start a personal Zoom meeting, turn on their camera, and share their screen while recording themselves taking the exam. These recordings were submitted and retained while the exams were being graded. If the grader noticed potential integrity concerns in a student's exam responses, they would review the recording. This still isn't a perfect solution, so we do not have any general recommendations except to point out that online proctoring of multiple-choice tests represents an attempt to preserve an old-fashioned assessment technique that is not well suited to the online environment. Whenever possible, we'd suggest eliminating online multiple-choice exams in favor of the kinds of assessments discussed in chapter 4. These assessments have their own challenges, but many can obviate the need for intrusive online proctoring tools. When online tests need to be proctored, for degree integrity, students could be given the option of taking their test in-person at a nearby testing center or using the remote proctoring software.

Even though similarity detection tools are much more ubiquitous than remote proctoring, they too are not without their critiques and challenges. First is the dreaded similarity score. If the two of us had a dollar for every time we've been asked what an acceptable percentage of similarity should be, we could retire. Why are similarity scores so problematic? For starters, similarity scores are not entirely accurate. One of us was recently evaluating a similarity report for a submission that included accurately cited and referenced block quotations which had been marked as similar. The lengthy quotations dramatically inflated the similarity score. Thus, the score by itself does not always reflect the true status of any given document. Setting aside actual errors, similarity scores are context dependent. Some similarity between documents is acceptable, even preferable. In some STEM disciplines, descriptions of laboratory methods should be consistent across papers to reflect identical methodologies. In law, we're told that it's often considered bad practice to create new material in a brief when tried-and-true language exists. Second, low similarity scores can create a false sense of confidence. Many graders interpret a low similarity score to mean that a paper is original and a high one to mean the opposite. A paper that is identical to source material but with a synonym substituted for each word might not be flagged as plagiarized by the tool, but surely most graders would consider it to be a breach of academic integrity (and others might see it as a failed attempt at paraphrasing). Graders must use similarity scores as one of many indicators of originality in combination with other strategies described in this chapter to make judgments about academic integrity or misconduct.

Beyond the limitations of similarity scores, current similarity detection engines focus on similarity of the surface text rather than the deeper structure or meaning. Some tools are better at recognizing paraphrasing than others, but none (at the time of writing) is able to identify structural plagiarism, in which a series of ideas or an entire argument is lifted from a source without attribution. This has two important consequences. First, some students repurpose similarity detection software in order to use minimal paraphrasing as a writing strategy. Rather than learning to incorporate source material into their own thinking, they rewrite a few words or sentences at a time until their similarity score is low enough to avoid scrutiny. Modern paraphrasing tools can also be used to defeat currently available similarity detection software. Students no longer need to do even basic paraphrasing themselves in order to defeat a similarity detection engine.

In sum, simple paraphrasing without understanding undermines the pedagogical purpose of teaching students to write.

The tools created to detect machine- versus human-generated text have received a tremendous amount of news coverage, with most of that coverage pointing out how flawed these tools appear to be.[14] According to the reports and our own informal tests, the tools can flag text generated solely by a human as machine text, and vice versa.

Tricia generated text using ChatGPT4 then ran it through a detector, which identified 50 percent of the text as coming from a machine (and consequently 50 percent as coming from a human). However, once Tricia ran the same output through what's known as a spinner (i.e., a paraphrasing tool such as QuillBot) the detector identified the text as 100 percent human generated. In addition, some tools also may tend to falsely detect text generated by an English language learner as machine generated.[15] At the time we are writing this book, AI detectors are in their infancy but improving rapidly. Recent studies have shown 95 percent accuracy in detecting AI-generated writing, with few false positives.[16] This is a major improvement in a short time and a qualitatively better outcome than humans can produce at scale. Studies conducted in mid-2024 indicate that the best detectors are reasonably good at identifying AI-generated text that is cut and pasted without editing while rarely generating false positive tests for AI. The tools seem particularly inaccurate when text generated by one machine is spun by another or manipulated using other adversarial techniques.[17] We hope that detection will grow in sophistication and capacity as research and development continues. We believe that having accurate detectors is useful—if not to ensure our students are learning, then to be able to detect dis- and misinformation being promulgated to threaten democracies.

So, should instructors use any preventative or detection tools as a strategy to enhance integrity and reduce cheating? That's a good question. Back in 2009, Davis and colleagues cautioned us against getting into a technological arms race with our students.[18] The rationale behind their warning was twofold: students (i.e., the younger generation) would likely outsmart faculty in such a competition, and also it would undermine the faculty-student relationships that are conducive to deep, meaningful learning. We can see the fruits of the technological arms race if we look closely at plagiarism. In the 1990s, similarity detection tools were created to help instructors identify plagiarism. Since that time, contract cheating, paraphrasing tools, and artificial intelligence have risen; since these methods produce "original work," they are not detected by similarity tools. In response, the tech industry is developing tools to detect work written by a contract cheater or by artificial intelligence. And so the cycle continues.

At the same time, we also acknowledge the very real need not only to secure the integrity of the degrees we confer, but also to assure students that we will do what we can to prevent cheating. Otherwise, "if enforcement is not robust, or if students come to believe that everyone is doing it—even if they are not—the tendency to cheat will increase."[19] On that basis, here are some fundamental principles we recommend for guiding the decision to use (or not use) anti-cheating technology.

1. *It should work*. This principle seems obvious, but as we pointed out, the technology is progressing so quickly that our standards for evaluating tools rapidly become slapdash. For example, when one leading ed-tech provider developed and released their tool to detect text written by ChatGPT-3 in March 2023, their internal testing indicated a 99 percent accuracy rate. Unfortunately, GPT-4 was released in the same month, immediately rendering all the testing obsolete. In the time between January and July 2023, the makers of ChatGPT created, tested, and quietly retracted their own AI writing detection tool, citing a lack of accuracy. This raises the question, does any tool, whether for AI detection or for any other academic integrity function, work in new contexts, with new datasets, or for different AI tools? At the time of this writing, the answers to these questions are still being debated because the pace of change

is so fast. Thus, instructors have the responsibility to evaluate the performance of any technology-based anti-cheating tool with a consistent and critical eye. Before you decide to use any tool, we suggest that you read the science (not the news headlines) on the tool and talk to your local educational technology expert. If your institution allows, you could also try out the tool yourself first. Put your own writing through a similarity detection software application to see whether it detects any plagiarism in your writing. Take a test in front of a remote proctor to see if it flags you for any suspicious activity. Generate some content from your favorite GenAI product and run it through an AI detector, then run your own writing through the same detector. (If you want to run student writing through it, make sure you obtain their knowledge and consent.) And remember, if you do use the tool, interpret the results in context; it provides you with only one piece of data and should never be considered foolproof or conclusive.

2. *It shouldn't exacerbate inequities.* Any technology that can be defeated by a product that costs money or by a contract cheating provider creates wealth-based inequities. For example, a lockdown browser for remote or online assessments can always be defeated by the use of a second device. Any student who can't afford two devices is therefore at a disadvantage. Technologies that require high-speed internet at home or lengthy travel to a testing center have similar problems.[20] Give serious thought as well to students with disabilities, who might well experience technologies quite differently than their peers do. AI-powered cheating detection based on video surveillance may well flag honest behavior in a student with motor control differences, to name only one example. As you decide to integrate security technology into your courses, be aware that new inequities can sneak in as well. Only you (or perhaps your educational institution) can determine whether the increased

security is worth any reduction in fairness created by a particular tool in a particular situation.

3. *It shouldn't undermine efforts to build community.* Include students in the discussion about anti-cheating technology, respect their concerns, and be willing to make changes if you determine that they have a point. Students expect some detection measures at most institutions (e.g., similarity detection software) but others, like AI-based video proctoring still feel very creepy to many students. Be aware of the cultural context surrounding assessment security at your institution and be sensitive to students' perceptions of your motivation. People are sensitive to being surveilled, and many students perceive blanket use of video proctoring, plagiarism checking, and AI detectors as a preemptive accusation of cheating. In this situation, the student-instructor relationship could become adversarial, leading to neutralizing attitudes and possibly even more cheating. Conversely, to the extent that honest students see your security efforts as protecting their honest efforts, these technologies can have a beneficial effect on their attitudes and behaviors. We are not against closely observing students performing a task or applying knowledge in order to evaluate their mastery of learning objectives; the trick is determining the line between a "trust but verify learning" and a "police state" mentality. Both formative observation and assessment security may be important, but the latter often feels tremendously different than the former and so should happen only as often as absolutely necessary (see principle 6 below).
4. *It should be developmental.* When students are given feedback about their work and a chance to self-correct it, then technology can be part of the learning process rather than "cop shit," as some have called it.[21] We should deploy anti-cheating tools with the understanding that substantial risks coexist with the benefits.

However, when an educational technology tool wraps anti-cheating features together with proactive learning opportunities, the balance may be tipped in favor of its use to simultaneously improve learning opportunities and the integrity of our courses. Of course, if the alternative is easy cheating, sometimes it's necessary to employ security measures even when they don't serve any other function.

5. *It should be easy to use properly.* As we've said, if we had a dollar for everyone who has asked one of us what the threshold for plagiarism should be on a similarity report, we could give this book away for free. The challenge is that no two reports are the same, and the similarity percentage isn't an indicator of cheating or plagiarism, but merely of similarities between two sources of text. More generally, technology is a tool to help instructors understand students' assignment-completion processes and identify those cases where they extend outside the bounds of the rules. It is just as much a fundamental failure of integrity for instructors to outsource this important work to a company as it is for students to outsource their essay writing to a contract cheating service. Any tool whose outputs are easy for instructors to interpret and integrate into their own judgments is to be preferred over one that treats its outputs as a fait accompli.
6. *It should be used sparingly and intentionally.* Not every assessment needs, or should be layered with, high levels of security. *Formative assessments* (such as practice problem sets, active problem solving, or case study analyses) are designed to facilitate learning. *Summative assessments* (such as tests, portfolios, or projects) are designed to certify that the student has acquired the knowledge and abilities the assessment was designed to measure. Formative assessments prepare students for summative assessments, and summative assessments measure the extent to which learning has occurred.

> The former are assessments *for* learning, whereas the latter are assessments *of* learning.[22] Assessment security measures should be deployed on these summative assessments that "qualify students for degrees and professions" and perhaps should occur most often at the program rather than the individual course level.[23]

On balance, no technology is inherently good or bad, even for a particular task. There are trade-offs and challenges to lockdown browsers, online proctoring, similarity detection, and AI writing detection. If a particular tool is able to achieve developmental benefits without undermining learning and does so in a fair and cost-effective way, we would endorse it. If not, then the risk of a compromised assessment must outweigh the cheating risk when making the difficult decision to add another layer of technology to the students' obligations

Create and Use a Cheating Detection Checklist for Grading

Contract cheating has become a growing concern in higher education. While the frequency of its occurrence is debated, estimates are that between 3 and 15 percent of students have submitted academic work created by someone else.[24] This percentage may seem small, but that impression can be deceiving. First, it may be an underestimate, since the research frequently relies on self-reports.[25] Second, the rates of contract cheating appear to be increasing,[26] so instructors must increase their vigilance even to maintain the status quo. Third, while contract cheating may, in fact, be restricted to a small number of students, for a subset of that group, it's their dominant schoolwork strategy. Consequently, the percentage may underestimate how many *assignments* were contracted and also the severity of the issue. These concerns were exacerbated in 2022 when ChatGPT-3 was released,[27] making it easy to generate humanlike writing in response to a natural language prompt, often for free. This isn't contract cheating *per se*, but it can be equivalent to contract cheating if students are outsourcing their thinking and work. Regardless, it raises serious concerns about the future ability to use written or out-of-class assignments as summative assessments.

Manual Approaches to Identifying Cheating

As we've discussed, technology-based strategies for detecting contract cheating and machine-generated text have limitations, so we advocate a hands-on approach. Once one is attuned to the characteristics of an outsourced assignment, they do become easier to detect.[28] Of course, no detection system, human or otherwise, is perfect, but the process of reflecting on what a good submission versus a suspicious one looks like can be useful in and of itself.

Sarah Eaton has compiled a useful resource on detecting contract cheating that relies on research by experts in the field, including Ann Rogerson, Cath Ellis, Kane Murdoch, and others.[29] Much of this advice describes criteria that demonstrate limited engagement with an assignment, which is characteristic of assessments created by someone not enrolled in the course (or by GenAI). When assignments are written by people or machines not taking the course, they tend to contain made-up facts, information, and references, or to use references that are not assigned in the course. Of course, these features can also be characteristic of disengagement more generally, so the possible indicators of cheating we describe next (with some exceptions) are not meant to be diagnostic but rather a flag for further investigation.

Substantial changes in tone, style, or content compared to a student's previous work suggest a different author. For example, one of us once viewed a paper where basic vocabulary words were misspelled in the first paragraph but later on terms such as "paradigm" were used properly. While these types of inconsistencies are more often seen between assignments, it turned out that this student had submitted work written by someone else and added their own introduction and conclusion. Of course, in order to make longitudinal comparisons of student work, one must have repeated examples generated in response to different assignments. For this reason, a single long paper at the end of a course is at higher risk for contract or machine cheating.

Deficits in research are common. For contract cheated papers, limited research occurs largely because rates are fixed by the word or page. Humans often do some cursory research, which can be apparent. Some qualities of research that can point toward contract cheating include the use of abstracts rather than full papers, consistent use of outdated sources, sources that are in unusual languages, sources that the student is unlikely to be able to access, citations that do not match the reference list, wholly fabricated citations or a complete lack of citations, or reliance on a reference list with no in-text citations. Chatbots can cite sources, but don't conduct scholarly research in the human sense; they are merely machines that generate content based on the next most predictable word in a sentence. Chatbot output may include made-up references and arguments or content that is widespread on the internet rather than associated with your class. A friend of ours recently asked for and received a perfectly formed paper in his area of expertise which contained references, but none that he recognized. It turns out that they were completely fabricated, as were some of the studies and logical points that the chatbot generated. Because contract cheating providers and chatbots are often competent writers but not knowledgeable about the content, there can be a dramatic mismatch between the quality of the writing and the quality of the research. In general, these traits are somewhat correlated in honest work, so notable discrepancies between the two is an indicator of outsourcing. Of course, our students do sometimes honestly make these mistakes, so it is imperative that we follow up on suspicious research patterns rather than assuming wrongdoing. It is also true that as GenAI is trained on domain-specific content, fewer and fewer of these blatant errors may occur (in fact, at the time of the writing of this book, ChatGPT-4 was already much better at referencing real works because it had been connected with Bing, an internet search engine).

The submitted work often does not fit the course content. Another hallmark of outsourcing is that the creator of the content (whether human or machine) is unable (or, for human providers, unwilling) to create an assignment that fits the context. So, the contracted human or machine relies on material that wasn't covered in class or isn't even related to the course topic. One of us recently handled an unusually blatant case in which a student submitted a narrative about shopping in response to an assignment calling for a business plan.[30]

The submitted work often does not meet the assignment criteria. We frequently see computer science assignments that are written in the wrong programming language, use plug-ins or other features that students don't have access to, or rely on techniques that the students have not been taught and are unlikely to know. Contract cheating providers often also cut corners with respect to instructions so that they can complete the work faster—for example, using the wrong citation style or failing to format properly. Similar problems can occur with chatbots if they are not trained on particular citation styles or formats.

The file properties may reveal contract cheating. Lastly, contract cheating providers and clients are often careless with document handling. The metadata (file properties) of student submissions can indicate contract cheating subtly or clearly. For instance, if a document has only been edited for two or three minutes, the default language is one the student is unlikely to use, or the document author is someone the student is unlikely to know (for example, an author in the English-speaking developing world), this offers strong evidence of misconduct.[31] Even plagiarism detection reports can be instructive. For example, the Turnitin cover page includes a time stamp and the time zone from which the paper was submitted. One of us had a student enrolled to attend in person, but her papers were being submitted from Kenya (a hot spot for contract cheating providers). On the other hand, a very short editing time can result from honest processes—such as copy and pasting from one word processor to another, downloading a

Google doc as a Word document, or renaming the file—so it is not always an indicator of contract cheating. It is, however, a good way to hide the original metadata of a dishonestly created assignment.

Information tracked in the LMS may reveal dishonest activity. Although many LMS systems scrub key metadata from student-submitted files, they also collect information that can help detect academic dishonesty. For example, many systems track the IP address from which submissions originate. Of course, a student might submit from an unfamiliar IP address for a myriad of reasons, but anomalies can indicate that the submission warrants further examination. In the same vein, many LMS quiz modules track browser use. When a quiz is submitted unusually quickly or slowly, or when multiple students submit identical answers at the same time or in the same sequence, these can be signs of collusion. Some LMSs even track when users leave the browser window to switch to or open another window. Even more telling, LMS activity logs can show each entry into the answer box in html format. The html coding will reveal whether the student is typing in or copying and pasting answers. Despite appearances, LMS logs are not completely reliable indicators of misconduct, but they can show suspicious activity for the instructor to follow up on.

How about impersonation? Contract cheating can be addressed by verifying the identity of a work's creator. If it were possible to know with some certainty who created the work a student submitted, then contract cheating would become much more difficult. Tools for verifying people's identity are fairly sophisticated as of this writing. Governments routinely use online identity verification technology such as CLEAR Verified and ID.me for immigration identification checks. Educational institutions could do likewise to ensure that the person completing an activity is actually the person receiving the grade or credential. Because identity verification is vitally important across multiple sectors, the technology to solve this problem is relatively advanced. These tools are quite expensive and are only useful for identifying an individual at a single point in time. Their usefulness for preventing cheating is thus limited to making sure that a test taker's identity is verifiable or that the person writing an assessment is the one enrolled in the course.[32]

Identifying the author of a document such as a paper, program, or problem set can be easy if the electronic document properties have not been altered. However, when they have been, document properties won't help identify contract cheating. Machine learning and AI tools can make detection easier, though. For example, forensic linguists have developed stylometric analysis techniques for comparing writing samples to assess the likelihood that they were created by the same author. As of this writing, one such product is commercially available, but as stylometry becomes more common, it will become more difficult to substitute the work of another author for one's own.[33]

Synchronous author identification tools such as keystroke recording are also available to supplement the identification tools described so far.[34] Although keystroke identification techniques are in their infancy, they can measure typing speed and patterns of pauses, errors, and key presses. These measurements are unique to each typist and can thus identify whether a text was typed by a particular individual. Unfortunately, these identification methods are not yet very effective for academic purposes, and countermeasures have already appeared. Over time, though, the wheel of technology will turn, and it could become more or less difficult to substitute another person's or machine's work for a student's own. Only time will tell which will happen.

How to Respond to Suspected Outsourcing

If after applying one or more of the detection techniques described so far you suspect a student may have outsourced their academic work to another human or a machine, we recommend having a conversation with your student—preferably in person (or in a synchronous online meeting). Don't ambush them; let them know in broad terms your concerns about their work when setting up the meeting. Don't be confrontational or even assume that they committed a policy violation; instead, ask about their work process.

Start by asking them to describe the process of completing the work broadly, then zoom in to particular references, turns of phrase, sections of code, or other content that seems suspicious. If the student can demonstrate their understanding of course readings and concepts and provides clear answers about process, use of sources, or other concerns, this evidence can go a long way toward alleviating concerns about outsourcing. Alternatively, at this point, many students will acknowledge that they used inappropriate methods to complete their work, particularly if they feel comfortable and respected during the discussion. They may not know that those methods are inappropriate, but often they acknowledge that as well. Other students may panic or double down on their dishonesty, providing no response or a response that does not account for your concerns. Document this and use it as supporting evidence for filing a violation report according to your institution's policy.

Understanding your own expectations for high-quality assessments, particularly those that rely on assumptions about the ethics, purpose, and mores of higher education, can be very helpful when evaluating student work for academic misconduct. When you are aware of your expectations and clearly communicate them to students, it becomes more obvious when those expectations are violated by contract cheating or through copying and pasting from an existing source. Furthermore, knowing and communicating your expectations helps your students to succeed authentically and thus avoid integrity violations in the first place.

Know Your Students (Personally, as Writers, as Scholars)

In light of the previous section, it should be clear that the best way to identify inauthentic student work is to know your students. When you are familiar with their skills and abilities, interests, and goals, you can see them as three-dimensional people, and you hope that they see you that way, too.

You can get to know your students through some simple mechanisms. Icebreakers are a reliable strategy for community building in face-to-face or online modalities. These can take the form of "name, rank, and serial number" introductory exercises, a discussion board, or any number of other activities. Of course, the purpose of these activities is to help you put a name with a face, but you can also use them to add a "voice" to your knowledge of your students. *Voice* can refer literally to the sound of a person's voice, which can create powerful connections, as well as to their voice as a writer. We use a simple introductory activity to gather data that can help customize our courses to the interests of our students and serve as a baseline for evaluating their later work for both growth and authenticity. In both online and in-person classes, David asks students to write a little bit about themselves on an LMS discussion board. This serves the introductory function but also provides a baseline writing sample that he can use to track progress or make comparisons to later work, if necessary.[35] Remember that you don't need to be able to recognize and converse with a given student at any point, you just need some background you can refer to later if questions of assignment authenticity arise.

Jennifer Gonzalez cautions that most icebreakers are superficial, are cheesy, and require students either to take big social risks or just make up stuff about themselves.[36] As one alternative, she suggests having students move around to get in "blobs or lines" based on particular characteristics. We love this idea and would add that making the characteristics relevant to the class can help students to identify their peers early. David has students in his research methods course move into groups based on "would you rather" questions: "Would you rather write an introduction section or a results section?" or "Would you rather give a ten-minute speech or run a two-by-two analysis of variance in R?" for example. These items remind students that they're not alone in their fears and concerns about the course and help them identify classmates who might be good partners, tutors, or listeners to their complaints.[37]

Intermediate scaffolded assignments are also useful benchmarks for establishing whether a student has outsourced a particular assignment. When the tone, voice, vocabulary, or overall quality of work changes from a draft to the final version, this can justify further examination. Similarly, when the topic of the final assignment is unrelated to the components, or is related in a surprising way, this can signal a change in author. This technique can also be used without the addition of scaffolded drafts. In any course in which writing or other creative work is submitted, including computer code, authorship can be established by an initial proctored assessment. Early in a course, students would be required to submit a short assignment that mirrors the later longer ones but doesn't require any content knowledge. The purpose of this assignment is for you to get to know the students' capabilities and also to document their writing style in a way that prevents plagiarism or outsourcing. It's then possible to use this sample as a baseline comparison to later work to ensure that authorship remains consistent throughout the course. This technique is easiest to implement in person, but it can work online as well by using remote proctoring or requiring students to complete the assignment at a testing center. We recommend that wholly online programs consider this option as part of onboarding students into their remote learning experience.

Another option for ensuring that students are the authors of their assignments is through the use of the viva, or oral, exam, as we discussed in chapter 4. Alan Turing based his eponymous test for determining whether a computer can think on conversational fluency.[38] The test requires a machine to be indistinguishable from a human interlocutor in a blinded test judged by other humans. He made this choice because conversational fluency was and still is a hallmark of complex cognition and understanding. We propose that Turing's logic can apply equally to determining whether the same mind was at work in two different contexts: the creation of a work and a discussion of it later. Just as a computer can easily fool humans in scripted situations, a simple presentation on the material is insufficient for determining whether the presenter is also the creator of the original work. We suggest a short (five or ten minutes), low-stakes conversation with each student about their work, covering the creation process, the content, their conclusions, and their logical extensions. Not all students will be able to have a clear and sophisticated conversation in this context, but in almost all cases when the student is the author of the work, the conversation will be easy to connect to their submission. When they are not the author, it's more likely that they will speak in broad generalizations, miss the topic entirely, or be unable to discuss it at all.[39]

Conducting an oral assessment for each student for a single assignment may not be feasible in large courses. However, UC San Diego engineering faculty have demonstrated that it isn't impossible if teaching assistants are trained to conduct these conversations along with the instructor.[40] If this isn't possible in your class (due to a shortage of teaching assistants, for example), you could also choose to randomly assign students to the viva once per semester for periodic assignments. Students will understand that they may be required to discuss their work on any activity and can prepare accordingly, but faculty only need to conduct a fraction of the conversations for each assignment. If each student is evaluated at least once per semester, fairness is maintained.

Assessment Security in the Age of GenAI

> *In today's digital age, students have harnessed the power of Artificial Intelligence (AI) in both honest and dishonest ways, reshaping the landscape of education. On the one hand, AI has revolutionized learning by providing personalized study recommendations, automating routine tasks, and offering instant access to a world of knowledge. Students now have intelligent tutors at their fingertips, helping them grasp complex concepts and excel academically. However, this technological advancement has also given rise to a darker side, where AI is used for plagiarism detection evasion, cheating on exams, or even generating essays with minimal effort. This book delves into the multifaceted relationship between students and AI, exploring its potential for genuine learning enhancement and the ethical dilemmas it poses in the pursuit of academic success.*

Why is this paragraph italicized? Because it was written by ChatGPT-3.5 in response to the prompt, "Write a paragraph for a book about the uses of AI by students, both honest and dishonest."

It's not bad, and it's better than the output we retrieved from version 3.0 (which gave us two paragraphs, despite the instructions). But as you can see, it is quite formulaic. ChatGPT is just one of many education-disruptive technologies. Free or inexpensive automated tools are available to solve mathematical problems, balance chemistry equations, translate from one language to another, generate images, write computer programming code, and more.

This is not new. As long as there has been academia, there have been technological disruptions that have threatened, or appeared to threaten, learning and assessment validity. Undoubtedly, the replacement of papyrus by paper, the printing press, and the ball-point pen have all been decried as the end of intellectual life in the academy. It's not difficult to imagine that teachers sought to ban each innovation for a time, until the technology became ingrained in academic work and was later mandated, as electronic calculators were. To think of the situation another way, for as long as there have been assignments, students have been seeking easier ways to complete those assignments and attempting to use technology to further this goal, often in nefarious ways. Plagiarism is as old as communication. It requires easy access to the words of others, so wax tablets, papyrus, paper, and the printing press have all enabled advances in plagiarism. Electronic documents with cut-and-paste functionality are an evolution of this process, not a revolution. Similarly, getting help from a friend once required being in the same place, but later the internet allowed for the sharing of old assessments virtually using computers, and now it can be done while on the move using a smartphone or smart watch. With the advent of online cheating marketplaces, paying someone to do one's work is easier than ever. Our point is not that cheating has become easier as the result of technology, but that all emerging technology should (and must) change expectations within academia, particularly around what and how we assess, and how we maintain the validity of our assessments.

Let's look at the challenge of securing assessments in the age of GenAI with an example from traditional language instruction. AI-based translation tools, which are readily available to students, perform consistently better than early language learners and are often as good as fairly advanced learners at straightforward person-to-person communication. Students in required language courses express frustration that they are made to complete translation tasks that technology can do faster and better. Any test of their language abilities that seems pointless and is not secure will likely be corrupted by using technology. The language instructor's first instinct in such a predicament may be to ban the technology. Yet, this is a fruitless effort for any out-of-class assessments since the use of translation tools is difficult to detect, thus making the ban impossible to enforce and the students' learning impossible to validate. Therefore, the only ways to enhance the validity of an assessment is to have the students complete it in a controlled environment (so they can't cognitively offload to GenAI), design a task that GenAI can't do, or rethink the learning objectives and redesign the assessment to allow students to cognitively offload. The question is, how do you decide which to do?

Assessment security is not just about ensuring that students don't cheat, but also ensuring that the assessment is a valid measure of the learning that students were expected to accomplish. As Phill Dawson notes, "When summative assessment does not meet its summative purpose well enough, there is little point in securing it."[41] So, when thinking about assessment security, first consider the validity of the learning objectives and the validity of the assessment for measuring the achievement of those learning objectives. If the learning objectives are still relevant, the assessment is still a good way to measure them, and cognitive offloading would undermine that validity, then securing the assessment is necessary. Otherwise, rethink and redesign. Let's look at some examples.

Computer programming is already much easier than it was just a few years ago because of AI-based debugging tools and large language models for coding like Codex and Github's Copilot will continue that trend. However, budding computer programmers will still need to understand how to structure a computing problem to generate code and be able to reality-check the results of their AI-driven coding. So, there may be assessments in an introductory computer programming class that must be secured to ensure that the students are not completing them with the aid of GenAI. However, once those students advance in their program, it could be that they can cognitively offload those basic tasks.[42] There may be other times, however, when computer programming can be cognitively offloaded to GenAI from the beginning. Leo Porter, a UC San Diego teaching professor, and Daniel Zingaro, an associate teaching professor at the University of Toronto, argue that people who want to learn how to program no longer need to "struggle with syntax, control flow, and the host of other Python concepts" in order to write code; instead, they only need to learn them enough to help "solve meaningful problems and interact productively with Github Copilot."[43]

This principle applies across disciplines. In mathematics, calculators are a cheap and easy alternative for solving complex problems or for those who have trouble with basic math. Therefore, out-of-class assessments that test a student's ability to do basic math manually will likely have no validity. And that's just with the ubiquitous access to a calculator. In addition, Photomath or a number of other websites and tools can answer basic and complex math questions for students. While a calculator doesn't give incorrect answers (unless there is a human entry error), GenAI frequently does. So, in math, the future-proofing skill may not be a person's ability to generate the answer on their own, but their ability to assess the correctness of GenAI output. Math instructors and others who teach math-based classes will need to figure out what are the new skills that students should be learning and how to assess those skills with validity.

Writing instructors are also struggling with these decisions. It's easy to see that writing straightforward prose will no longer be required for communication any more than knowing how to spell is. Spellcheck and its relatives are so ubiquitous that most of us don't consider it inappropriate for use by college students (if we consider the question at all). Of course, today's students are often much less proficient in spelling, grammatical construction, and stylistic writing than their predecessors were, but their final product is less likely to have spelling errors. As AI becomes more sophisticated, it will be able to generate theses based on topic inputs, produce examples, and link them to the thesis with effective logical transitions. So, in thinking about assessment security and validity, writing instructors have to consider what part of the writing process should be the next part cognitively offloaded to GenAI. And to do that, they need to think about the learning objectives and what is lost in the process of that offloading.

John Warner, in *Why They Can't Write* (2020) has argued that the fundamental challenges to teaching writing arise when writing is taught as a rote process using inflexible scaffolds. When students aren't given practice in creating and organizing prose followed by feedback and revision, they develop into writers who are uncomfortable with structure, argument, and creative use of language. Artificial intelligence will make this problem exponentially worse, because it serves as the ultimate scaffold. Students will lose the opportunity to use writing as a learning tool. This seems problematic. Similarly, an electric scooter is a more efficient form of transportation than a bicycle, but it also leads to a dramatic reduction in fitness unless the eliminated exercise is replaced.

The impact of GenAI on the capacity of people to write or solve math problems may be scary, but even scarier are the implications for critical thinking. As David's undergraduate mentor J. Frank Yates used to say, "Writing is nature's way of telling you how unclear your ideas are." The writing process is often more important than the product itself because it is in the process of writing where thinking gets done. This is why David is fond of saying that the point of an assignment is not to get the work done, but to *do* the work. Many writing (and other) assignments are intended to engage students' critical thinking and argumentation skills just as much as their ability to communicate their conclusions. When students don't learn the *process* of writing (or statistical calculations or any other skill), they lose an essential strategy for critical thinking and general problem solving. It may be true that future students will be able to organize arguments and understand complex systems without writing about them, but because human academic history is intertwined with our written tradition, a whole new set of techniques for critical thinking will need to be developed. This reinvention will be painful as the intellectual community grapples with a completely new way of developing arguments that won't be fully developed for a generation.

Final Thoughts

The key to assessment validity in the age of GenAI, then, is to examine whether the learning objectives are still valid, and if so, whether the assessment is still a valid measure of that learning. If both are true and the use of GenAI would threaten that validity, then the security strategies we covered in this chapter need to be applied.[44] On the other hand, if they are not, then instructors need to change the way we teach and assess. In particular, we need to change in ways that enable us to emphasize process over product. Chapter 4 contains our guide for how we all can think about making these changes. Dawson, for example, has argued that "if a computer can do something and we can't tell if the computer did it, we need a very good reason to continue to assess students without the computer's help."[45] We mostly agree with this notion but wish to note that there is a very good reason to continue to assess unaided work. Many of the skills we teach benefit our students through the process of learning them and by serving as building blocks for more complex tasks. By allowing students to use technological scaffolds, we deprive them of opportunities to practice basic skills. As David tells his students, "You don't lift weights because you need the weights to be higher up, you lift weights because it's good for your body." Similarly, people write, do arithmetic, write computer programs, and perform other tasks that AI can do easily because they are good for us and serve as the building blocks of more complex tasks. Maybe this means that instructors shouldn't assess these tasks summatively, but it doesn't mean we should abandon them entirely.

Second, as a profession, we need to harness the power of technology to help faculty to adapt, students to learn, and postsecondary degrees to retain their integrity. Institutions need to adopt technologies that help faculty generate dynamically changing summative assessments to evaluate and provide feedback on students' performance. Adaptive practice testing software already exists that leverages the "testing effect" (self-testing as a form of learning) to help students achieve mastery of material through repeated practice tests. As students demonstrate proficiency with certain concepts, the software directs their attention to those aspects of the material that require more practice. Automated feedback on formative assessments could enable overworked instructors to assign more, and more varied, writing assignments rather than relying on static multiple-choice exams. This shift might yield fairer assessments since biases can be addressed systematically. Such technologies can help instructors create mastery-based assessments and courses that support students' intrinsic motivation and self-efficacy. When combined with an understanding of course goals, AI technology can be harnessed to improve student outcomes, reduce cheating, and enhance assessment validity.

The future of assessment security is not simply a blanket acquiescence to utilizing more technology and more surveillance, but a balanced approach to rethinking course and assessment design and using security only when necessary to ensure that the work being submitted for certification of knowledge and abilities was completed by the student receiving that certification.

Next Steps

1. Interrogate your learning objectives to determine which are still valid and which need to be updated given the existence of GenAI.
2. Examine your assessments in light of what you have decided about your learning objectives. Are the assessments still valid or do you need to redesign any of them? Which are assessments of learning (summative rather than formative) and thus need to be secured?
3. For any assessment you are redesigning, consider whether any part of it can or should be cognitively offloaded to GenAI.
4. For summative assessments or assessments that students need to complete without the aid of GenAI,

choose at least one of the following strategies for securing them:
   a. Generating new questions every term
   b. Using randomization techniques
   c. Deploying technology (e.g., lockdown browsers)
   d. Proctoring students as they complete the assessment
5. For administrators, consider the value of closely examining assessment security tools that your instructors might use. Make sure that the tools you're considering meet the criteria we've outlined before buying or renewing your contracts.
6. Also for institutional leaders, examine the value of establishing a computer-based testing facility on your campus that provides students with consistent and secure testing conditions, as well as of purchasing assessment software like PrairieLearn that enables instructors to individualize and randomize assessment questions.[46]

7

INFUSING ETHICS INTO TEACHING AND LEARNING

If you implement some of the strategies in this book, you're likely going to feel disappointed the next time a student cheats in your class. Yes, despite improving your teaching and the conditions for learning, and enhancing assessment security, you will still experience occasional cheating episodes. There is really only one reason for this: students are human beings. Our colleague Jason Stephens, in an excellent piece written for *Change: The Magazine of Higher Education*, discussed the natural reasons why animals and humans cheat: "From an evolutionary perspective, academic misconduct is best understood as a contemporary, context-specific expression of a highly developed capacity to deceive in order to survive and succeed."[1]

This doesn't mean that cheating is inevitable—Jason argues it is actually evitable. But it is a strategy that has proven—through thousands of years of evolution—to be a successful way to survive. For students, this means finding successful strategies to survive the challenges of schooling, in particular how to pass their classes and ultimately receive that degree. While instructors might hope that they would see learning as a successful strategy to meet those end goals, too often the environment that students are in conveys that it is grades, not learning, that makes them successful. Their admission to university is based on grades. Honors distinctions are based on grades. Academic success is based on grades. The awarding of a degree is determined based on the cumulation of grades. Of course, grades are supposed to represent learning, but if students don't believe that they can achieve the necessary grade through learning, there are workarounds that will still ensure their academic survival. We are not attempting to morally justify the choice to cheat, but rather to explain it and to argue that cheating cannot be boiled down to bad people choosing to do bad things. Rather, cheating is more likely the result of relatively good (or at least normal) people choosing to put some needs ahead of others; that is, putting surviving school ahead of their own intrinsic need for growth and desire to see themselves as honest.

The key here is that many students mistakenly act as if every point on every assessment is critical to their survival. The good news is that because fairness is so evolutionarily important and cheating is so effective as a strategy, primates, including humans, have evolved a range of cognitive tools to detect and prevent it.[2] Therefore, instructors may be able to leverage that desire for fairness to help students choose honest learning, even when they perceive that their academic survival is at stake. But first, recall the caveat we mentioned back in chapter 1: the suggestions we provide in this chapter will likely not change the hearts, minds, or actions of those with the dark triad of personality traits (sociopathy, Machiavellianism, and narcissism). That is why chapter 6 on securing assessment integrity is so critical. Cheating must be detected to create a teachable moment for the majority of our students (as detailed in this chapter), to ensure a level playing field for those who are working authentically, and also to ensure that we are not graduating students who have cheated their way to their higher education certification. This chapter is focused on the majority of students who cheat because they made an error in judgment or action. This chapter also differs from the previous ones in that we don't recommend particular strategies. Rather, this chapter is geared to developing a shared philosophy for why and how we, as educators, should respond to integrity violations when they occur.

The False Dichotomy of Good versus Bad

Children are socialized to learn right from wrong through their observation of adults' behaviors and adults' responses to the children's actions.[3] This is known as *inductive learning*. If a child sees an adult speed while driving, they may learn that it's acceptable to break the rules of the road. If that child then becomes a student driver who speeds, but an adult condemns the behavior, they may deduce that rules can only be broken by some people or in some situations. One consequence of this inductive learning strategy is that it doesn't equip people to apply their learned moral rules in novel situations.[4] The challenge can be particularly difficult when one is faced not with a choice of right versus wrong but with a choice among competing goods that are in conflict. As an example, imagine a student who has been powerfully socialized to help friends when they're in trouble, but also not to cheat in school. What is a good person to do, then, when a friend who is failing a class asks to copy their paper? In those cases, people often notice only one good (help the friend!) and completely overlook the ethical challenge posed by the situation.

It's also true that people sometimes perceive that they're on the horns of an ethical dilemma when they are actually trapped within the language of dichotomy. The overuse of dichotomous language like good versus bad and right versus wrong presents the false impression that (1) we *can* choose between the two; (2) that we *must* choose between the two; (3) that it is always clear which is good and which is bad; and (4) it is always clear which to choose. Rushworth Kidder, author of "How Good People Make Tough Choices," challenges the belief that we are often forced to choose between two actions or options.

The false dichotomous thought pattern says, "I can either help my friend by giving them my paper, or I can tell them no." However, if I break that pattern with a critical ethical analysis, then I could actually explore other options for helping without violating integrity. For example, I could help my friend by teaching them the concepts they are struggling to understand, or I could help my friend by advising them to ask the instructor for help, or I could help my friend by referring them to the writing center, and so on.

This ability to think beyond the dichotomy, beyond the forced choice between two alternatives, is what Kidder refers to as a "trilemma"—a third option that upholds the two values that appear to be in conflict. The trilemma option puts the situation into perspective—giving my friend my homework would not be helping them at all but hurting them. I am potentially hurting them because I am interfering with their learning and their growth as a writer, or even setting them up to make a bad decision to cheat. So, if I initially perceive that I have a forced choice between loyalty (to the friend) and integrity (to self or the university), I can reframe the situation to discover a multiple of other choices that would allow me to help my friend *with* integrity. The problem is that students are not taught how to make, and act on, good ethical decisions in either their formal educational experiences or their personal lives. But they should be.

Why Teaching Ethical Decision Making Matters

When Tricia was teaching the academic integrity seminar that she designed for UC San Diego, she had an interesting conversation with a group of students who had been reported for plagiarism. This was early in Tricia's career, and she was very curious about students' reasoning about plagiarizing. This was around 2008 or 2009, when there was a lot of debate among theorists and researchers about whether student plagiarism was a matter of ethics, a natural progression in the process of learning how to write, or a result of ignorance or cultural norms.[5] Tricia intuitively understood that students could make a citation mistake because they didn't yet understand the mechanics of citation. After all, citation mechanics are not ethically right or wrong; they are arbitrary rules created by experts and expected to be followed by novices. Of course, students could also make citation mistakes because they weren't critically reading for understanding or didn't know how to paraphrase properly. So, Tricia decided to explore the origins of plagiarism with this group of students (who had all submitted their plagiarized papers to Turnitin):

Tricia: Do you understand what Turnitin does?
Students: Yes, it compares our papers to all other papers submitted and to everything on the internet and then highlights when material looks copied.
Tricia: So, why would you submit a paper with plagiarism in it to Turnitin?

Tricia grouped the answers she received into three basic explanations:

- *The 3 a.m. syndrome*: It was late, I had only so much more time until the paper was due. I was exhausted and fed up, so I made a bad choice. I plagiarized to finish the paper so that I could go to sleep. (These students made a choice between two needs.)
- *Disbelief in detection*: There are, like, one hundred people in the class. There is no way they're going to check the Turnitin reports of every student. (These students engaged in a more calculated cost-benefit analysis.)
- *Integrity isn't really important*: Whenever the professor talked about the paper, he just went on and on about how many pages it had to be, the font and margin sizes, and how many references we needed to cite. I had written seven pages, and I was quite happy with them and felt "done," but the teacher harped so much on the ten-page requirement that I got frustrated and plagiarized the last three pages. (Here's the impact of an instructor's modeling: a done-to-specs paper is better than an honest paper.)

Thus, even though they understood plagiarism and (relatively correctly) the processes that Turnitin uses to detect similarities, these students cheated. You likely see in their reasoning that many of the strategies recommended in this book—including course and assessment design as well as clear communication of integrity—may have prevented them from plagiarizing. However, the point we'd like to highlight for the purpose of this chapter is this: behind all these explanations is an expressed lack of ethical reasoning or an inability or unwillingness to act ethically in the face of frustrated needs. Are we saying that all plagiarism, or even all cheating, can be boiled down to ethical choices? No, of course not. However, neither is it correct to say that plagiarism, or even cheating, is always the result of unintentional mistakes resulting from a lack of academic skills.

Instead, we posit that integrity violations should be categorized as errors, whether ethical or otherwise. To explore this, we turn to the learning from errors at work literature, which outlines a helpful causal typology of how errors are made:[6]

- A lack of knowledge and skills
- An intent to violate standards
- A deviation from standards for some reason other than intent or a lack of knowledge or skills

In education, we see the first type of error a lot. A lack of knowledge or skills might lead to content errors (because the student misunderstood a course concept) or plagiarism (because they do not understand citation practices). We have also seen students who seem intent on violating the academic integrity standards by, for example, outsourcing the completion of their schoolwork to a contract cheating provider. And we have seen other students who had the knowledge and skills, but deviated from the standards for reasons such as procrastination or failure to recognize that their choice of action was a violation.

In institutions around the world, the unhelpful dichotomous thinking that plagues students also plagues faculty and administrators: it's bad students who cheat or it's bad institutions that encourage cheating. The truth is that higher education institutions are like any other organization; the people within it will err from time to time, so we should have a strategy for catching and correcting mistakes before they cause (real) harm.[7]

In this chapter, we explore what individual instructors and institutions can do to minimize these cheating errors, or minimize their recurrence, by teaching ethics before and after an error occurs. We cannot simply talk about what individual instructors can do because the acquisition of ethical reasoning and the courage to choose ethical actions takes time and repeated learning opportunities. Also, because we are resolute advocates for "leveraging the cheating moment as a teachable moment,"[8] an institutional rather than individual approach is necessary to ensure students receive equal opportunities for education that are intentionally and thoughtfully designed.

Education before the Error

Here is one of the most common challenges we receive when speaking to faculty: "Cheating is morally wrong and students know that, so they must be punished." These colleagues tend to mistake our teaching and learning approach for being laissez faire, and they ask us why we don't want students to be punished. This position is juxtaposed with the challenge from others who accuse us of wanting to police students and of being too focused on punishment. Both sides seemingly fail to appreciate the other position and the moral consequences of their own position. Faculty often have strongly held moral positions that are based on emotions or intuition and therefore require a conscious cognitive process outside of the moral decision itself to fully understand.[9] If faculty have trouble seeing the moral dimensions of punishment or nonpunishment of cheating, how do we realistically expect our students to reason through their ethical positions without help?

On the rare occasions where this kind of help is offered, it usually comes in the form of a one-time, online training for incoming or new students. This training usually consists of tutorials that define various academic integrity violations and set out some expectations for norms in higher education. Students are "supposed to know this" from their secondary education, but we retrain them to ensure consistency. Unfortunately, this training fails to account for three key problems:

1. Even when presented as vignettes, the situations we describe are abstract and disconnected from students' intuitions about their own academic lives. Unless they

are faced with a very similar dilemma, there will be little transfer of moral principles from the example to real life because students' moral intuitions simply don't engage.

2. Moral consequences are often delayed, while practical consequences are immediate. Humans, particularly those whose frontal lobes are still developing, engage in *temporal discounting*, which means that they give less weight to later consequences than immediate ones.[10] Therefore, doing the right thing may seem to be of lesser value in the moment than it will seem later.
3. Even when students engage their morals and decide that doing the right thing is worth it, they sometimes fail to act because they don't know what to do. They have never practiced the difficult skills of saying no to a friend, of scrapping an evening's work and starting again, or of asking for help.

In short, as educators we expect our students to know what is ethical, when to act ethically, and how to act ethically, but we don't give them any training or knowledge about how to do those things. Why not? It turns out that in the twentieth century, there was a "values war," a disagreement over who—families, churches, or schools—should teach ethics.[11] This disagreement was never resolved, so in the end, no one really assumed the responsibility. In the 1990s, some ethics education started to appear in elementary and secondary schools in the form of character education. Again, however, this education focused on how to be a good person, rather than on teaching students ethical reasoning and behavior skills. We contend that this unresolved values war has left a gaping hole in our higher education curriculum, wherein we teach students the skills of an academic discipline without teaching them how to ethically practice that discipline.

The English writer Samuel Johnson—who often wrote about morality, the pursuit of happiness, and the quest for fulfillment—once warned that "integrity without knowledge is weak and useless, and knowledge without integrity is dangerous and dreadful."[12] We don't disagree, although we would modernize

Johnson's use of the word "integrity" with the phrase "ethical reasoning." As a new age of artificial intelligence dawns, it is more important than ever to ask not *if* we can build smarter machines, but *whether* we should and *how* we should do so. For example, the developers of GenAI tools are alleged to have stolen the data they used to train their machines and to have paid less than living wages to Kenyans to refine the training data set.[13] Would the people running these companies have approached the innovation differently had they had more exposure to and training in ethical reasoning? We'll never know, but we argue that ethical reasoning and acting must be integrated into the educational curriculum if we aim to prepare graduates for a life in which ethical conduct is expected and necessary.[14] This is particularly relevant now because the ability to act ethically may be one of the few skills that distinguish humans from machines. We are not arguing that every student should have to take an ethics course in the philosophy department, but rather that ethics education should be fully and seamlessly integrated into the four-year higher education curricula across all disciplines. This type of education could take a variety of forms, some easier to implement than others. Following, we offer two ideas.

Implement the Giving Voice to Values Curriculum

In *Normal Organizational Wrongdoing*, Donald Palmer tells the story of two different companies as a way to illuminate the dangers of a lack of ethical oversight in corporate America. Parmalat and Enron were two very successful companies but both had a tremendous amount of misconduct hidden in plain sight. Parmalat had been overstating its profits and assets for decades, while Enron was hiding its losses to make the company appear more profitable than it was. Apparently, there were people who knew (or at least suspected) that misconduct was occurring, but they failed to do or say anything about it. Arthur Andersen, the accounting firm for Enron, continued to approve Enron's accounts without comment. Deloitte and others affiliated with Parmalat did the same. Individuals either lacked the courage to act or engaged in rationalizing to fade the ethics of the situation from their consciousness so they could live peacefully with their failure to act.

The rise and fall of major organizations as a result of ethical misconduct has led to the development of training programs such as the Giving Voice to Values (GVV) curriculum.[15] The GVV curriculum is free and designed to be incorporated into almost any course in any discipline. At the core of GVV is the notion that people generally understand the difference between right and wrong, but they lack the courage and skills to act on that knowledge—to voice their values in the face of opposition. The overall learning goal of GVV is not ethical judgment or reasoning, but communication competence and skill. There are four learning objectives that build toward that communication competence and skill:

1. Understand the most common rationalizations for not acting.
2. Articulate what's at stake for those involved in the situation, including yourself.
3. Identify and utilize the levers of influence on those who disagree with you.
4. Develop and apply powerful and persuasive responses to the rationalizations.

The curriculum gives students the opportunity to script and practice responses to rationalizations and enhances those responses through feedback and coaching to build the resilience needed to act according to their values in real life. The goal is to help them find a method for voicing their values in a way that is authentic to them and effective for the situation at hand. GVV is well designed and easy to implement within existing courses (with stand-alone 1.5–2-hour workshops or functional/topic modules) or as a standalone course. Plenty of material is available for free, and prepared modules can be purchased at a discounted price.[16]

Teach Ethical Decision Making

A college student's friend asks to copy an assignment. The student says, "No, I'm not going to do that; it would be wrong." The friend responds, "But you owe me! I lent you my ride the other day when you had to get to work. The least you could do is give me your assignment!" Is this a right-versus-wrong or mostly-right versus mostly-right decision? What if the scenario involves a final exam, and the friend asks the student protagonist to let him copy from her exam because if she doesn't, he'll fail the class and won't get into med school! Is this now a right-versus-wrong or right-versus-right decision for the protagonist?

As we mentioned at the outset of this chapter, humans are often taught to choose good over bad and right over wrong, but they are not taught how to recognize these dichotomies, let alone what to do in the face of them. While the GVV curriculum starts at the moment of action; that is, helping people act on their decision, the majority of ethical reasoning instruction starts three steps back. Such instruction starts with teaching students how to recognize ethical issues, so that they can then proceed to make ethical judgments, stimulate their ethical motivation, and finally, take ethical action.[17] Why is that? Many ethical transgressions are caused by the failure of the involved actors to recognize they were facing an ethical situation in the first place.[18] After all, one cannot act in accordance with one's own (or one's institutional) values if one does not recognize that those values are under threat. Ethical awareness, then, is the critical stimulus moment of ethical decision-making and acting. Therefore, teaching students to recognize an ethical issue might have some power to mitigate their future cheating behaviors. This is the premise behind UC San Diego's Academic Integrity Seminar.

In this seminar, students are taught that they can improve their ethical awareness by using three simple tests to analyze any situation they might be facing:[19]

1. Does the situation undermine honesty, respect, responsibility, fairness, trustworthiness, and/or courage (values test)?
2. Does the situation run afoul of standards, laws, or rules (standards test)?

3. What would happen if this situation were exposed to others, particularly those in the public or those in authority (exposure test)?

This simple framework is transferable to other classes. Instructors in any discipline could provide the framework to students, which they then apply to either generic or discipline-specific case studies of the students' or professor's choice. Generic case studies involve academic integrity violations according to the International Center for Academic Integrity's six fundamental values.[20] Discipline-specific case studies could use examples from real-life professionals and researchers, as well as the values and standards applicable to the discipline (e.g., the IEEE Code of Ethics for professional engineers).[21] Repeated exposure to such real-life case studies could help students develop their ethical sensitivity so that they could recognize an ethical issue when they're facing one.

Developing ethical awareness is just the first step. Once someone has awareness, they need to be able to determine the most appropriate course of action. There is quite a bit of existing research that elucidates how an ethical reasoning lesson can be incorporated into any course.[22] The process starts with teaching students an ethical decision-making model—a process for thinking clearly and critically to reach a conclusion. Teaching students a process for thinking clearly through ethical decisions is not dissimilar to teaching them the scientific method. While the scientific method is not without its critics, it remains a useful way to walk novice scientists through the four basic steps of doing science: observe, hypothesize, test, and analyze.[23] The most common ethical decision-making models follow a similar logic: identify the issue (through observation), gather information, brainstorm possible solutions, evaluate possible solutions from various ethical perspectives, make a decision, and reflect on the ethical implications after the decision is executed.[24] Even a cursory look at this model makes it clear that critical thinking—rather than specific ethical values—is what is being taught. Critical thinking, a purported goal of higher education, is not outside the realm of a professor in any discipline.

It is often the prospect of helping students evaluate possible solutions from various ethical perspectives that makes most professors nervous, but it need not. For example, Subbian, Shaw, and Halpin suggest a non-discipline-specific evaluation method, known as COVER, which stands for Code, Outcomes, Values, Editorial, and Rule.[25] Following is the process for deciding the best course of action out of all of the possible courses of action:

1. Look at rules, standards, codes of ethics, and laws for guidance (Code).
2. Consider which action would elicit the greatest amount of good with the least amount of harm (Outcomes).
3. Contemplate which action would uphold one's own values, as well as those of all stakeholders (Values).
4. Distinguish which action would survive the "front page of the newspaper test"; that is, which action you would be proud to have publicly known (Editorial).
5. Distinguish which action you would be willing to have set as the precedent for all actions to follow in similar situations (Rule).

For those familiar with philosophical foundations of ethics, you might recognize the Outcomes portion as reflecting utilitarianism, Values as reflecting virtue ethics, and the Rule portion as reflecting Kantian ethics. But to teach ethical decision making, you do not need to teach your students about the philosophers behind these principles or the complexities of their theories. We are not advocating that all professors become philosophers (even though many of us have doctorates in philosophy!), but that we leverage the genius of ethicists and philosophers to normalize critical ethical decision making in everyday life and in everyday professional and personal challenges.

How Can Ethical Decision Making Be Taught?

Teaching ethical decision making can be quite simple. Present students with a scenario, but instead of asking them to solve it from a disciplinary perspective, have them solve it from an ethical perspective. In a business class, a professor could ask, "Should we sell this product or not?" and guide students away from thinking simply about economic or supply-chain concerns and toward thinking about the question from an ethical perspective. In an engineering class, a professor could ask, "Should we make this product or not?" and similarly guide students away from thinking simply in engineering design terms and toward the ethical implications of the product. In a first-year experience course or a psychology course, perhaps there is even room to have students develop their own case study of an ethical dilemma they have identified (with their newfound ethical awareness). Preferably, these cases would come from their own lived experiences so the situation is meaningful and not prone to abstraction or hypothetical analyses. Those case studies could be anonymized and shared within the class for collective problem solving using a provided ethical framework. These example exercises within three different disciplines (business, engineering and psychology) are authentic, relevant, and relatable. The point is that students should learn that there is an ethical implication to almost all the decisions they make, and that this is a lesson worthy of teaching. We are not arguing that college faculty are responsible for teaching students the right decision to make (although some would argue that), but we are definitely arguing that we are responsible for teaching students that they should think critically before making personal or professional decisions.

Education in Response to the Error

Everyone has heard stories of a professor who witnessed cheating during an exam and became so incensed that they took the test out of the student's hands, yelled at them, kicked them out of the exam, and gave them an F in the course. Maybe that professor was you. There are also stories of professors who, when they see plagiarism on a paper, sigh, get a glass of wine, then write a note to the student expressing their sadness and disappointment that the student plagiarized after all the work the professor did to teach them about proper citation practices. Maybe that professor was you. You have also likely heard that some professors, after detecting cheating, decide to handle it personally rather than following university policy if the student expresses remorse or worry about the impact of a report on their future career. Perhaps that professor was you.

How faculty react to cheating matters. If, as in the first story, you react in the moment in anger and as judge, jury, and executioner, you risk teaching the student that retribution rather than justice is the way to respond to someone who errs in judgment. If, as in the second story, you act like the victim, the wounded, the injured party, you risk teaching the student that cheating or plagiarism is only wrong if the professor cares or it caused an immediate and demonstrated injury or harm. If, as in the third story, you bypass university policy because the student states that they will never cheat again, you risk teaching the student that the remedy for one integrity violation is another integrity violation (that two wrongs make a right) and that if the student says just the right thing, they can escape the justice that might befall others. This last scenario is particularly concerning given that students are differently gifted when it comes to communicating, and communicating in the same language as the instructor, so such an approach would likely primarily continue to advantage the already advantaged.

There are many different, legitimate ways to react to cheating and plagiarism; we wouldn't be so arrogant as to tell you how you should react. You are a unique individual who must figure out how best to react in the moment in a way that feels authentic to you but also follows your institutional policy. However, we do have some tips for how you may decide how to react, tips that emerge from experience as well as from research.

Be thoughtful and intentional in responding to ethical errors your students make. First and foremost, we recommend that you find and read your institution's academic integrity policy. It's important that the faculty at an institution works together to respond to academic integrity violations, and it is to everyone's detriment when colleagues are pulling in different directions. Once you've read the policy, there may be aspects of it that contradict your own beliefs or the recommendations we make. Please work hard to change the policy before acting unilaterally, especially if you are someone with some power and authority, such as a professor with tenure. Why make a difference for only a few students when you can effect change that impacts everyone?

Once you understand your institution's policy, we propose that you choose to respond to ethical errors as teachable moments rather than exclusively as occasions for punishment. This doesn't mean that there should not be consequences for ethical errors, but that the consequences should be designed to be developmental rather than punitive (at least for the first violation).[26] For you as an instructor, keep your educator hat on when you respond to cheating. As an educator, you see a student, not a scoundrel or criminal, which means you see a person who has the capacity to learn. In other words, try responding to students' ethical errors the same way you might respond to a student's honest error. Academic institutions exist so that students may learn, and achieving that mission for all students depends on your ability to overcome your own emotional responses to cheating and focus on the goal, which is to help as many students as possible to become authentically educated graduates of your institution.

When a student makes an honest error in your class (say an error of content), you might be disappointed in them or perhaps even in yourself for not reaching them. It's also likely that you'll think something along the lines of "That's pretty normal. Students often make this sort of error," and you'll give them feedback to help them learn from their error. When you notice multiple students making the same errors, you take the time to reflect on your lesson plans, perhaps alter your pedagogical strategy, and reteach in order to help more students learn the concepts or skills they're struggling with.

Faculty know how to deal with honest errors. When students act to demonstrate their learning in an assessment, faculty have a rubric by which to evaluate the student learning and they have a point system for addressing errors. Errors mean a loss of points (or a failure to gain points). More errors equate to a lower grade in the course. But there is often no rubric by which faculty can respond to ethical errors, other than a simple statement like, "Cheat in my class and you'll get an F."

To that end, here is our suggested rubric for responding to ethical errors. Remember that your purpose or function as the instructor is to facilitate and assess learning. When a student cheats on a particular assessment, it means you cannot honestly and fairly assess their accomplishment of the assessment's learning objectives. So, we suggest you give a simple 0 on the assessment in question. This advice assumes that it would be difficult to get a 0 by submitting an authentic but terrible attempt. The structural consequences of misconduct should always be worse than those of giving the assignment an honest but unsuccessful try. Otherwise, students receive the message that they might as well cheat since there's some chance that they won't be caught, and if they are, the consequence is the same as if they didn't do the work in the first place. If a 0 isn't worse than the honest outcome would have been, it's a good time to rethink your grading system more broadly. Cheating should also have more serious consequences than simply not doing the assignment. Therefore, we recommend implementing a rule that allows partial credit for late or revised work but forbids late or redo assignments in cases of academic misconduct.

We also suggest that you acknowledge the ethical error, model your ethical and professional obligation to respond per institutional policy, and invite the student to remain as an engaged learner in the remainder of the class. Any consequences beyond these should be dependent on the broader context and dictated by your institutional policy.

Now is a good time to address the option of allowing the student who cheats to redo the assessment for full or partial credit. We know of faculty who do this, and with the best of intentions. This approach seems especially common in cases of plagiarism, where the student is given a chance to rewrite the assignment without the plagiarized material. We get it. If the point is to help the student learn from their mistake, shouldn't we enable them to continue to advance toward mastery of the learning objective? Perhaps. We would just caution you with this: make your approach fair and in accordance with institutional policy. If you allow all students an opportunity to rewrite or redo an assignment to eliminate errors, then allow the same to the student whose mistake was of the ethical nature. We both have known faculty who allow students to revise and resubmit after plagiarizing, but not after submitting a poorly but honestly completed assignment. That sounds not only unfair, but almost like an invitation to plagiarize! If you plagiarize, don't worry, you'll get extra time on the assignment to get it right, but if you just do the assignment poorly, too bad!

Of course, there are many who would argue that plagiarism isn't the result of an ethical error, but of an error in critical reading or a lack of writing ability. We will not get into that debate here because it is not a useful tangent, but if that is true (and we're not saying it isn't), it only serves to prove our point. If any revise and resubmit is allowed, it should be allowed across the board, regardless of the nature or reason for the error. Revision based on error should also be graded appropriately to your learning goals. You don't want to encourage cheating by allowing a penalty-free rewrite option. Students, especially extrinsically motivated students, are exquisitely attuned to the incentive structures inherent in our syllabi. If there's no consequence for attempting to submit an easy-to-obtain, learning-free assessment, they will attempt it. To them, it's a sensible time-management strategy.

There is, of course, more that a student can learn from an ethical violation, but that responsibility should hardly fall on the shoulders of individual instructors. Thus, we end this chapter with some notes about what should happen at the institutional level as well.

Education after the Error

If cheating is "normal but evitable," as Stephens argues (and we agree),[27] why is it that most instructors and higher education institutions treat cheating as something either to be ignored or responded to with punishment?

It's tempting for educators to ignore cheating. We ignore it because we'd rather not know. We ignore it because that feels easier than preventing it or responding to it. We ignore it because we rationalize the misconduct for the students: "It's just cheating on this one small homework assignment. I shouldn't make a capital case out of it." We ignore it because it makes us sad, we feel bad for the student, or we don't want to ruin their academic career by reporting them. Oftentimes we ignore it because our institutional systems and procedures for responding to it are complicated or overly cumbersome. And frankly, most faculty are not rewarded for any time or effort they spend on academic integrity, and no adjunct instructor is paid for work they do outside of their contracted time (usually from the first to last day of class).[28]

It's also tempting to respond with punishment. After all, it can be maddening when a student cheats, especially if you have executed strategies to deter misconduct. You put in the effort to create an environment that is conducive to learning and assessments that encourage integrity, yet a student still cheats in your class. We have heard our fair share of professors who believe that the student's punishment is the instructor's reward for the hard work they put in to detect and report the cheating. "Why should I report any student cheating in the future if this is the only punishment they get?" is an example of one such refrain. "Are you kidding me? It took me hours to prepare this report, show up at a hearing, and then all they get is a warning? That's not right!" is another example. We have also heard from instructors that the process should be swifter and expulsion more common, essentially denying students the right to due process and amplifying the message that integrity mistakes are grave academic wrongs.[29] And, of course, there are those who believe that punishment will serve as a deterrent, both for that student and also for other students in the future.

However, this sentiment seems antithetical to the purpose and philosophy of higher education, does it not? Are educators merely gatekeepers or enforcers of social hierarchy? Should they be in the business of punishing students who err, or should they be in the business of helping students learn from their errors? We believe that educational institutions should see cheating as a teachable moment,[30] an opportunity to help a student learn an ethical way forward. And let's do that at the institutional level, rather than put yet another responsibility on individual faculty members.

At the institutional level, administrators can turn a cheating moment into a teachable moment by applying experiential learning theory.[31] Experiential learning theory suggests that people can learn from their experiences if the appropriate conditions and structures are afforded to them. They need time for reflection on the experience, followed by opportunities to share that reflection with others. They need time for abstract conceptualization so that they can generalize and visualize their learning from one experience to how it might inform them in possible future experiences. Then they need time for active experimentation, to try out different ways of acting in the future in a safe and nonjudgmental space.

Consider the process of learning how to ride a bike. It would be extraordinarily difficult to learn how to do so simply by reading a book or watching a video. You might theoretically understand the physics of riding a bike and be able to hypothesize an action-reaction-action in such a scenario, but you're still unlikely to get on a bike and ride it perfectly without an incident. Now, you might argue that this analogy is not relevant. Riding a bike is a physical activity, so of course, one can only learn by doing. But learning how to make ethical decisions is intellectual or moral, and that is very different. Good point. Counterpoint: ethical decision making is physical because it leads, or doesn't lead, to ethical actions. What better way is there to learn about the impact and importance of ethical decision making than by experiencing the consequences of failed decision making?

Tricia and Jason Stephens proposed that learning from ethical failure can be structured in four steps: assess, assign, educate, and evaluate.[32] Because each learner and each ethical error is different, the first step is to assess what it is the student needs to learn. What was lacking that led to the error? For example, did the student lack knowledge of proper citation practices or the ability to recognize the ethical issue they were facing? Tricia and Jason argue that this assessment should be done with, not for, the student. Then, once this assessment is complete, intentionally targeted educational opportunities can be assigned, completed, and evaluated.

We won't spend a lot of space in this book detailing what these educational opportunities might look like, given that this book is written primarily for instructors rather than educational administrators. However, we will provide two examples to illustrate the lesson and perhaps provide fodder for broaching this approach with institutional leaders. Restorative justice (RJ) is one model for how this can be done. RJ is a form of nonpunitive accountability—holding students accountable for their actions but in a fashion that is about learning, growth, and repairing the harm, rather than about punishment.[33] The best book to read to learn more about RJ in higher education is David Karp's *The Little Book of Restorative Justice for Colleges and Universities.* Briefly, RJ requires that members of the community join the student in a discussion of the student's violation and the harm it caused, then together come up with solutions for repairing that harm. Those solutions may include education or development for the student, but educating the student isn't the focus; the focus is on restoring the harm that befell the community.

What Tricia and her team do at the UC San Diego Academic Integrity Office (United States) is quite different. After assessing a student's learning and developmental needs, the team has a menu of educational offerings that can be assigned to the student.[33] The educational offerings range from developing a student's writing skills to their ethical reasoning skills. Student learning is facilitated through reflective assignments, one-on-one coaching and mentoring, group discussions, and application assignments. Although conversations about harm are woven into these activities, restoring harm to the community is not the primary focus. Rather, the focus is on the student and what they can do to learn from their experience and develop whatever academic and ethical decision-making skills they need to avoid future errors.

We offer just these two examples to illustrate that institutions can take different approaches to leverage an ethical error into a teachable moment. To reiterate, by advocating for treating the cheating moment as a teachable moment, we are not advocating for a consequence-free environment. Consequences are the natural outcome of actions; for every action, there is a reaction. But as Tricia and Jason Stephens point out, the goal should not be consequences for the sake of punishment, but meaningful, relevant consequences for the sake of learning and eventually, if needed, for degree integrity. So, from the academic point of view, this can mean a zero on the assignment in which cheating occurred. From the institutional point of view, it can mean something like a notation in a disciplinary record, just as there might be for an employee in their personnel file. Consequences do have value; they demonstrate the importance of making tough ethical choices, even when it is tempting not to, and they help students to foresee that cheating is not worth it because of the risk of consequences. However, the consequences do not always need to be overly harsh, especially on a first violation. What is important is that students perceive that a response is likely and that it's at least somewhat aversive to them (even if we know that it's also educational). If students believe that a response will happen and that reasonable consequences will flow from that response, cheating will seem like a less desirable behavior to those inclined to do it, and the students who are not likely to cheat will recognize that their institution is supporting their decision as well.

Final Thoughts

Erring is a normal and inevitable part of being human. Of course, you might argue that when a student buys a paper written by someone else to submit as their own, this isn't an error but an intentional act of deception. It is truc that sometimes cheating results from an intentional decision to subvert the purpose of the assignment, circumvent the learning, or simply to survive under pressure. But as the learning from errors at work literature suggests, the intent to deviate from standards is, indeed, still an error. When our children err, even if they do so with a seeming intent to do something wrong, we usually try to guide them toward a new action or judgment; in other words, we coach them and help them develop so that they can learn and make fewer mistakes (at least in the same arena) in the future. So, we suggest that you do the same for other people's children too—your students. But let us be clear. We are not suggesting that colleges and universities should allow students to cheat repeatedly throughout their educational career by responding to the instances only with educational opportunities. Quite the opposite. We are advocating that when cheating occurs, faculty and administrators react as educators, rather than as victims or police officers, by centering on the learning that could occur from accountability. However, if after working with the student to help them learn and grow from their errors, they continue to make the same bad choices and engage in the same dishonest actions, the institution acknowledges that the teacher-learner relationship is not working out as designed and makes the decision to end the relationship. The termination should not be framed with the intent to punish the student, but with a statement of fact: This isn't working out for either of us, you are either unable or unwilling to be accountable for the integrity and learning standards here, so we're letting you go. And, in the end, this experience is about learning as well.

Next Steps

1. Can you think of one thing you could do to proactively infuse ethics into your course curriculum, using either the Giving Voices to Values curriculum or the case-study approach for developing ethical reasoning?
2. Reflect on how you typically respond to cheating when it occurs. Is this response aiding or harming (you, your students, and your relationships with all students)? How might you react differently?
3. What does your institution currently do to leverage the teachable moment when cheating occurs? Could you advocate for change or development in this area?
4. Administrators, work with faculty to develop an across-the-curriculum ethical thinking requirement that goes beyond mere academic integrity tutorials. Do current

institutional responses to cheating offer students an opportunity to learn from their ethical error and further advance their ethical reasoning and acting skills?

5. Also for administrators, do you have an AI policy that specifies how faculty should respond to this type of integrity violation? If so, examine it and revise it as necessary to make reporting and responding to AI policy violations as easy and transparent as possible for faculty, while still ensuring students receive the appropriate level of due process.

CONCLUSION

The world is changing rapidly. It's a cliché because it's true, so we won't apologize for saying it. At the time of writing this book, we were introduced to the next greatest thing to disrupt the status quo in education—generative artificial intelligence. Perhaps that is why the age of AI feels as if a paradigm shift is under way. Unlike other recent disruptors to education, artificial intelligence—machine deep learning in particular—will continue to grow and evolve, causing disruption at a record pace. Think about this. When we started writing this book in mid-2022, ChatGPT hadn't been released. While we were writing it, ChatGPT-3.5 and then ChatGPT-4 were released, along with Google Bard (which became Gemini), Bing Chat, Anthropic Claude, and thousands of other tools. Then, less than two years later, as we were working on the final edits to the book in May 2024, ChatGPT-4o was unveiled, offering users multimodal capabilities that make it possible for every person to have their own live-time AI assistant.

What's the solution? We could retreat into what Phill Dawson calls "assessment conservatism," as faculty largely did during the COVID-19 pandemic, conserving traditional ways of assessment and adding ever more prohibitions and surveillance to them. One solution to artificial intelligence and contract cheating could be to retreat back to in-person, invigilated exams as summative assessments and maintain homework and paper writing as either low-stakes or formative assessments, with tight prevention and detection controls in place. Dawson calls this "assessment security theatre"—it makes us look like "we are doing something about cheating," even though there are "no proven anti-cheating benefits."[1]

That path is tempting, and secure assessments are definitely needed in some situations. However, securing assessments is often used as an excuse not to change the course design. After all, many postsecondary instructors are neither rewarded nor encouraged and supported in redesigning their courses and assessments. Plus, maybe some are convinced that they already have the best-designed course or the best-designed assessments for their discipline or for the content they are teaching. Yet, there is evidence that the status quo is not only failing to minimize cheating, but is also not preparing students for their lives as twenty-first-century professionals.[2]

It is time for a change. Yes, we've changed before. Math instructors made changes when the calculator was invented. Some instructors changed when the internet emerged, and still others changed as a result of the pandemic, but the change that is required now in the age of AI is foundational. The times do not call for a tinkering around the edges, but for a fundamental rethinking and reframing of what we as educators identify as knowledge, how we teach knowledge, and how we assess knowledge—and, of course, how we define and conceptualize cheating and academic integrity.

The changes we advocate in this book all require us to move toward a learner- and learning-centered approach and away from the notion that faculty teach and students learn (or cheat). We must acknowledge that every aspect of our courses, from learning objectives to the syllabus, is subject to revision in the coming years, including class time, out-of-class experiences, and whether there even is a class per se. Perhaps most importantly, we will be required to change our assessment strategy from static to dynamic to reflect a shift from passive to active teaching and learning.

So, to close out *The Opposite of Cheating*, we summarize the eight guideposts that we hope will help you navigate your journey as you make the necessary changes for the AI age.

Revise How You Think and Talk about Integrity

Given that the reasons for cheating are complex, and that students cheat because they are human beings, revise how you talk about cheating and integrity, as well as the rules that you set in place. Talking *with* rather than *at* your students about academic integrity is a first step. Be active and strive to make integrity matter as much to them as it does to you. Getting on the same page with your students is the second step. You learned under different conditions and in different contexts than all or most of your students. You most likely see technology and tools differently than they do. And they will almost always know more about the latest and greatest tools for cognitive offloading than you will. Have honest conversations with your students about these tools. Connect their desire for learning and skill development with their desire to act with integrity, but do not be naive about the human propensity to cheat or cognitively offload. Be honest with yourself—you too have offloaded cognitive tasks, as well as at times been dishonest, disrespectful, untrustworthy, unfair, and irresponsible—and then be honest with your students. This is a not a you-against-them scenario. This is an us-with-us scenario. In the age of AI, it is more important than ever for us to remember that we humans have to stick together.

Refocus on Learning

Higher education has become commodified in the last half century or so. Politicians and policymakers talk about the importance of a college diploma rather than a university education. Jobs and livelihoods all over the world depend more on academic attainment than the knowledge and skills that degrees and diplomas represent. As long as commodification continues, it's hard to see how to address the other challenges facing higher education. Cheating has many causes, but the disconnect between students, faculty, and society as to the purpose of higher education sits very close to the heart of the matter. As an instructor, administrator, or citizen, you must work to reposition learning as a public good and one worthy of the tremendous investment required to achieve it.

This problem is obviously much larger than any one faculty member can address, but just because "you are not expected to complete the work, neither are you free to desist from it."[3] There are many ways to rethink university education, as we've discussed in depth throughout the book. However, they all refocus attention on learning, whether that be facilitating learning or assuring the valid assessment of learning. The good news is, and we reiterate here, that what's good for learning is also good for integrity and other cherished values like equity and inclusion. Here we say be as bold as your class, teaching, and institutional context allows. Tenured colleagues, please lead the way. If not you, then who? Our call to courage means you must have an evidence-based plan to support your changes. We hope that this book has provided a guide to some of the outstanding academic integrity research that grounds the suggestions we make.

Rethink Your Educational Persona

You have choices in the design of your classes. Will you center yourself or the students? Will you center teaching or learning? Will your students be actively constructing knowledge or passively regurgitating information? Students are more likely to cheat if you design with your needs and your convenience in mind than if you design with their learning in mind. Do they know what they're in your class to learn and why it's of value? Do they see fairness and transparency in deadlines and grading procedures? Do they see the relevancy between your choice of content to cover, activities to engage in, and assessments to complete, and do they see a connection between any of those things and the real world? Education does not always have to be immediately practical, but it does have to be immediately relevant and meaningful. Is the way in which you are educating relevant and meaningful for the twenty-first century, in the age of AI and contract cheating?

Reconsider the Nature and Point of Assessment

Not all assessments are equal, nor do they all fulfill the same purpose. Both formative and summative assessments tend to focus on external evaluative judgments—what others (usually the instructor) think of the student's knowledge. However, there also need to be "sustainable assessments"—those that involve the student's evaluative judgment of their own work and the work of others.[4] In higher education, faculty have traditionally focused primarily on summative assessments and secondarily on formative assessments. Now, with grading movements like specs grading, contract grading, and ungrading, we are starting to incorporate sustainable assessments. With the advance of artificial intelligence, we are called to consider cheating differently in each of these types of assessments. Perhaps in your formative assessments you consider the use of tools as cognitive offloading rather than cheating, and invite students to reflect on their use of cognitive offloading and its impact on their learning (engendering metacognition). In sustainable assessments, ask students to incorporate artificial intelligence, evaluate the quality of its work, and critically extrapolate what the chatbot did and did not do well. What is fake and real evidence in the piece it produced, and how would the student edit and expand the output to improve it? Summative assessments—those that will eventually be used to grant the credential—must have integrity, which means you must know what each student knows and can do under particular conditions and in what context. This is when assessment security comes into play. In other words, think carefully about which assessments require security and which do not.

Reimagine How You Show Up for Your Students

How you show up (your *presence*) in the classroom—physical or virtual—matters. Classes are diverse. Students' abilities are varied, their experiences rich, and their goals unique. Whether you are teaching a class of twenty students or six hundred, and whether you are teaching synchronously or asynchronously, virtually or in person, you can choose to show up in a way that creates connection, a sense of belonging, and a deeper commitment to learning with integrity. Your first step here is to develop your own teacher cognition—your own metacognition of how you think about teaching, teachers, students, and learning. Then, you can leverage that awareness to be present with and for your students, to model integrity, and to be enthusiastic and intentional about your choices. Do you want your class to be teacher or learner centered? Do you choose to ignore or attend to at-risk students? Showing up for your students is a choice that you can make when you first design the course, and then every day that you teach and engage in assessment.

Revisit Assessment Security for a New Era

Even though we wrote the majority of this book in a proactive and optimistic tone, we are also practical. There are threats to assessment security like never before. It is way too easy for students to arrange for someone else to complete one assessment for them, let alone an entire course or degree. Plus, the ease will soon be met with affordability; advances in artificial intelligence are already augmenting, and may someday replace, the human contract cheating provider, making contract cheating cheaper and way, way faster. This, along with the increasing prevalence of remote or online assessments, will exacerbate the temptations and opportunities to cheat. You cannot proceed toward the opposite of cheating without thinking about assessment security and integrity. But what does that look like? Some assessment security can be achieved by all the strategies we mention in the book, which can be summed up as *teaching better*. By teaching better, you enhance students' intrinsic motivations for learning and for integrity. However, making teaching better your only strategy would be naive. Collectively, we faculty owe it to society to ensure that, at the very least, our summative assessments are completed by the enrolled student and in the manner and context expected. As Phill Dawson eloquently points out, "We need to move beyond all-or-nothing and dichotomous thinking, and carefully balance assessment security and academic integrity."[5]

Reframe How You Respond to Cheating

On a scale of 1 (not at all) to 10 (extremely), how mentally and emotionally exhausting is it for you to respond to cheating? If you said anything higher than 6, then you need to reframe how you respond to cheating. Our guess is that you experience a painful emotion (e.g., anger, sadness, disappointment, despair) or you attempt to overanalyze the situation to find a reason or explanation for what went wrong. Instead, we encourage you to reframe cheating as an opportunity to educate and as an excellent opportunity for learning. Think of cheating as a mistake, an error, or even a failure. Mistakes, errors, and failures are not things to be ashamed of or ostracized for. Rather, they should be leveraged for the power they give to experiential learning—or learning from experience—the most powerful type of learning there is. Have a clear process for responding to cheating that follows your institution's policies and procedures. Although it's challenging, hold difficult conversations with the student, then move on. For your own learning and development, sometime later, maybe after the term has ended, reflect on whether you could have done anything differently. But don't harp on it. To err is human, after all. The trick is to forgive, learn, and grow forward.

Provide Quality Teaching, Learning, and Assessment Resources

This item is for the institutional leaders and administrators who are reading this book. Your instructors are limited in their ability to follow any of these guideposts or implement any of the changes we recommend throughout this book without your support. We often hear institutional leaders say, "We value undergraduate education," for example, but then we do not see any (or only limited) training, support, or funding provided to faculty to design or redesign their courses, pedagogy, and assessments. We also see a rise in the hiring of adjunct or contingent faculty who are expected to develop courses and assessments on their own (unpaid) time. If you truly value quality teaching, learning, and assessment, you will provide the infrastructure to support it. This goes beyond the typical supports such as student success coaches, student learning and writing centers, and academic tutoring for students. It means creating physical and virtual environments that are conducive to active and engaged teaching and learning. It means course design and pedagogical training and support (via, for example, instructional designers) for instructors. It means paid time to do course design, and rewards through the tenure and promotion system for well-designed instruction. It means rewarding faculty who attend to academic integrity and actively supporting faculty who deter, detect, and report cheating. It means establishing mechanisms, such as computer-based testing facilities, to ensure the validity of assessments and the integrity of degrees.

As we said in the introduction, even when people wish for change, they hope that it will happen without their having to change. The ways in which faculty teach, assess, and respond to cheating are choices. Perhaps even habits. James Clear, author of *Atomic Habits,* suggests that "habits are the small decisions you make and actions you perform every day."[6] The first step to changing your decisions and actions is to break your current way of doing things and create new ways.

NOTES

Acknowledgments

1. Bertram Gallant, "Academic Integrity in the Twenty-First Century."
2. Lang, *Cheating Lessons.*

Introduction

1. We use "GenAI" throughout this book as an umbrella term to refer to any artificial intelligence tool, including ChatGPT, that generates content (text, code, images, music) in response to a user's prompt.

2. We use "instructor," "faculty," "lecturer," and "professor" as appropriate when we're telling a particular person's story; otherwise, we use the terms interchangeably to be inclusive of geographic regions, institutional types, and institutional roles.

3. Dan Glaiser, "University Uproar over Heiress Who 'Cheated,'" *The Guardian,* November 30, 2004, https://www.theguardian.com/world/2004/nov/30/usa.internationaleducationnews.

4. Davis, Drinan, and Bertram Gallant, *Cheating in School.*

5. Based on research in Australia, as much as 5 to 10 percent of people enrolled in postsecondary education worldwide are not authentic students, at least not in all of their courses (personal communications on X, formerly Twitter).

6. Throughout this book, we use "class" or "classrooms" to refer to online, hybrid, or in-person modes of instruction. We believe that the majority of strategies presented in this book are relevant to all instructional venues, but in the case where we think a strategy is not generic to all situations, we will make that evident. Otherwise, assume you can try the strategy in your class, no matter whether it is virtual, physical, or both.

7. A note about instructor agency. Obviously, it is not absolute. Your agency is shaped by the situational factors of your course(s). In *Creating Significant Learning Experiences,* L. Dee Fink identified four factors that live outside of you:

1. The specific classroom context (e.g., class size; online, hybrid, or in-person modality; lower-division, upper-division, or graduate level; length and frequency of class meetings; synchronous or asychronous instruction; lab or classroom format; and physical/technological conditions.
2. Learning context (e.g., learning outcomes or conditions set by others).
3. Subject characteristics (e.g., theoretical versus practical; survey versus in-depth.
4. Students' characteristics (e.g., their life situations, prior knowledge, feelings about the class, their expectations).

This construct of situational factors will appear throughout this book with regard to issues to consider.

8. Bertram Gallant, "Academic Integrity as a Teaching & Learning Issue."

9. We follow the International Center for Academic Integrity definition of *academic integrity* as the courage to uphold honest, respect, responsibility, fairness and trustworthiness even when it is difficult to do so.

10. Fink, *Creating Significant Learning Experiences.*

Chapter 1. Why Students Cheat

1. Stephens, "How to Cheat and Not Feel Guilty."

2. Esteves et al., "Dark Triad Predicts Academic Cheating."

3. See, e.g., Rettinger and Bertram Gallant, *Cheating Academic Integrity*; Bertram Gallant and Rettinger, "Introduction to 30 Years of Research on Academic Integrity"; Eaton, "Academic and Research Integrity."

4. Anderman and Koenka, "Relation between Academic Motivation and Cheating"; Waltzer and Dahl, "Why Do Students Cheat?"

5. Bandura, "Exercise of Human Agency through Collective Efficacy."

6. Alt, "Assessing the Connection between Self-Efficacy for Learning."

7. Fouad and Smith, "Test of a Social Cognitive Model for Middle School Students."

8. Dweck, "Can Personality Be Changed?"

9. Herdian and Rahayu, "'I Don't Want to Commit Academic Dishonesty'"; Dweck, "Motivational Processes Affecting Learning."

10. Dweck, "Power of Believing You Can Improve."

11. David A. Rettinger, unpublished data, 2022.

12. Warner, *Why They Can't Write.*

13. Some readers might be curious about what David did in this situation. He doesn't actually remember. But if a similar situation happened again, he would probably determine that, despite having committed plagiarism, the student didn't violate his institution's honor code, which requires intent or disregard of policies. Under that policy, true ignorance would require remediation not punishment. David would now require the student to rewrite the draft with

the understanding that future plagiarism would be considered disregard of the rules and warrant a report under the honor system.

14. Roig, "Can Undergraduate Students Determine Whether Text Has Been Plagiarized?"

15. Roig, "Plagiarism and Paraphrasing Criteria of College and University Professors."

16. Waltzer, DeBernardi, and Dahl, "Student and Teacher Views on Cheating in High School."

17. 2021 statistics from footballdb.com

18. McCabe, Butterfield, and Treviño, *Cheating in College.*

19. Waltzer, DeBernardi, and Dahl, "Student and Teacher Views on Cheating in High School."

20. McCabe, Butterfield, and Treviño, *Cheating in College.*

21. Stephens, "Bridging the Divide."

22. Stephens, "Bridging the Divide."; Sykes and Matza, "Techniques of Neutralization."

23. This is not to say that systems, procedures, or policies are always fair so if you hear this claim, it is always a neutralization rather than a statement of fact. This is the power of neutralizations—the facts behind them could actually be true. Here, however, we are focused on the power of neutralizations used after the fact to justify cheating, not on critiquing or defending systems or policies.

24. Sykes and Matza, "Techniques of Neutralization."

25. Tenbrunsel and Messick, "Ethical Fading."

26. Alonso, "Simple Interventions Can Curb Cheating, Study Finds."

27. Waltzer and Dahl, "Students' Perceptions and Evaluations of Plagiarism."

28. We purposefully do not cite our sources for these quotations; the contract cheating companies do not need our free advertising.

29. Learning Strategies Center, "Successful Students Ask for Help When They Need It!" Cornell University accessed December 28, 2023, https://lsc.cornell.edu/successful-students-ask-for-help-when-they-need-it/; Student Life, "Academic Success Requires Asking for Help, accessed December 28, 2023, https://studentlife.umich.edu/parents/article/academic-success-requires-asking-help; "Maximizing Student Learning," Columbia Online, accessed December 28, 2023, https://online.columbia.edu/students/.

30. Tenbrunsel and Messick, "Ethical Fading," 226.

31. Tenbrunsel and Messick, "Ethical Fading," 228.

32. Young, "How the 'Contract Cheating' Industry Has Gotten More Aggressive."

33. John Ross, "Australia Blocks Access to Biggest Contract Cheating Websites," *Times Higher Education (THE)*, August 5, 2022. https://www.timeshighereducation.com/news/australian-regulator-forces-mass-blocking-cheating-websites.

34. Social learning theory explains that organisms (in this case, students) need not experience reinforcement themselves to increase the chances of a behavior that leads to positive outcomes. Bandura, "Observational Learning."

35. Ciranka and van den Bos, "Social Influence in Adolescent Decision-Making."

36. O'Rourke et al., "Imitation Is the Sincerest Form of Cheating"; Carrell, Malmstrom, and West, "Peer Effects in Academic Cheating."

37. McCabe, Butterfield, and Treviño, "Academic Dishonesty in Graduate Business Programs."

38. Stephens, Young, and Calabrese, "Does Moral Judgment Go Offline?"

39. McCabe, "Cheating among College and University Students."

40. Longoni, Tully, and Shariff, "Plagiarizing AI-Generated Content."

41. Esteves et al., "Dark Triad Predicts Academic Cheating."

42. Anderman and Koenka, "Relation Between Academic Motivation and Cheating."

43. Kerr and Wood, "A Look at 20 Years of Tuition Costs at National Universities."

44. Sethi, "Mystery of India's Deadly Exam Scam."

45. Stephens and Gehlbach, "6—Under Pressure and Underengaged."

46. Jordan, "College Student Cheating."

47. Anderman and Koenka, "Relation between Academic Motivation and Cheating."

48. Roig and DeTommaso, "Are College Cheating and Plagiarism Related to Academic Procrastination?"

49. Beasley, "Students Reported for Cheating."

50. "American Time Use Survey," US Bureau of Labor Statistics, https://www.bls.gov/tus/charts/students.htm.

51. Carnevale et al., *Learning while Earning.*

52. McCabe, Butterfield, and Treviño, *Cheating in College.*

53. Pulvers and Diekhoff, "Relationship between Academic Dishonesty and College Classroom Environment."

54. Jordan, "College Student Cheating."

55. Rundle, Curtis, and Clare, "Why Students Do Not Engage in Contract Cheating"; Rettinger, "Role of Emotions and Attitudes."

56. When talking about responses to cheating, we use three different terms: "consequence," "penalty," and "sanction." Generally, we use "consequence" as an umbrella term—there are consequences imposed by others and also natural consequences that come in the form of a reaction to an action. We use "penalty" and "sanction" more precisely when we're referring to a punishment for cheating imposed by an instructor or institution.

57. Rettinger, unpublished data, 2012; Dench and Joyce, "Information and Credible Sanctions in Curbing Online Cheating among Undergraduates."

58. Dench and Joyce, "Information and Credible Sanctions."
59. Nagin and Pogarsky, "Experimental Investigation of Deterrence."
60. Charness and Schram, "Social and Moral Norms in the Laboratory."
61. Tatum, "Honor Codes and Academic Integrity."

Chapter 2. Communicating Integrity

1. McCabe, Butterfield, and Treviño, *Cheating in College*.
2. Longoni, Tully, and Shariff, "Plagiarizing AI-Generated Content."
3. Bretag, "About Academic Integrity"; University of Auckland, "Academic Integrity Course"; UC San Diego, "Academic Integrity Tutorial."
4. For example, using Google Translate may be considered cheating in a language course but not in a chemistry course.
5. These are direct quotations from syllabi found on the internet and spun through QuillBot to protect the innocent.
6. ICAI, "Fundamental Values."
7. See Perkins et al., " AI Assessment Scale," for one example of how you might do this.
8. For a guide on crafting your GenAI policy, see Bertram Gallant, "Crafting Your GenAI & AI Policy."
9. Hansen, "U.S. Education System Isn't Giving Students What Employers Need."
10. Brooks, "In the Age of A.I., Major in Being Human."
11. Gilbert, "If Only Gay Sex Caused Global Warming."
12. Tappin and McKay, "Illusion of Moral Superiority."
13. Green, "Storytelling in Teaching."
14. Uribarri, "Ethics Case Studies."
15. Ethics Unwrapped, "Armstrong's Doping Downfall."
16. https://www.shrs.pitt.edu/sites/default/files/library/documents/him/Academic%20Integrity%20Pledge%202020.pdf
17. https://www.marquette.edu/provost/integrity-pledge.php
18. https://itali.uq.edu.au/teaching-guidance/assessment/academic-integrity
19. Mazar, Amir, and Ariely, "Dishonesty of Honest People."
20. Thaler and Sunstein, *Nudge*.
21. Bryan et al., "Motivating Voter Turnout by Invoking the Self"; Shu, Gino, and Bazerman, "Dishonest Deed, Clear Conscience."
22. Shu, Gino, and Bazerman, "Dishonest Deed, Clear Conscience."
23. Lee, "Scientists Are Scrutinizing Their Work with Francesca Gino."
24. Kristal et al., "Signing at the Beginning versus at the End."
25. Bertram Gallant, Brownstone, and Minnes, "Can Nudges Reduce Student Cheating?"

26. Bryan et al., "Motivating Voter Turnout by Invoking the Self."

27. Bryan et al., "Motivating Voter Turnout by Invoking the Self."

28. Pettigrew and Mays, "What Role Is There for 'Nudging' Clinicians?"

29. Waltzer, DeBernardi, and Dahl, "Student and Teacher Views on Cheating in High School."

30. Pettigrew and Mays, "What Role Is There for 'Nudging' Clinicians?"

31. Cagala, Glogowsky, and Rincke, "Detecting and Preventing Cheating in Exams."

32. Heyman et al., "Eliciting Promises from Children Reduces Cheating."

33. McCabe, Treviño, and Butterfield, "Honor Codes and Other Contextual Influences."

34. Shu, Gino, and Bazerman, "Dishonest Deed, Clear Conscience."

35. Bertram Gallant, Brownstone, and Minnes, "Can Nudges Reduce Student Cheating?"

36. Heyman et al., "Eliciting Promises from Children Reduces Cheating."

37. See, respectively, Meiselman, "Ghostbusting in Detroit"; Bryan et al., "Motivating Voter Turnout by Invoking the Self"; Geller, "Buckle-up Promise Card." Evans and Lee, "Promising to Tell the Truth."

38. "Adidas Fair Play Code of Conduct," accessed March 21, 2024, https://www.adidas-group.com/en/investors/corporate-governance/adidas-fair-play-code-of-conduct; Samsung Biologics, "Business Ethics," accessed March 1, 2024, https://samsungbiologics.com/esg/social/ethics.

39. ICAI, "Fundamental Values."

40. Adams, Tashchian, and Shore, "Codes of Ethics as Signals for Ethical Behavior."

41. Sezer, Gino, and Bazerman, "Ethical Blind Spots."

42. Somers, "Ethical Codes of Conduct and Organizational Context."

43. ICAI, "Fundamental Values."

44. Team-Based Learning Collaborative, "Team-Based Learning."

45. Bazerman and Tenbrunsel, *Blind Spots.*

Chapter 3. Designing Courses for Integrity

1. Lang, *Cheating Lessons.*

2. We use "learning goals" to refer to big-picture aims that instructors have for a course. "Learning objectives" are specific and measurable ways that those goals are achieved. "Learning outcomes" refers to the behaviors that students exhibit if they have achieved a particular learning objective.

3. Anderson and Krathwohl, *Taxonomy for Learning, Teaching, and Assessing.*

4. Fink, *Creating Significant Learning Experiences.*

5. Berkeley Center for Teaching & Learning, "Establish Course-Level Learning Objectives."

6. Paraphrased from text generated by ChatGPT, OpenAI, February 3, 2024, https://chat.openai.chat.

7. We flesh out the concept of good instruction in chapter 4

8. Fulmer, "Weekly Digest #64."

9. Richmond et al., "Can a Learner-Centered Syllabus Change Students' Perceptions?"

10. Fulmer, "Weekly Digest #64."

11. Online personal communications.

12. EmersonCentral.com. "Emerson's Self-Reliance," accessed January 16, 2024, https://emersoncentral.com/texts/essays-first-series/self-reliance/.

13. Hills and Peacock, "Replacing Power with Flexible Structure."

14. Lalley and Gentile, "Classroom Assessment and Grading"; Blum, *Ungrading*; Nilson, "Yes, Virginia, There's a Better Way to Grade."

15. Anderman and Koenka, "Relation between Academic Motivation and Cheating."

16. Tversky and Kahneman, "Framing of Decisions and the Psychology of Choice."

17. Shampanier, Mazar, and Ariely, "Zero as a Special Price."

18. Levy et al., "A Quantitative Review of Overjustification Effects."

19. Pintrich, "Role of Metacognitive Knowledge."

20. Reisberg, *Cognition*.

21. Reisberg, *Cognition*.

22. Roediger and Karpicke, "Test-Enhanced Learning."

23. Ebbinghaus, "Memory."

24. Bloom and Shuell, "Effects of Massed and Distributed Practice."

25. Susser and McCabe, "From the Lab to the Dorm Room."

26. Zilles et al., "Making Testing Less Trying."

27. Mazar, Amir, and Ariely, "Dishonesty of Honest People."

28. See Caitlin Kelley, "News: Making the Grade: EECS Professors Develop 'A's for All' Pilot," Berkeley Engineering, December 1, 2023, https://engineering.berkeley.edu/news/2023/12/making-the-grade/.

29. Hogan and Pressley, *Scaffolding Student Learning*.

30. Caruana, "Scaffolding Student Learning."

31. Dweck, "Motivational Processes Affecting Learning."

32. Caruana, "Scaffolding Student Learning."

33. Perusall home page. Accessed January 22, 2024. https://www.perusall.com.

34. Cervini, "Cheating No Credit to Open Course Students."

35. Gray, "Biggest Cheating Scandals in Call of Duty History."

36. Poindexter, "How a Huge Cheating Scandal Altered the Chess World."

37. Stephens, "Natural and Normal, but Unethical and Evitable."

38. Campbell, Clark, and OShaughnessy, "Introduction to the Special Issue."

39. Slavin, "Mastery Learning Re-Reconsidered"; Kulik, Kulik, and Bangert-Drowns, "Effectiveness of Mastery Learning Programs."

40. Maier and Seligman, "Learned Helplessness at Fifty."

41. Nilson and Stanny, *Specifications Grading.*

42. Based on Nilson, "Yes, Virginia, There's a Better Way to Grade."

43. Nilson and Stanny, *Specifications Grading*; Sykes and Matza, "Techniques of Neutralization."

44. Blum, *Ungrading.*

45. Stephens, "Natural and Normal, but Unethical and Evitable," 201; Northcutt, Ho, and Chuang, "Detecting and Preventing 'Multiple-Account' Cheating."

46. Pulvers and Diekhoff, "Relationship between Academic Dishonesty and College Classroom Environment."

47. Zilles et al., "Every University Should Have a Computer-Based Testing Center."

Chapter 4. Designing Assessments for Integrity

1. Furze, "Teaching AI Ethics."

2. Bazerman and Tenbrunsel, *Blind Spots.*

3. National Society of Professional Engineers, "NSPE Code of Ethics for Engineers," accessed December 30, 2023. https://www.nspe.org/resources/ethics/code-ethics.

4. For example, Santa Clara University, "A Framework for Ethical Decision Making," accessed December 30, 2023, https://www.scu.edu/ethics/ethics-resources/a-framework-for-ethical-decision-making/.

5. See, e.g., Kidder, "How Good People Make Tough Choices."

6. Center for Teaching and Learning, "Types of Rubrics."

7. Eberly Center. "Grading and Performance Rubrics," Example 2: Psychology Assignment, Undergraduate Cognitive Psychology, Anne L. Fay, Carnegie Mellon University, accessed June 16, 2023, https://www.cmu.edu/teaching/designteach/teach/rubrics.html.

8. Fitzpatrick, Fox, and Weinstein, *AI Classroom.*

9. Assignment overview and associated learning goals are from https://teach.genetics.utah.edu/content/heredity/.

10. McCabe, Butterfield, and Treviño, *Cheating in College.*

11. Salend, "Addressing Test Anxiety."

12. Individual followed by team testing is a structure within Team-Based Learning (TBL). For more information, see https://www.teambasedlearning.org/. Team testing might also serve the mastery-based goals we talked about in the previous chapter. So, retesting, whether with teams or with assessment platforms like PrairieLearn (www.prairielearn.com), is a form of revision as well.

13. Team-Based Learning Collaborative. "Team-Based Learning."

14. This pedagogy works for both virtual and in-person classes. See, e.g., Anas et al., "Effect of Online and In-Person Team-Based Learning."

15. Langer, "Illusion of Control."

16. Bertram Gallant, ed., special issue, *ASHE Higher Education Report*

17. Lund, 1997, as cited in Ashford-Rowe, Herrington, and Brown, "Establishing the Critical Elements."

18. Wiggins, "Authenticity in Assessment."

19. Ajjawi et al., "From Authentic Assessment to Authenticity in Assessment"; Gulikers, Bastiaens, and Kirschner, "Five-Dimensional Framework for Authentic Assessment."

20. Ashford-Rowe, Herrington, and Brown, "Establishing the Critical Elements."

21. Messier, "Authentic Assessments."

22. Quantitative Analysis Center, "Passion-Driven Statistics."

23. Dawson, "Cognitive Offloading and Assessment"; Dawson, Carless, and Lee, "Authentic Feedback."

24. "About Us," Grammarly, accessed January 9, 2024, https://www.grammarly.com/about.

25. Baghdadchi et al., "Student Perceptions of Oral Exams."

26. Luckie et al., "Verbal Final Exam in Introductory Biology."

27. Joughin, "Dimensions of Oral Assessment."

28. Qi and Schurgers, "Oral Exams in Support of Academic Integrity."

29. Baghdadchi et al., "Student Perceptions of Oral Exams."

30. Styler, "Will's Oral Exam Procedures and Policies."

31. Durning et al., "Feasibility, Reliability, and Validity of a Post-Encounter Form."

32. As of this writing, AI software to replace the image of a human in a video is just coming online, so stay tuned for modified procedures for recorded oral assessments in the near future.

33. Grez, Valcke, and Roozen, "How Effective Are Self- and Peer Assessment?"

Chapter 5. Classroom Strategies That Promote Success with Integrity

1. Breed and Sanchez, "Both Environment and Genetic Makeup."

2. Fowler and Christakis, "Social Contagion Theory."

3. Burgess et al., "Influence of Social Contagion within Education."

4. Kenney et al., "Poor Mental Health."

5. Anderman et al., "Academic Motivation and Cheating"; Braxton, "Improprieties in Teaching and Learning"; Carson, Goldman, and Simonds, "It's in the Pedagogy."

6. "Charles Barkley on LGBTQ+ Community: 'If You Have a Problem with Them, F**k You,' CNN, accessed July 26, 2023, https://www.cnn.com/videos/us/2023/07/20/charles-barkley-lgbtq-bud-light-cprog-orig-alw.cnn.

7. Cruess, Cruess, and Steinert, "Role Modelling."

8. Burgess et al., "Influence of Social Contagion within Education."

9. Bandura and McDonald, "Influence of Social Reinforcement."

10. Christian, *Alignment Problem.*

11. Ahn, Hu, and Vega, "'Do as I Do, Not as I Say.'"

12. Ahn, Hu, and Vega, "'Do as I Do, Not as I Say.'"

13. Ahn, Hu, and Vega.

14. Ahn, Hu, and Vega.

15. Ahn, Hu, and Vega, p. 4.

16. Ahn, Hu, and Vega.

17. Ahn, Hu, and Vega.

18. Rettinger, unpublished data, 2021.

19. Anderman et al., "Academic Motivation and Cheating," 82, 79.

20. Harrison and Spencer, "Beyond Doing Integrity Online."

21. Garrison and Arbaugh, "Researching the Community of Inquiry Framework."

22. Harrison and Spencer, "Beyond Doing Integrity Online."

23. Castellanos-Reyes, "20 Years of the Community of Inquiry Framework"; Garrison and Arbaugh, "Researching the Community of Inquiry Framework."

24. Immordino-Yang and Damasio, "We Feel, Therefore We Learn."

25. Hammer, "From the Laboratory to the Classroom"; Keeley, Smith, and Buskist, "Teacher Behaviors Checklist"; Komarraju, Musulkin, and Bhattacharya, "Role of Student–Faculty Interactions."

26. Garrison and Arbaugh, "Researching the Community of Inquiry Framework."

27. Garrison, Anderson, and Archer, "Critical Inquiry in a Text-Based Environment."

28. Wilson and Ryan, "Professor-Student Rapport Scale."

29. Anderman et al., "Academic Motivation and Cheating," 82.

30. Doo and Bonk, "Effects of Self Efficacy."

31. Edwards and Taasoobshirazi, "Social Presence and Teacher Involvement."

32. Murdock and Anderman, "Motivational Perspectives on Student Cheating."

33. Garrison and Arbaugh, "Researching the Community of Inquiry Framework."

34. Team-Based Learning Collaborative, "Team Based Learning."

35. Garrison, Anderson, and Archer, "Critical Inquiry in a Text-Based Environment."

36. POGIL website, https://pogil.org.

37. Richardson et al., "Using the Community of Inquiry Framework."

38. Carson, Goldman, and Simonds, "It's in the Pedagogy."

39. See, respectively, Denial, "Introduction to a Pedagogy of Kindness"; McGee Banks and Banks, "Equity Pedagogy"; Carson, Goldman, and Simonds, "It's in the Pedagogy."

40. Bernstein, "The Mentor Who Taught Me to See Students as People First."

41. Denial, "Introduction to a Pedagogy of Kindness."

42. Stephens, "Natural and Normal, but Unethical and Evitable."

43. Burgstahler and Cory, *Universal Design in Higher Education.* Quotation from College of Design, "Center for Universal Design."

44. Inclusive Education Initiative, "Introductory Series on Universal Design for Learning."

45. Kolb and Kolb, "Learning Styles and Learning Spaces."

46. Adriano Pianesi, "Teachable Moments of Leadership," accessed December 30, 2023, http://caseinpointmethod.com/.

47. Hativa and Goodyear, "Research on Teacher Thinking"; Kagan, "Ways of Evaluating Teacher Cognition."

48. Trimboli, *Deep Listening.*

Chapter 6. Protecting Assessment Integrity

1. Dawson, *Defending Assessment Security in a Digital World,* 19.

2. As described by Thaler and Sunstein, *Nudge.*

3. The more literal translation is closer to, "Don't place stumbling blocks before the blind." The intent of the passage is to prohibit us from creating situations that unfairly penalize weakness. Because blindness does not equate with weakness, we've used an updated if less literal translation.

4. Ellis and Murdoch, "Educational Integrity Enforcement Pyramid."

5. Rettinger et al., "Assessing Academic Integrity."

6. Tesler, "Assigning Seats at UC San Diego Using Canvas."

7. "PrairieLearn," accessed January 22, 2024, https://www.prairielearn.com/.

8. Jenkins et al., "When Opportunity Knocks."

9. Bowman, "Scanning Students' Rooms during Remote Tests Is Unconstitutional."

10. Balash et al., "Examining the Examiners."

11. Swauger, "What's Worse Than Remote School?"

12. Bowman, "Scanning Students' Rooms during Remote Tests Is Unconstitutional."

13. Dendir and Maxwell, "Cheating in Online Courses."

14. Fowler, "We Tested a New ChatGPT-Detector for Teachers"; Jimenez, "Professors Are Using ChatGPT Detector Tools"; Klee, "Professor Flunks All His Students."

15. Myers, "AI-Detectors Biased against Non-native English Writers."

16. Weber-Wulff et al., "Testing of Detection Tools."

17. Perkins et al., "GenAI Detection Tools."

18. Davis, Drinan, and Gallant, *Cheating in School.*

19. Davis, Drinan, and Gallant, *Cheating in School,* 52.

20. The leaders of educational institutions could resolve at least one part of this problem—the distance to a trusted testing center. If the majority of colleges and universities instituted testing centers—and opened them up to all students from any institution—then travel to such centers wouldn't be unreasonable for most students.

21. Waters, "Hack Education."

22. Carless, "Scaling Up Assessment for Learning," as cited in Dawson, *Defending Assessment Security in a Digital World.*

23. Dawson, *Defending Assessment Security in a Digital World*, 221.

24. Newton, "How Common Is Commercial Contract Cheating?"

25. Curtis et al., "Moving beyond Self-Reports."

26. Newton, "How Common Is Commercial Contract Cheating?"

27. https://chat.openai.com/.

28. Dawson and Sutherland-Smith, "Can Training Improve Marker Accuracy?"

29. Eaton, "15 Strategies to Detect Contract Cheating"; Rogerson, "Detecting Contract Cheating."

30. Now that one can upload files for GenAI tools to incorporate into the output, students can prompt the tool to produce work that does fit the course context. Still, at the time of this writing, we're finding that students typically are not investing that much time in getting the machines to do their work. But humans hired as contract cheaters might be using the machines in this manner.

31. In "Brave New World," Kane Murdoch offers several tips for identifying the author of a document, including analyzing the metadata and interrogating LMS logs.

32. It's important to point out here that, for now, the government requires identity verification only for online programs. Why should we care only about enrolled persons fraudulently receiving online degrees when we know the same can happen in in-person programs as well?

33. Ison, "Detection of Online Contract Cheating."

34. Stewart et al., "Investigation of Keystroke and Stylometry Traits."

35. Of course, affluent students can fake this by hiring the contract cheating provider to complete all aspects of the course. Remember the Walmart heiress story at the beginning of this book?

36. Gonzalez, "Icebreakers That Rock."

37. Gonzalez.

38. Turing, "Computing Machinery and Intelligence."

39. Sotiriadou et al., "Role of Authentic Assessment."

40. Lubarda et al., "Oral Exams for Large-Enrollment Engineering Courses."

41. Dawson, *Defending Assessment Security in a Digital World*, 129.

42. This is why Phill Dawson encourages assessment redesign at the programmatic level to establish coherency and appropriate scaffolding from lower- to higher-level courses.

43. Porter and Zingaro, *Learn AI-Assisted Python Programming.*

44. Bertram Gallant, "Crafting Your GenAI & AI Policy."

45. Dawson, *Defending Assessment Security in a Digital World*, 189.

46. Zilles et al., "Making Testing Less Trying."

Chapter 7. Infusing Ethics into Teaching and Learning

1. Stephens, "Natural and Normal, but Unethical and Evitable."
2. Brosnan and de Waal, "Evolution of Responses to (Un)Fairness."
3. Bandura and McDonald, "Influence of Social Reinforcement"; Robichaud et al., "Role of Logical Consequences."
4. Waltzer and Dahl, "Why Do Students Cheat?"
5. On plagiarism as part of learning to write, see Moore Howard, "Plagiarisms, Authorships, and the Academic Death Penalty"; on cultural norms, see Introna et al., "Cultural Attitudes towards Plagiarism."
6. Harteis and Bauer, "Learning from Errors at Work."
7. Listen to this Hidden Brain podcast for more ideas along this line: Hidden Brain Media, "Learning from Your Mistakes," accessed January 22, 2024, https://hiddenbrain.org/podcast/learning-from-your-mistakes/.
8. Bertram Gallant, "Academic Integrity as a Teaching & Learning Issue."
9. Haidt, "Emotional Dog and Its Rational Tail."
10. Chapman, "Temporal Discounting and Utility for Health and Money."
11. Davis, Drinan, and Bertram Gallant, *Cheating in School.*
12. Johnson, *History of Rasselas, Prince of Abissinia*, chap. 41.
13. Cerullo, "ChatGPT Maker OpenAI Sued for Allegedly Using 'Stolen Private Information,'" CBS News, June 30, 2023, https://www.cbsnews.com/news/chatgpt-open-ai-lawuit-stolen-private-information/; Billy Perrigo, "Exclusive: The $2 Per Hour Workers Who Made ChatGPT Safer," *TIME*, January 18, 2023. https://time.com/6247678/openai-chatgpt-kenya-workers/.
14. Christensen Hughes and Bertram Gallant, "Infusing Ethics and Ethical Decision Making."
15. Gentile, "Giving Voice to Values."
16. Darden School of Business, "Giving Voice to Values."
17. Instruction is often based on a neo-Kohlbergian four-component model of ethical decision making; see Rest et al., *Postconventional Moral Thinking.*
18. Bazerman and Tenbrunsel, *Blind Spots.*
19. Stephens and Bertram Gallant, "Enhancing Moral Sensitivity."
20. Denney and Roberts, *Building Honor in Academics.*
21. IEEE. "7.8. IEEE Code of Ethics," accessed December 31, 2023, https://www.ieee.org/about/corporate/governance/p7-8.html.
22. Christensen Hughes and Bertram Gallant, "Infusing Ethics and Ethical Decision Making."
23. Blystone and Blodgett, "WWW"; Castillo, "Scientific Method."
24. Subbian, Shaw, and Halpin, "Ethical Decision-Making Frameworks."
25. Subbian, Shaw, and Halpin, "Ethical Decision-Making Frameworks."
26. Bertram Gallant and Stephens, "Punishment Is Not Enough."
27. Stephens, "Natural and Normal."

28. For more on the challenges that integrity violations pose for part-time or contingent faculty, see Bertram Gallant, "Part-Time Integrity?"

29. By "due process," we mean giving students notice that they are suspected of an integrity violation and a chance to be heard. Typically, the harsher the consequence for the integrity violation, the more due process the student should be afforded.

30. Bertram Gallant, "Leveraging the Teachable Moment."

31. Kolb and Kolb, "Learning Styles and Learning Spaces."

32. Bertram Gallant and Stephens, "Punishment Is Not Enough."

33. Eerkes et al., *Essential Elements for Non-punitive Accountability.*

34. UCSD, "Academic Integrity Training."

Conclusion

1. Dawson, *Defending Assessment Security in a Digital World,* 145.
2. AAC&U, "How College Contributes to Workforce Success."
3. *Pirkei Avot* 2:21.
4. Dawson, "Cognitive Offloading and Assessment."
5. Dawson, Carless, and Lee, "Authentic Feedback," 142.
6. Quotation from Clear, "Habits Guide"; also see Clear, *Atomic Habits.*

BIBLIOGRAPHY

Adams, Janet S., Armen Tashchian, and Ted H. Shore. "Codes of Ethics as Signals for Ethical Behavior." *Journal of Business Ethics* 29, no. 3 (2001): 199–211. https://doi.org/10.1023/A:1026576421399.

Ahn, Janet N., Danfei Hu, and Melissa Vega. "'Do As I Do, Not As I Say': Using Social Learning Theory to Unpack the Impact of Role Models on Students' Outcomes in Education." *Social and Personality Psychology Compass* 14, no. 2 (2020): e12517. https://doi.org/10.1111/spc3.12517.

Ajjawi, Rola, Joanna Tai, Mollie Dollinger, Phillip Dawson, David Boud, and Margaret Bearman. "From Authentic Assessment to Authenticity in Assessment: Broadening Perspectives." *Assessment & Evaluation in Higher Education* (October 19, 2023): 1–12. https://doi.org/10.1080/02602938.2023.2271193.

Alonso, Johanna. "Simple Interventions Can Curb Cheating, Study Finds." *Inside Higher Ed*, November 10, 2022. https://www.insidehighered.com/news/2022/11/10/low-effort-interventions-can-combat-student-cheating.

Alt, Dorit. "Assessing the Connection between Self-Efficacy for Learning and Justifying Academic Cheating in Higher Education Learning Environments." *Journal of Academic Ethics* 13, no. 1 (2015): 77–90. https://doi.org/10.1007/s10805-015-9227-5.

American Association of Colleges and Universities (AAC&U). "How College Contributes to Workforce Success." April 1, 2021. https://www.aacu.org/liberaleducation/articles/how-college-contributes-to-workforce-success.

Anas, Shafeena, Ioannis Kyrou, Mariann Rand-Weaver, and Emmanouil Karteris. "The Effect of Online and In-Person Team-Based Learning (TBL) on Undergraduate Endocrinology Teaching during COVID-19 Pandemic." *BMC Medical Education* 22, no. 1 (2022): 120. https://doi.org/10.1186/s12909-022-03173-5.

Anderman, Eric M., and Alison C. Koenka. "The Relation between Academic Motivation and Cheating." *Theory into Practice* 56, no. 2 (2017): 95–102. https://doi.org/10.1080/00405841.2017.1308172.

Anderman, Eric M., Shantanu Tilak, Andrew H. Perry, Jacqueline von Spiegel, and Arianna Black. "Academic Motivation and Cheating: A Psychological Perspective." In *Cheating Academic Integrity: Lessons Learned from 30 Years of Research*, edited by David A. Rettinger and Tricia Bertram Gallant, 65–98. San Francisco, CA: Jossey-Bass, 2022.

Anderson, Lorin W., and David R. Krathwohl, eds. *A Taxonomy for Learning, Teaching, and Assessing: A Revision of Bloom's Taxonomy of Educational Objectives.* Complete ed. New York: Longman, 2001.

Ashford-Rowe, Kevin, Janice Herrington, and Christine Brown. "Establishing the Critical Elements That Determine Authentic Assessment." *Assessment & Evaluation in Higher Education* 39, no. 2 (2014): 205–22. https://doi.org/10.1080/02602938.2013.819566.

Baghdadchi, Saharnaz, Diya Qi, M. Lubarda, Alex Phan, and N. Delson. "Student Perceptions of Oral Exams in Undergraduate Engineering Classes and Implications for Effective Oral Exam Design." *ASEE Annual Conference & Exposition Proceedings* (2022). https://www.semanticscholar.org/paper/Student-perceptions-of-oral-exams-in-undergraduate-Baghdadchi-Qi/6d08802c1d4144987d6a987c080a4f5a44b98865.

Balash, David G., Dongkun Kim, Darika Shaibekova, Rahel A. Fainchtein, Micah Sherr, and Adam J. Aviv. "Examining the Examiners: Students' Privacy and Security Perceptions of Online Proctoring Services." Paper presented at USENIX Symposium on Usable Privacy and Security, George Washington University, August 10, 2021, https://www.usenix.org/conference/soups2021/presentation/balash.

Bandura, Albert. "Exercise of Human Agency through Collective Efficacy." *Current Directions in Psychological Science* 9, no. 3 (2000): 75–78. https://doi.org/10.1111/1467-8721.00064.

———. "Observational Learning." In *The International Encyclopedia of Communication.* New York: John Wiley & Sons, 2008. https://doi.org/10.1002/9781405186407.wbieco004.

Bandura, Albert, and Frederick J. McDonald. "Influence of Social Reinforcement and the Behavior of Models in Shaping Children's Moral Judgment." *Journal of Abnormal and Social Psychology* 67, no. 3 (1963): 274–81. https://doi.org/10.1037/h0044714.

Bazerman, Max H., and Ann E. Tenbrunsel. *Blind Spots.* Paperback ed. Princeton, NJ: Princeton University Press, 2013.

Beasley, Eric M. "Students Reported for Cheating Explain What They Think Would Have Stopped Them." *Ethics and Behavior* 24, no. 3 (2014): 229–52. https://doi.org/10.1080/10508422.2013.845533.

Berkeley Center for Teaching & Learning, "Establish Course-Level Learning Objectives." Accessed January 8, 2024. https://teaching.berkeley.edu/teaching-guides/designing-your-course/establish-course-level-learning-objectives.

Bernstein, Jill. "The Mentor Who Taught Me to See Students as People First." *Hechinger Report,* June 24, 2019. http://hechingerreport.org/the-mentor-who-taught-me/.

Bertram Gallant, Tricia. "Academic Integrity as a Teaching & Learning Issue: From Theory to Practice." *Theory into Practice* 56, no. 2 (2017): 88–94. https://doi.org/10.1080/00405841.2017.1308173.

———, ed. "Academic Integrity in the Twenty-First Century: A Teaching and Learning Imperative." Special issue, *ASHE Higher Education Report* 33, no. 5 (2008): 1–143. https://doi.org/10.1002/aehe.3305.

———. "Crafting Your GenAI & AI Policy: A Guide for Instructors." Google doc. San Diego, CA, 2023. https://docs.google.com/presentation/d/1miPTdRU8YNoJBc_zcLLr1KIhLxIkZu6xx1155zebXJo/edit?usp=sharing.

———. "Leveraging the Teachable Moment: What, If Anything, Can Students Learn from Cheating?" In *A Research Agenda for Academic Integrity*, edited by Tracey Bretag, 55–68. Northampton, MA: Edward Elgar, 2020. https://www.elgaronline.com/edcollchap/edcoll/9781789903768/9781789903768.00011.xml.

———. "Part-Time Integrity? Contingent Faculty and Academic Integrity." *New Directions for Community Colleges* 2018, no. 183 (2018): 45–54. https://doi.org/10.1002/cc.20316.

Bertram Gallant, Tricia, Steven Brownstone, and Mia Minnes. "Can Nudges Reduce Student Cheating?" *Change: The Magazine of Higher Learning* 54, no. 4 (2022): 50–56. https://doi.org/10.1080/00091383.2022.2078157.

Bertram Gallant, Tricia, and David Rettinger. "An Introduction to 30 Years of Research on Academic Integrity." *Journal of College and Character* 23, no. 1 (2022): 1–5. https://doi.org/10.1080/2194587X.2021.2017975.

Bertram Gallant, Tricia, and Jason M. Stephens. "Punishment Is Not Enough: The Moral Imperative of Responding to Cheating with a Developmental Approach." *Journal of College and Character* 21, no. 2 (2020): 57–66. https://doi.org/10.1080/2194587X.2020.1741395.

Bloom, Kristine C., and Thomas J. Shuell. "Effects of Massed and Distributed Practice on the Learning and Retention of Second-Language Vocabulary." *Journal of Educational Research* 74, no. 4 (1981): 245–48. https://doi.org/10.1080/00220671.1981.10885317.

Blum, Susan D. *Ungrading: Why Rating Students Undermines Learning*. 1st ed. Morgantown: West Virginia University Press, 2020.

Blystone, Robert V., and Kevin Blodgett. "WWW: The Scientific Method." *CBE—Life Sciences Education* 5, no. 1 (2006): 7–11. https://doi.org/10.1187/cbe.05-12-0134.

Bowman, Emma. "Scanning Students' Rooms during Remote Tests Is Unconstitutional, Judge Rules." *NPR*, August 26, 2022, https://www.npr.org/2022/08/25/1119337956/test-proctoring-room-scans-unconstitutional-cleveland-state-university.

Braxton, John M. "Improprieties in Teaching and Learning." In *Creating the Ethical Academy: A Systems Approach to Understanding Misconduct and Empowering Change*, edited by Tricia Bertram Gallant. New York: Routledge, 2011.

Breed, Michael, and Leticia Sanchez. "Both Environment and Genetic Makeup Influence Behavior." *Nature Education Knowledge* 3, no. 10 (2010): 68.

Bretag, Tracey, lead advisor. "About Academic Integrity." Epigeum. Published March 2019. https://www.epigeum.com/courses/studying/academic-integrity/.

Brooks, David. "In the Age of A.I., Major in Being Human." *New York Times*, Opinion, February 3, 2023. https://www.nytimes.com/2023/02/02/opinion/ai-human-education.html.

Brosnan, Sarah F., and Frans B. M. de Waal. "Evolution of Responses to (Un) Fairness." *Science* 346, no. 6207 (2014): 1251776. https://doi.org/10.1126/science.1251776.

Bryan, Christopher J., Gregory M. Walton, Todd Rogers, and Carol S. Dweck. "Motivating Voter Turnout by Invoking the Self." *Proceedings of the National Academy of Sciences* 108, no. 31 (2011): 12653–56. https://doi.org/10.1073/pnas.1103343108.

Buehler, Roger, Dale Griffin, and Johanna Peetz. "Chapter One—The Planning Fallacy: Cognitive, Motivational, and Social Origins." In *Advances in Experimental Social Psychology*, edited by Mark P. Zanna and James M. Olson, 43:1–62. Cambridge, MA: Academic Press, 2010. https://doi.org/10.1016/S0065-2601(10)43001-4.

Burgess, Laura G., Patricia M. Riddell, Amy Fancourt, and Kou Murayama. "The Influence of Social Contagion within Education: A Motivational Perspective." *Mind, Brain, and Education* 12, no. 4 (2018): 164–74. https://doi.org/10.1111/mbe.12178.

Burgstahler, Sheryl E., and Rebecca C. Cory. *Universal Design in Higher Education: From Principles to Practice*. Cambridge, MA: Harvard Education Press, 2008.

Cagala, Tobias, Ulrich Glogowsky, and Johannes Rincke. "Detecting and Preventing Cheating in Exams: Evidence from a Field Experiment." *Journal of Human Resources* 59, no. 1 (2024): 210–41. https://doi.org/10.3368/jhr.0620-10947R1.

Campbell, Robert, David Clark, and Jessica OShaughnessy. "Introduction to the Special Issue on Implementing Mastery Grading in the Undergraduate Mathematics Classroom." *PRIMUS* 30, nos. 8–10 (2020): 837–48. https://doi.org/10.1080/10511970.2020.1778824.

Carless, David. "Scaling Up Assessment for Learning: Progress and Prospects." In *Scaling Up Assessment for Learning in Higher Education*, edited by David Carless, Susan M. Bridges, Cecilia Ka Yuk Chan, and Rick Glofcheski, 3–17. The Enabling Power of Assessment, vol. 5. Singapore: Springer, 2017. https://doi.org/10.1007/978-981-10-3045-1_1.

Carnevale, Anthony P., Nicole Smith, Michelle Melton, and Eric W. Price. *Learning while Earning: The New Normal*. Washington, DC: Center on Education and the Workforce, Georgetown University, 2015. https://cew.georgetown.edu/wp-content/uploads/Working-Learners-Report.pdf.

Carrell, Scott E., Frederick V. Malmstrom, and James E. West. "Peer Effects in Academic Cheating." *Journal of Human Resources* 43, no. 1 (2008): 173–207. https://doi.org/10.3368/jhr.43.1.173.

Carson, Mariko, Jacqueline Goldman, and Jennifer Simonds. "It's in the Pedagogy: Evidence-Based Practices to Promote Academic Integrity." In *Cheating Academic Integrity: Lessons from 30 Years of Research*, edited by David A. Rettinger and Tricia Bertram Gallant, 131–68. New York: John Wiley & Sons, 2022.

Caruana, V. "Scaffolding Student Learning: Tips for Getting Started," 2012. https://www.semanticscholar.org/paper/Scaffolding-Student-Learning%3A-Tips-for-Getting-Caruana/0ca8349f35b7f6e20232e10a05a89cfa803f0b83.

Castellanos-Reyes, Daniela. "20 Years of the Community of Inquiry Framework." *TechTrends* 64, no. 4 (2020): 557–60. https://doi.org/10.1007/s11528-020-00491-7.

Castillo, M. "The Scientific Method: A Need for Something Better?" *American Journal of Neuroradiology* 34, no. 9 (2013): 1669–71. https://doi.org/10.3174/ajnr.A3401.

Center for Teaching and Learning. "Types of Rubrics." DePaul Teaching Commons. Accessed December 30, 2023. https://resources.depaul.edu/teaching-commons/teaching-guides/feedback-grading/rubrics/Pages/types-of-rubrics.aspx.

Cervini, Erica. "Cheating No Credit to Open Course Students." *Sydney Morning Herald*, August 27, 2012. https://www.smh.com.au/education/cheating-no-credit-to-open-course-students-20120827-24w7v.html.

Chapman, Gretchen B. "Temporal Discounting and Utility for Health and Money." *Journal of Experimental Psychology: Learning, Memory, and Cognition* 22, no. 3 (1996): 771–91. https://doi.org/10.1037/0278-7393.22.3.771.

Charness, Gary, and Arthur Schram. "Social and Moral Norms in the Laboratory." University of California at Santa Barbara, Economics Working Paper Series qt6rv7x0tf, Department of Economics, UC Santa Barbara (2012). https://ideas.repec.org/s/cdl/ucsbec.html

Christensen Hughes, Julia, and Tricia Bertram Gallant. "Infusing Ethics and Ethical Decision Making into the Curriculum." In *Handbook of Academic Integrity*, edited by Tracey Bretag, 1055–73. Singapore: Springer, 2016. https://doi.org/10.1007/978-981-287-098-8_12.

Christian, Brian. *The Alignment Problem: Machine Learning and Human Values*. New York: W. W. Norton, 2020.

Ciranka, Simon, and Wouter van den Bos. "Social Influence in Adolescent Decision-Making: A Formal Framework." *Frontiers in Psychology* 10 (2019). https://www.frontiersin.org/articles/10.3389/fpsyg.2019.01915.

Clear, James. *Atomic Habits: Tiny Changes, Remarkable Results: An Easy & Proven Way to Build Good Habits & Break Bad Ones*. New York: Avery, 2018.

———. "The Habits Guide: How to Build Good Habits and Break Bad Ones." Blog post. Accessed December 31, 2023. https://jamesclear.com/habits.

College of Design. "Center for Universal Design." NC State University. Accessed December 30, 2023. https://design.ncsu.edu/research/center-for-universal-design/.

Cruess, Sylvia R., Richard L. Cruess, and Yvonne Steinert. "Role Modelling—Making the Most of a Powerful Teaching Strategy." *BMJ* (Clinical Research Ed.) 336, no. 7646 (2008): 718–21. https://doi.org/10.1136/bmj.39503.757847.BE.

Curtis, Guy J., Margot McNeill, Christine Slade, Kell Tremayne, Rowena Harper, Kiata Rundle, and Ruth Greenaway. "Moving beyond Self-Reports to Estimate the Prevalence of Commercial Contract Cheating: An Australian Study." *Studies in Higher Education* 47, no. 9 (2022): 1844–56. https://doi.org/10.1080/03075079.2021.1972093.

Darden School of Business. *Giving Voice to Values.* Charlottesville, VA: Darden Business Publishing. Accessed December 31, 2023. https://store.darden.virginia.edu/giving-voice-to-values?_gl=1*1h65mee*_ga*MTc5NDEyNjgyLjE2Njc2ODQ3Mzg.*_ga_SLY12CWTWF*MTY2ODM2ODIwNi4zLjEuMTY2ODM2ODIxMC41Ni4wLjA.&_ga=2.49254758.1156198513.1668368206-179412682.1667684738.

Davis, Stephen F., Patrick F. Drinan, and Tricia Bertram Gallant. *Cheating in School: What We Know and What We Can Do.* New York: John Wiley & Sons, 2011.

Dawson, Phillip. "Cognitive Offloading and Assessment." In *Reimagining University Assessment in a Digital World,* edited by Margaret Bearman, Phillip Dawson, Rola Ajjawi, Joanna Tai, and David Boud, 37–48. The Enabling Power of Assessment, vol. 7. Cham, Switzerland: Springer International, 2020. https://doi.org/10.1007/978-3-030-41956-1_4.

———. *Defending Assessment Security in a Digital World: Preventing E-Cheating and Supporting Academic Integrity in Higher Education.* London: Routledge, 2021. https://doi.org/10.4324/9780429324178.

Dawson, Phillip, David Carless, and Pamela Pui Wah Lee. "Authentic Feedback: Supporting Learners to Engage in Disciplinary Feedback Practices." *Assessment & Evaluation in Higher Education* 46, no. 2 (2021): 286–96. https://doi.org/10.1080/02602938.2020.1769022.

Dawson, Phillip, and Wendy Sutherland-Smith. "Can Training Improve Marker Accuracy at Detecting Contract Cheating? A Multi-Disciplinary Pre-Post Study." *Assessment & Evaluation in Higher Education* 44, no. 5 (2019): 715–25. https://doi.org/10.1080/02602938.2018.1531109.

Dench, Daniel, and Theodore Joyce. "Information and Credible Sanctions in Curbing Online Cheating among Undergraduates: A Field Experiment." *Journal of Economic Behavior & Organization* 195 (March 2022): 408–27. https://doi.org/10.1016/j.jebo.2022.01.018.

Dendir, Seife, and R. Stockton Maxwell. "Cheating in Online Courses: Evidence from Online Proctoring." *Computers in Human Behavior Reports* 2 (August–December 2020): 100033. https://doi.org/10.1016/j.chbr.2020.100033.

Denial, Catherine. "Introduction to a Pedagogy of Kindness." OneHE. Accessed May 11, 2023. https://onehe.org/courses/introduction-to-a-pedagogy-of-kindness/.

Denney, Valerie P., and Camilla J. Roberts. *Building Honor in Academics: Case Studies in Academic Integrity*. 1st ed. San Francisco: Jossey-Bass, 2023.

Doo, Min Young, and Curtis J. Bonk. "The Effects of Self-Efficacy, Self-Regulation, and Social Presence on Learning Engagement in a Large University Class Using Flipped Learning." *Journal of Computer Assisted Learning* 36, no. 6 (2020): 997–1010. https://doi.org/10.1111/jcal.12455.

Durning, Steven, Anthony Artino, John Boulet, Jeffrey Larochelle, Cees Van der Vleuten, Bonnie Arze, and Lambert Schuwirth. "The Feasibility, Reliability, and Validity of a Post-Encounter Form for Evaluating Clinical Reasoning." *Medical Teacher* 34, no. 1 (2012): 30–37. https://doi.org/10.3109/0142159X.2011.590557.

Dweck, Carol S. "Can Personality Be Changed? The Role of Beliefs in Personality and Change." *Current Directions in Psychological Science* 17, no. 6 (2008): 391–94. https://doi.org/10.1111/j.1467-8721.2008.00612.x.

———. "Motivational Processes Affecting Learning." *American Psychologist* 41, no. 10 (1986): 1040–48. https://doi.org/10.1037/0003-066X.41.10.1040.

———. "The Power of Believing You Can Improve." *TEDxNorrkoping*. November 2014. https://www.ted.com/talks/carol_dweck_the_power_of_believing_that_you_can_improve.

Eaton, Sarah Elaine. "Academic and Research Integrity as Transdisciplinary Fields of Scholarship and Professional Practice." In *Handbook of Academic Integrity*, edited by Sarah Elaine Eaton, 1–18. Singapore: Springer Nature, 2020. https://doi.org/10.1007/978-981-287-079-7_165-1.

———. "15 Strategies to Detect Contract Cheating." Taylor Institute for Teaching and Learning. Accessed December 30, 2023. https://taylorinstitute.ucalgary.ca/resources/15-strategies-to-detect-contract-cheating.

Ebbinghaus, Hermann. "Memory: A Contribution to Experimental Psychology." *Annals of Neurosciences* 20, no. 4 (2013): 155–56. Originally published 1885. https://doi.org/10.5214/ans.0972.7531.200408.

Edwards, Ordene V., and Gita Taasoobshirazi. "Social Presence and Teacher Involvement: The Link with Expectancy, Task Value, and Engagement." *Internet and Higher Education* 55 (October 2022): 100869. https://doi.org/10.1016/j.iheduc.2022.100869.

Eerkes, Deborah, Jessica Ketwaroo-Green, Sam Pearson, Imre Juurlink, Bailey Reid, Imre Juurlink, Sarah Scanlon, Leah Martin, and Samantha Bokma. *Essential Elements for Non-punitive Accountability: A Workbook for Understanding Alternative Responses to Gender-Based Violence*. Accessed December 31, 2023. https://genderequitylke.org/resource/essential-elements-for-non-punitive-accountability-a-workbook-for-understanding-alternative-responses-to-gender-based-violence/.

Ellis, Cath, and Kane Murdoch. "The Educational Integrity Enforcement Pyramid: A New Framework for Challenging and Responding to Student Cheating." *Assessment & Evaluation in Higher Education*, (2024), 1–11. https://doi.org/10.1080/02602938.2024.2329167.

Esteves, Germano Gabriel Lima, Letícia Sousa Oliveira, Josemberg Moura de Andrade, and Mariana Peres Menezes. "Dark Triad Predicts Academic Cheating." *Personality and Individual Differences* 171 (March 2021): 110513. https://doi.org/10.1016/j.paid.2020.110513.

Ethics Unwrapped. "Armstrong's Doping Downfall." McCombs School of Business, University of Texas. Accessed December 27, 2023. https://ethicsunwrapped.utexas.edu/video/armstrongs-doping-downfall.

Evans, Angela D., and Kang Lee. "Promising to Tell the Truth Makes 8- to 16-Year-Olds More Honest." *Behavioral Sciences & the Law* 28, no. 6 (2010): 801–11. https://doi.org/10.1002/bsl.960.

Fink, L. Dee. *Creating Significant Learning Experiences: An Integrated Approach to Designing College Courses.* Rev. and updated ed. Jossey-Bass Higher and Adult Education Series. San Francisco: Jossey-Bass, 2013.

Fitzpatrick, Dan, Amanda Fox, and Brad Weinstein. *The AI Classroom: The Ultimate Guide to Artificial Intelligence in Education.* N.p.: TeacherGoals, 2023.

Fouad, Nadya A., and Philip L. Smith. "A Test of a Social Cognitive Model for Middle School Students: Math and Science." *Journal of Counseling Psychology* 43 (1996): 338–46. https://doi.org/10.1037/0022-0167.43.3.338.

Fowler, Geoffrey A. "We Tested a New ChatGPT-Detector for Teachers. It Flagged an Innocent Student." *Washington Post,* April 14, 2023. https://www.washingtonpost.com/technology/2023/04/01/chatgpt-cheating-detection-turnitin/.

Fowler, James H., and Nicholas A. Christakis. "Social Contagion Theory: Examining Dynamic Social Networks and Human Behavior." *Statistics in Medicine* 32, no. 4 (2013): 556–77. https://doi.org/10.1002/sim.5408.

Fulmer, Sara. "Weekly Digest #64: Preparing a Learning-Focused Syllabus." Blog post. Learning Scientists, June 18, 2017. https://www.learningscientists.org/blog/2017/6/18/weekly-digest-64.

Furze, Leon. "Teaching AI Ethics." Blog post. January 26, 2023. https://leonfurze.com/2023/01/26/teaching-ai-ethics/#teaching-ai-ethics-suggested-activity

Garrison, D. Randy, Terry Anderson, and Walter Archer. "Critical Inquiry in a Text-Based Environment: Computer Conferencing in Higher Education." *Internet and Higher Education* 2, nos. 2–3 (1999): 87–105. https://doi.org/10.1016/S1096-7516(00)00016-6.

Garrison, D. Randy, and J. B. Arbaugh. "Researching the Community of Inquiry Framework: Review, Issues, and Future Directions." *Internet and Higher Education* 10, no. 3 (2007): 157–72. https://doi.org/10.1016/j.iheduc.2007.04.001.

Geller, E. S. "The Buckle-Up Promise Card: A Versatile Intervention for Large-Scale Behavior Change." *Journal of Applied Behavior Analysis* 24, no. 1 (1991): 91–94. https://doi.org/10.1901/jaba.1991.24-91.

Gentile, Mary C. "Giving Voice to Values: An Overview." Darden Ideas to Action. Accessed December 31, 2023. https://ideas.darden.virginia.edu/giving-voice-to-values-an-overview.

Gilbert, Daniel. “If Only Gay Sex Caused Global Warming.” *Los Angeles Times*, July 2, 2006. https://www.latimes.com/archives/la-xpm-2006-jul-02-op-gilbert2-story.html.

Gonzalez, Jennifer. “Icebreakers That Rock.” Cult of Pedagogy, July 23, 2015. https://www.cultofpedagogy.com/classroom-icebreakers/.

Gray, Gabran. “The Biggest Cheating Scandals in Call of Duty History.” SVG, January 25, 2022. https://www.svg.com/746994/the-biggest-cheating-scandals-in-call-of-duty-history/.

Green, Melanie C. “Storytelling in Teaching.” *APS Observer* 17 (April 2004). https://www.psychologicalscience.org/observer/storytelling-in-teaching.

Grez, Luc, Martin Valcke, and Irene Roozen. “How Effective Are Self- and Peer Assessment of Oral Presentation Skills Compared with Teachers' Assessments?” *Active Learning in Higher Education* 13 (June 2012): 129–42. https://doi.org/10.1177/1469787412441284.

Gulikers, Judith T. M., Theo J. Bastiaens, and Paul A. Kirschner. “A Five-Dimensional Framework for Authentic Assessment.” *Educational Technology Research and Development* 52, no. 3 (2004): 67–86. https://doi.org/10.1007/BF02504676.

Haidt, Jonathan. “The Emotional Dog and Its Rational Tail: A Social Intuitionist Approach to Moral Judgment.” *Psychological Review* 108, no. 4 (2001): 814–34. https://doi.org/10.1037/0033-295X.108.4.814.

Hammer, Elizabeth Yost. “From the Laboratory to the Classroom and Back: The Science of Interpersonal Relationships Informs Teaching.” *Journal of Social and Clinical Psychology* 24, no. 1 (2005): 3–10. https://doi.org/10.1521/jscp.24.1.3.59168.

Hansen, Michael. “The U.S. Education System Isn't Giving Students What Employers Need.” *Harvard Business Review*, May 18, 2021. https://hbr.org/2021/05/the-u-s-education-system-isnt-giving-students-what-employers-need.

Harrison, Douglas, and Sharon Spencer. “Beyond Doing Integrity Online: A Research Agenda for Authentic Online Education.” In *Cheating Academic Integrity: Lessons Learned from 30 Years of Research*, edited by David A. Rettinger and Tricia Bertram Gallant, 201–32. San Francisco, CA: Jossey-Bass, 2022.

Harteis, Christian, and Johannes Bauer. “Learning from Errors at Work.” In *International Handbook of Research in Professional and Practice-Based Learning*, edited by Stephen Billett, Christian Harteis, and Hans Gruber, 699–732. Springer International Handbooks of Education. Dordrecht: Springer Netherlands, 2014. https://doi.org/10.1007/978-94-017-8902-8_26.

Hativa, Nira, and Peter Goodyear. “Research on Teacher Thinking, Beliefs, and Knowledge in Higher Education: Foundations, Status and Prospects.” In *Teacher Thinking, Beliefs, and Knowledge in Higher Education*, edited by Nira Hativa and Peter Goodyear, 335–59. Dordrecht: Springer Netherlands, 2002. https://doi.org/10.1007/978-94-010-0593-7_15.

Herdian, Herdian, and Euis Rahayu. "'I Don't Want to Commit Academic Dishonesty': The Role of Grit and Growth Mindset in Reducing Academic Dishonesty." *Journal of Learning Theory and Methodology* 3, no. 1 (2022): 25–33. https://doi.org/10.17309/jltm.2022.1.04.

Heyman, Gail D., Genyue Fu, Jianyan Lin, Miao K. Qian, and Kang Lee. "Eliciting Promises from Children Reduces Cheating." *Journal of Experimental Child Psychology* 139 (November 2015): 242–48. https://doi.org/10.1016/j.jecp.2015.04.013.

Hills, Melissa, and Kim Peacock. "Replacing Power with Flexible Structure: Implementing Flexible Deadlines to Improve Student Learning Experiences." *Teaching and Learning Inquiry* 10 (July 11, 2022). https://doi.org/10.20343/teachlearninqu.10.26.

Hogan, Kathleen, and Michael Pressley. *Scaffolding Student Learning: Instructional Approaches and Issues.* Cambridge, MA: Brookline Books, 1997.

Immordino-Yang, Mary Helen, and Antonio Damasio. "We Feel, Therefore We Learn: The Relevance of Affective and Social Neuroscience to Education." *Mind, Brain, and Education* 1, no. 1 (2007): 3–10. https://doi.org/10.1111/j.1751-228X.2007.00004.x.

Inclusive Education Initiative. "Introductory Series on Universal Design for Learning (UDL)." Accessed December 30, 2023. https://www.inclusive-education-initiative.org/events/introductory-series-universal-design-learning-udl.

International Center for Academic Integrity (ICAI). "Fundamental Values." Accessed December 27, 2023. https://academicintegrity.org/resources/fundamental-values.

Introna, Lucas, Elspeth Wood, Niall Hayes, and Lynne Blair. "Cultural Attitudes towards Plagiarism." Department of Organisations, Work, and Technology, University of Lancaster, August 2003. https://www.academia.edu/1362321/Cultural_attitudes_towards_plagiarism.

Ison, David. "Detection of Online Contract Cheating through Stylometry: A Pilot Study." *Online Learning* 24, no. 2 (2020). https://doi.org/10.24059/olj.v24i2.2096.

Jenkins, Baylee D., Jonathan M. Golding, Alexis M. Le Grand, Mary M. Levi, and Andrea M. Pals. "When Opportunity Knocks: College Students' Cheating amid the COVID-19 Pandemic." *Teaching of Psychology* 50, no. 4 (2023): 407–19. https://doi.org/10.1177/00986283211059067.

Jimenez, Kayla. "Professors Are Using ChatGPT Detector Tools to Accuse Students of Cheating. But What If the Software Is Wrong?" *USA Today*, April 12, 2023. https://www.usatoday.com/story/news/education/2023/04/12/how-ai-detection-tool-spawned-false-cheating-case-uc-davis/11600777002/.

Johnson, Samuel. *The History of Rasselas, Prince of Abissinia.* Mineola, NY: Dover, 2005.

Jordan, Augustus. "College Student Cheating: The Role of Motivation, Perceived Norms, Attitudes, and Knowledge of Institutional Policy." *Ethics & Behavior* 11 (2001): 233–47. https://doi.org/10.1207/S15327019EB43_3.

Joughin, Gordon. "Dimensions of Oral Assessment." *Assessment & Evaluation in Higher Education* 23, no. 4 (1998): 367–78. https://doi.org/10.1080/0260293980230404.

Kagan, Dona M. "Ways of Evaluating Teacher Cognition: Inferences Concerning the Goldilocks Principle." *Review of Educational Research* 60, no. 3 (1990): 419–69. https://doi.org/10.3102/00346543060003419.

Karp, David R. *The Little Book of Restorative Justice for Colleges and Universities: Repairing Harm and Rebuilding Trust in Response to Student Misconduct.* Little Books of Justice & Peacebuilding. Intercourse, PA: Good Books, 2013.

Keeley, Jared, Dale Smith, and William Buskist. "The Teacher Behaviors Checklist: Factor Analysis of Its Utility for Evaluating Teaching." *Teaching of Psychology* 33, no. 2 (2006): 84–91. https://doi.org/10.1207/s15328023top3302_1.

Kenney, Shannon R., Graham T. DiGuiseppi, Matthew K. Meisel, Sara G. Balestrieri, and Nancy P. Barnett. "Poor Mental Health, Peer Drinking Norms, and Alcohol Risk in a Social Network of First-Year College Students." *Addictive Behaviors* 84 (September 2018): 151–59. https://doi.org/10.1016/j.addbeh.2018.04.012.

Kerr, Emma, and Sarah Wood. "A Look at 20 Years of Tuition Costs at National Universities." *US News & World Report*, September 22, 2023. https://www.usnews.com/education/best-colleges/paying-for-college/articles/see-20-years-of-tuition-growth-at-national-universities.

Kidder, Rushworth. "How Good People Make Tough Choices: Resolving the Dilemmas of Ethical Living." *Semantic Scholar*, January 24, 1995. https://www.semanticscholar.org/paper/How-Good-People-Make-Tough-Choices%3A-Resolving-the-Kidder/3a880bbc63930785921e74150d81f8e5110183ad.

Klee, Miles. "Professor Flunks All His Students after ChatGPT Falsely Claims It Wrote Their Papers." *Rolling Stone*, May 17, 2023. https://www.rollingstone.com/culture/culture-features/texas-am-chatgpt-ai-professor-flunks-students-false-claims-1234736601/.

Kolb, Alice Y., and David A. Kolb. "Learning Styles and Learning Spaces: Enhancing Experiential Learning in Higher Education." *Academy of Management Learning & Education* 4, no. 2 (2005): 193–212. https://doi.org/10.5465/amle.2005.17268566.

Komarraju, Meera, Sergey Musulkin, and Gargi Bhattacharya. "Role of Student-Faculty Interactions in Developing College Students' Academic Self-Concept, Motivation, and Achievement." *Journal of College Student Development* 51, no. 3 (2010): 332–42. https://doi.org/10.1353/csd.0.0137.

Kristal, Ariella S., Ashley V. Whillans, Max H. Bazerman, Francesca Gino, Lisa L. Shu, Nina Mazar, and Dan Ariely. "Signing at the Beginning versus at the End Does Not Decrease Dishonesty." *Proceedings of the National Academy of Sciences* 117, no. 13 (2020): 7103–7. https://doi.org/10.1073/pnas.1911695117.

Kulik, Chen-Lin C., James A. Kulik, and Robert L. Bangert-Drowns. "Effectiveness of Mastery Learning Programs: A Meta-Analysis." *Review of Educational Research* 60, no. 2 (1990): 265–99. https://doi.org/10.3102/00346543060002265.

Lalley, James P., and J. Ronald Gentile. "Classroom Assessment and Grading to Assure Mastery." *Theory into Practice* 48, no. 1 (2009): 28–35. https://doi.org/10.1080/00405840802577577.

Lang, James M. *Cheating Lessons: Learning from Academic Dishonesty*. Cambridge, MA: Harvard University Press, 2013.

Langer, Ellen J. "The Illusion of Control." *Journal of Personality and Social Psychology* 32 (1975): 311–28. https://doi.org/10.1037/0022-3514.32.2.311.

Lee, Stephanie, M. "Scientists Are Scrutinizing Their Work with Francesca Gino. Here's What They've Found So Far." *Chronicle of Higher Ed*, November 6, 2023. https://www.chronicle.com/article/scientists-are-scrutinizing-their-work-with-francesca-gino-heres-what-theyve-found-so-far.

Levy, Allison, Iser G. DeLeon, Catherine K. Martinez, Nathalie Fernandez, Nicholas A. Gage, Sigurdur Óli Sigurdsson, and Michelle A. Frank-Crawford. "A Quantitative Review of Overjustification Effects in Persons with Intellectual and Developmental Disabilities." *Journal of Applied Behavior Analysis* 50, no. 2 (2017): 206–21. https://doi.org/10.1002/jaba.359.

Longoni, Chiara, Stephanie Tully, and Azim Shariff. "Plagiarizing AI-Generated Content Is Seen As Less Unethical and More Permissible." PsyArXiv Preprints, June 18, 2023. https://doi.org/10.31234/osf.io/na3wb.

Lubarda, Marko, Nathan Delson, Curt Schurgers, Maziar Ghazinejad, Saharnaz Baghdadchi, Alex Phan, Mia Minnes, et al. "Oral Exams for Large-Enrollment Engineering Courses to Promote Academic Integrity and Student Engagement during Remote Instruction." In *2021 IEEE Frontiers in Education Conference (FIE)*, 1–5. Lincoln, NE: IEEE, 2021. https://doi.org/10.1109/FIE49875.2021.9637124.

Luckie, Douglas B., Aaron M. Rivkin, Jacob R. Aubry, Benjamin J. Marengo, Leah R. Creech, and Ryan D. Sweeder. "Verbal Final Exam in Introductory Biology Yields Gains in Student Content Knowledge and Longitudinal Performance." *CBE—Life Sciences Education* 12, no. 3 (2013): 515–29. https://doi.org/10.1187/cbe.12-04-0050.

Maier, Steven F., and Martin E. P. Seligman. "Learned Helplessness at Fifty: Insights from Neuroscience." *Psychological Review* 123, no. 4 (2016): 349–67. https://doi.org/10.1037/rev0000033.

Mazar, Nina, On Amir, and Dan Ariely. "The Dishonesty of Honest People: A Theory of Self-Concept Maintenance." *Journal of Marketing Research* 45, no. 6 (2008): 633–44.

McCabe, Donald L. "Cheating among College and University Students: A North American Perspective." *International Journal for Educational Integrity* 1, no. 1 (2005). https://doi.org/10.21913/IJEI.v1i1.14.

McCabe, Donald L., Kenneth D. Butterfield, and Linda Klebe Treviño. "Academic Dishonesty in Graduate Business Programs: Prevalence, Causes, and Proposed Action." *Academy of Management Learning & Education* 5, no. 3 (2006): 294–305. https://doi.org/10.5465/amle.2006.22697018.

———. *Cheating in College*. Baltimore: Johns Hopkins University Press, 2012. https://doi.org/10.1353/book.18818.

McCabe, Donald L., Linda Klebe Treviño, and Kenneth D. Butterfield. "Honor Codes and Other Contextual Influences on Academic Integrity: A Replication and Extension to Modified Honor Code Settings." *Research in Higher Education* 43, no. 3 (2002): 357–78. https://doi.org/10.1023/A:1014893102151.

McGee Banks, Cherry A., and James A. Banks. "Equity Pedagogy: An Essential Component of Multicultural Education." *Theory into Practice* 34, no. 3 (1995): 152–58. https://doi.org/10.1080/00405849509543674.

Meiselman, Ben S. "Ghostbusting in Detroit: Evidence on Nonfilers from a Controlled Field Experiment." *Journal of Public Economics* 158 (February 2018): 180–93. https://doi.org/10.1016/j.jpubeco.2018.01.005.

Messier, Nicole. "Authentic Assessments." Center for the Advancement of Teaching Excellence, University of Illinois, Chicago. April 15, 2022. https://teaching.uic.edu/resources/teaching-guides/assessment-grading-practices/authentic-assessments/.

Moore Howard, Rebecca. "Plagiarisms, Authorships, and the Academic Death Penalty." *College English* 57, no. 7 (1995): 788. https://doi.org/10.2307/378403.

Murdoch, Kane. "Brave New World?" ICAI blog post. June 12, 2023. https://academicintegrity.org/resources/blog/114-2023/june-2023/442-brave-new-world.

Murdock, Tamera B., and Eric M. Anderman. "Motivational Perspectives on Student Cheating: Toward an Integrated Model of Academic Dishonesty." *Educational Psychologist* 41, no. 3 (2006): 129–45.

Myers, Andrew. "AI-Detectors Biased against Non-native English Writers," May 15, 2023. Stanford University Human-Centered Artificial Intelligence. https://hai.stanford.edu/news/ai-detectors-biased-against-non-native-english-writers.

Nagin, Daniel S., and Greg Pogarsky. "An Experimental Investigation of Deterrence: Cheating, Self-Serving Bias, and Impulsivity." *Criminology* 41, no. 1 (2003): 167–94. https://doi.org/10.1111/j.1745-9125.2003.tb00985.x.

Newton, Philip M. "How Common Is Commercial Contract Cheating in Higher Education and Is It Increasing? A Systematic Review." *Frontiers in Education* 3 (2018). https://www.frontiersin.org/articles/10.3389/feduc.2018.00067.

Nilson, Linda B. "Yes, Virginia, There's a Better Way to Grade." *Inside Higher Ed*, January 19, 2016. https://www.insidehighered.com/views/2016/01/19/new-ways-grade-more-effectively-essay.

Nilson, Linda B., and Claudia J. Stanny. *Specifications Grading: Restoring Rigor, Motivating Students, and Saving Faculty Time*. Sterling, VA: Stylus, 2015.

Northcutt, Curtis G., Andrew D. Ho, and Isaac L. Chuang. “Detecting and Preventing ‘Multiple-Account’ Cheating in Massive Open Online Courses.” *Computers & Education* 100 (September 2016): 71–80. https://doi.org/10.1016/j.compedu.2016.04.008.

O’Rourke, Jillian, Jeffrey Barnes, Anna Deaton, Kristopher Fulks, Kristina Ryan, and David A. Rettinger. “Imitation Is the Sincerest Form of Cheating: The Influence of Direct Knowledge and Attitudes on Academic Dishonesty.” *Ethics & Behavior* 20, no. 1 (2010): 47–64. https://doi.org/10.1080/10508420903482616.

Palmer, Donald. *Normal Organizational Wrongdoing: A Critical Analysis of Theories of Misconduct in and by Organizations*. Paperback ed. Oxford: Oxford University Press, 2013.

Perkins, Mike, Leon Furze, Jasper Roe, and Jason MacVaugh. “Navigating the Generative AI Era: Introducing the AI Assessment Scale for Ethical GenAI Assessment.” ArXiv, December 12, 2023. https://arxiv.org/abs/2312.07086.

Perkins, Mike, Jasper Roe, Binh H. Vu, Darius Postma, Don Hickerson, James McGaughran, and Huy Q. Khuat. “GenAI Detection Tools, Adversarial Techniques and Implications for Inclusivity in Higher Education.” ArXiv, March 28, 2024. http://arxiv.org/abs/2403.19148.

Pettigrew, Luisa M., and Nicholas Mays. “What Role Is There for ‘Nudging’ Clinicians?” *British Journal of General Practice* 71, no. 703 (2021): 82–85. https://doi.org/10.3399/bjgp21X714857.

Pintrich, Paul R. “The Role of Metacognitive Knowledge in Learning, Teaching, and Assessing.” *Theory into Practice* 41, no. 4 (2002): 219–25. https://doi.org/10.1207/s15430421tip4104_3.

Poindexter, Owen. “How a Huge Cheating Scandal Altered the Chess World.” *Front Office Sports*. Blog post. November 20, 2022. https://frontofficesports.com/how-a-huge-cheating-scandal-altered-the-chess-world/.

Porter, Leo, and Daniel Zingaro. *Learn AI-Assisted Python Programming*. Shelter Island, NY: Manning, 2023. https://www.oreilly.com/library/view/learn-ai-assisted-python/9781633437784/.

Pulvers, Kim, and George M. Diekhoff. “The Relationship between Academic Dishonesty and College Classroom Environment.” *Research in Higher Education* 40, no. 4 (1999): 487–98.

Qi, Huihui, and Curt Schurgers. “Oral Exams in Support of Academic Integrity: From Catching Dishonesty to Promoting Excellence.” *Integrity Matters*. Blog post. December 11, 2022. https://academicintegrity.org/resources/blog/106-2022/december-2022/417-oral-exams-in-support-of-academic-integrity-from-catching-dishonesty-to-promoting-excellence.

Quantitative Analysis Center. “Passion-Driven Statistics.” Wesleyan University. Accessed July 17, 2023. https://passiondrivenstatistics.wescreates.wesleyan.edu/.

Reisberg, Daniel. *Cognition: Exploring the Science of the Mind.* 8th ed. New York: W. W. Norton, 2021.

Rest, James, Darcia Narvaez, Muriel J. Bebeau, and Stephen J. Thoma. *Postconventional Moral Thinking: A Neo-Kohlbergian Approach.* Mahwah, NJ: Lawrence Erlbaum Associates, 1999.

Rettinger, David A. "The Role of Emotions and Attitudes in Causing and Preventing Cheating." *Theory into Practice* 56, no. 2 (2017): 103–10. https://doi.org/10.1080/00405841.2017.1308174.

Rettinger, David A., Eric M. Anderman, Tricia Bertram Gallant, D. McNally, M. McTernan, Jason M. Stephens, and Holly E. Tatum. "Assessing Academic Integrity: The ICAI/McCabe Survey 2.0." Portland, OR, 2020.

Rettinger, David A., and Tricia Bertram Gallant. *Cheating Academic Integrity: Lessons from 30 Years of Research.* 1st ed. New York: John Wiley & Sons, 2022.

Richardson, Jennifer C., J. Ben Arbaugh, Martha Cleveland-Innes, Philip Ice, Karen P. Swan, and D. Randy Garrison. "Using the Community of Inquiry Framework to Inform Effective Instructional Design." In *The Next Generation of Distance Education: Unconstrained Learning,* edited by Leslie Moller and Jason B. Huett, 97–125. Boston, MA: Springer, 2012. https://doi.org/10.1007/978-1-4614-1785-9.

Richmond, Aaron S., Jeanne M. Slattery, Nathanael Mitchell, Robin K. Morgan, and Jared Becknell. "Can a Learner-Centered Syllabus Change Students' Perceptions of Student–Professor Rapport and Master Teacher Behaviors?" *Scholarship of Teaching and Learning in Psychology* 2, no. 3 (2016): 159–68. https://doi.org/10.1037/stl0000066.

Robichaud, Jean-Michel, Joannie Lessard, Laurence Labelle, and Geneviève A. Mageau. "The Role of Logical Consequences and Autonomy Support in Children's Anticipated Reactions of Anger and Empathy." *Journal of Child and Family Studies* 29, no. 6 (2020): 1511–24. https://doi.org/10.1007/s10826-019-01594-3.

Roediger, Henry L., and Jeffrey D. Karpicke. "Test-Enhanced Learning: Taking Memory Tests Improves Long-Term Retention." *Psychological Science* 17, no. 3 (2006): 249–55. https://doi.org/10.1111/j.1467-9280.2006.01693.x.

Rogerson, Ann M. "Detecting Contract Cheating in Essay and Report Submissions: Process, Patterns, Clues and Conversations." *International Journal for Educational Integrity* 13, no. 1 (2017): 10. https://doi.org/10.1007/s40979-017-0021-6.

Roig, Miguel. "Can Undergraduate Students Determine Whether Text Has Been Plagiarized?" *Psychological Record* 47, no. 1 (1997): 113–22. https://doi.org/10.1007/BF03395215.

———. "Plagiarism and Paraphrasing Criteria of College and University Professors." *Ethics & Behavior* 11, no. 3 (July 1, 2001): 307–23. https://doi.org/10.1207/S15327019EB1103_8.

Roig, Miguel, and Lauren DeTommaso. "Are College Cheating and Plagiarism Related to Academic Procrastination?" *Psychological Reports* 77, no. 2 (1995): 691–98. https://doi.org/10.2466/pro.1995.77.2.691.

Rundle, Kiata, Guy J. Curtis, and Joseph Clare. "Why Students Do Not Engage in Contract Cheating." *Frontiers in Psychology* 10 (October 2019). https://www.frontiersin.org/articles/10.3389/fpsyg.2019.02229.

Salend, Spencer J. "Addressing Test Anxiety." *Teaching Exceptional Children* 44, no. 2 (2011): 58–68. https://doi.org/10.1177/004005991104400206.

Sethi, Aman. "The Mystery of India's Deadly Exam Scam." *The Guardian*, December 17, 2015. https://www.theguardian.com/world/2015/dec/17/the-mystery-of-indias-deadly-exam-scam.

Sezer, Ovul, Francesca Gino, and Max H. Bazerman. "Ethical Blind Spots: Explaining Unintentional Unethical Behavior." *Current Opinion in Psychology* 6 (December 2015): 77–81. https://doi.org/10.1016/j.copsyc.2015.03.030.

Shampanier, Kristina, Nina Mazar, and Dan Ariely. "Zero As a Special Price: The True Value of Free Products." *Marketing Science* 26, no. 6 (2007): 742–57. https://doi.org/10.1287/mksc.1060.0254.

Shu, Lisa L., Francesca Gino, and Max H. Bazerman. "Dishonest Deed, Clear Conscience: When Cheating Leads to Moral Disengagement and Motivated Forgetting." *Personality and Social Psychology Bulletin* 37, no. 3 (2011): 330–49. https://doi.org/10.1177/0146167211398138.

Slavin, Robert E. "Mastery Learning Re-Reconsidered." *Review of Educational Research* 60, no. 2 (1990): 300–2. https://doi.org/10.3102/00346543060002300.

Somers, Mark John. "Ethical Codes of Conduct and Organizational Context: A Study of the Relationship between Codes of Conduct, Employee Behavior, and Organizational Values." *Journal of Business Ethics* 30, no. 2 (2001): 185–95. https://doi.org/10.1023/A:1006457810654.

Sotiriadou, Popi, Danielle Logan, Amanda Daly, and Ross Guest. "The Role of Authentic Assessment to Preserve Academic Integrity and Promote Skill Development and Employability." *Studies in Higher Education* 45, no. 11 (2020): 2132–48. https://doi.org/10.1080/03075079.2019.1582015.

Stephens, Jason M. "Bridging the Divide: The Role of Motivation and Self-Regulation in Explaining the Judgment-Action Gap Related to Academic Dishonesty." *Frontiers in Psychology* 9 (February 2018). https://www.frontiersin.org/articles/10.3389/fpsyg.2018.00246.

———. "How to Cheat and Not Feel Guilty: Cognitive Dissonance and Its Amelioration in the Domain of Academic Dishonesty." *Theory into Practice* 56 (March 8, 2017): 1–10. https://doi.org/10.1080/00405841.2017.1283571.

———. "Natural and Normal, but Unethical and Evitable: The Epidemic of Academic Dishonesty and How We End It." *Change: The Magazine of Higher Learning* 51, no. 4 (2019): 8–17. https://doi.org/10.1080/00091383.2019.1618140.

Stephens, Jason M., and Tricia Bertram Gallant. "Enhancing Moral Sensitivity in the Aftermath of Academic Misconduct: Results from a Quasi-Experimental Field Study." *Journal of Moral Education* (2023), 1–16. https://doi.org/10.1080/03057240.2023.2268298.

Stephens, Jason M., and Hunter Gehlbach. "6—Under Pressure and Underengaged: Motivational Profiles and Academic Cheating in High School." In *Psychology of Academic Cheating*, edited by Eric M. Anderman and Tamera B. Murdock, 107–34. Cambridge, MA: Academic Press, 2007. https://doi.org/10.1016/B978-012372541-7/50009-7.

Stephens, Jason M., Michael F. Young, and Thomas Calabrese. "Does Moral Judgment Go Offline When Students Are Online? A Comparative Analysis of Undergraduates' Beliefs and Behaviors Related to Conventional and Digital Cheating." *Ethics & Behavior* 17, no. 3 (2007): 233–54. https://doi.org/10.1080/10508420701519197.

Stewart, John C., John V. Monaco, Sung-Hyuk Cha, and Charles C. Tappert. "An Investigation of Keystroke and Stylometry Traits for Authenticating Online Test Takers." 2011 International Joint Conference on Biometrics (IJCB), Washington, DC, October 11–13, 2011, 1–7. https://doi.org/10.1109/IJCB.2011.6117480.

Styler, Will. "Will's Oral Exam Procedures and Policies." Accessed December 30, 2023. https://wstyler.ucsd.edu/oralexam/.

Subbian, Vignesh, Linda R. Shaw, and Colleen Lynel Halpin. "Ethical Decision-Making Frameworks for Engineering Education: A Cross-Disciplinary Review." Paper presented at the 129th ASEE Annual Conference and Exposition: Excellence through Diversity, Minneapolis, MN, June 26–29, 2022. http://www.scopus.com/inward/record.url?scp=85138253019&partnerID=8YFLogxK.

Susser, Jonathan A., and Jennifer McCabe. "From the Lab to the Dorm Room: Metacognitive Awareness and Use of Spaced Study." *Instructional Science* 41, no. 2 (2013): 345–63. https://doi.org/10.1007/s11251-012-9231-8.

Swauger, Shea. "What's Worse Than Remote School? Remote Test-Taking with AI Proctors." NBC News, November 7, 2020. https://www.nbcnews.com/think/opinion/remote-testing-monitored-ai-failing-students-forced-undergo-it-ncna1246769.

Sykes, Gresham M., and David Matza. "Techniques of Neutralization: A Theory of Delinquency." *American Sociological Review* 22 (1957): 664–70. https://doi.org/10.2307/2089195.

Tappin, Ben M., and Ryan T. McKay. "The Illusion of Moral Superiority." *Social Psychological and Personality Science* 8, no. 6 (2017): 623–31. https://doi.org/10.1177/1948550616673878.

Tatum, Holly E. "Honor Codes and Academic Integrity: Three Decades of Research." *Journal of College and Character* 23, no. 1 (2022): 32–47. https://doi.org/10.1080/2194587X.2021.2017977.

Team-Based Learning Collaborative. "What is TBL?" Accessed April 20, 2024. https://www.teambasedlearning.org/definition/.

Tenbrunsel, Ann E., and David M. Messick. "Ethical Fading: The Role of Self-Deception in Unethical Behavior." *Social Justice Research* 17, no. 2 (2004): 223–36. https://doi.org/10.1023/B:SORE.0000027411.35832.53.

Tesler, Glenn. "Assigning Seats at UC San Diego Using Canvas." Accessed December 30, 2023. https://mathweb.ucsd.edu/~gptesler/assigningseats.html.

Thaler, Richard H., and Cass R. Sunstein. *Nudge: The Final Edition*. Rev. ed. New York: Penguin Books, 2021.

Trimboli, Oscar. *Deep Listening: Impact beyond Words*. N.p.: Oscar Trimboli, 2019. https://www.oscartrimboli.com/.

Turing, Alan M. "Computing Machinery and Intelligence." In *Parsing the Turing Test: Philosophical and Methodological Issues in the Quest for the Thinking Computer*, edited by Robert Epstein, Gary Roberts, and Grace Beber, 23–65. Dordrecht: Springer Netherlands, 2009. https://doi.org/10.1007/978-1-4020-6710-5_3.

Tversky, Amos, and Daniel Kahneman. "The Framing of Decisions and the Psychology of Choice." *Science* 211, no. 4481 (1981): 453–58.

University of Auckland. "Academic Integrity Course." University of Auckland. Accessed December 27, 2023. https://www.auckland.ac.nz/en/students/forms-policies-and-guidelines/student-policies-and-guidelines/academic-integrity-copyright/academic-integrity-course.html.

University of California, San Diego (UCSD). "Academic Integrity Tutorial." Academic Integrity, UC San Diego. Accessed December 27, 2023. https://academicintegrity.ucsd.edu/excel-integrity/learn-more.html#Take-the-Academic-Integrity-Tut.

Uribarri, Adrian. "The *Times* and Jayson Blair." Ethics Case Studies, Society of Professional Journalists. Accessed December 27, 2023. https://www.spj.org/ecs13.asp.

Waltzer, Talia, and Audun Dahl. "Students' Perceptions and Evaluations of Plagiarism: Effects of Text and Context." *Journal of Moral Education* 50, no. 4 (2021): 436–51. https://doi.org/10.1080/03057240.2020.1787961.

———. "Why Do Students Cheat? Perceptions, Evaluations, and Motivations." *Ethics & Behavior* 33, no. 2 (2023): 130–50. https://doi.org/10.1080/10508422.2022.2026775.

Waltzer, Talia, Fiona C. DeBernardi, and Audun Dahl. "Student and Teacher Views on Cheating in High School: Perceptions, Evaluations, and Decisions." *Journal of Research on Adolescence* 33, no. 1 (2023): 108–26. https://doi.org/10.1111/jora.12784.

Warner, John. *Why They Can't Write*. Baltimore: Johns Hopkins University Press, 2020. https://doi.org/10.1353/book.61976.

Watters, Audrey. "Hack Education: Cheating, Policing, and School Surveillance." National Education Policy Center. October 21, 2020. https://nepc.colorado.edu/blog/cheating-policing.

Weber-Wulff, Debora, Alla Anohina-Naumeca, Sonja Bjelobaba, Tomáš Foltýnek, Jean Guerrero-Dib, Olumide Popoola, Petr Šigut, and Lorna Waddington. "Testing of Detection Tools for AI-Generated Text." *International Journal for Educational Integrity* 19, no. 1 (2023): 26. https://doi.org/10.1007/s40979-023-00146-z.

Wiggins, Grant. "Authenticity in Assessment, (Re-)Defined and Explained." Authentic Education. Blog post. January 26, 2014. https://authenticeducation.org/authenticity-in-assessment-re-defined-and-explained/.

Wilson, Janie H., and Rebecca G. Ryan. "Professor-Student Rapport Scale: Six Items Predict Student Outcomes." *Teaching of Psychology* 40, no. 2 (2013): 130–33. https://doi.org/10.1177/0098628312475033.

Worthen, Molly. "If It Was Good Enough for Socrates, It's Good Enough for Sophomores." *New York Times*, Opinion, December 2, 2022. https://www.nytimes.com/2022/12/02/opinion/college-oral-exam.html.

Young, Jeffrey R. "How the 'Contract Cheating' Industry Has Gotten More Aggressive in Recruiting Students" *EdSurge*, January 23, 2020. https://www.edsurge.com/news/2020-01-23-how-the-contract-cheating-industry-has-gotten-more-aggressive-in-recruiting-students.

Zilles, Craig, Matthew West, Geoffrey Herman, and Timothy Bretl. "Every University Should Have a Computer-Based Testing Facility." In *Proceedings of the 11th International Conference on Computer Supported Education*, edited by H. Chad Lane, Susan Zvacek, and James Uhomoibhi, 414–42. Setúbal, Portugal: SciTePress, 2019. https://doi.org/10.5220/0007753304140420.

Zilles, Craig, Matthew West, David Mussulman, and Tim Bretl. "Making Testing Less Trying: Lessons Learned from Operating a Computer-Based Testing Facility." In *2018 IEEE Frontiers in Education Conference (FIE)*, 1–9. San Jose, CA: IEEE, 2018. https://doi.org/10.1109/FIE.2018.8658551.

INDEX